NAVY STAFF
OFFICER'S
GUIDE

TITLES IN THE SERIES

THE U.S. NAVAL INSTITUTE

Blue & Gold Professional Library

For more than 100 years, U.S. Navy professionals have counted on specialized books published by the Naval Institute Press to prepare them for their responsibilities as they advance in their careers and to serve as ready references and refreshers when needed. From the days of coal-fired battleships to the era of unmanned aerial vehicles and laser weaponry, such perennials as *The Bluejacket's Manual* and *Watch Officer's Guide* have guided generations of Sailors through the complex challenges of naval service. As these books are updated and new ones are added to the list, they will carry the distinctive mark of the Blue & Gold Professional Library series to remind and reassure their users that they have been prepared by naval professionals and meet the exacting standards that Sailors have long expected from the U.S. Naval Institute.

BLUE & GOLD
PROFESSIONAL LIBRARY

PRAISE FOR *NAVY STAFF OFFICER'S GUIDE*

"A beautifully written, well-organized, and up-to-date gold mine of vital data and wise advice. Particularly focused on the new naval era of fleet-centered operations. Will improve the quality of Navy staff work and decisions by Navy commanders, and empower officers new to a Navy staff to hit the ground running."

> —**CAPT Peter M. Swartz, USN (Ret.),** senior CNA strategy analyst and former Cold War U.S. Navy strategist

"An excellent read that would be very valuable for anyone reporting to a staff! Very readable with historical context that enlightens today's staff constructs. Dale succinctly and accurately captures the essence of a Navy staff and provides experienced insights on how to succeed in your inevitable staff assignment."

> —**VADM Phil Sawyer, USN (Ret.)**

"Rielage's book reminds me of working with him optimizing a large staff to take on the even larger challenge presented by PRC actions in the Indo-Asia-Pacific. Reading his masterfully constructed book will serve you well working on and with staffs, inside as well as outside the Navy."

> —**ADM Scott H. Swift, USN (Ret.),** former Commander, U.S. Pacific Fleet, and founder of The Swift Group LLC, national security consultancy

"A one-of-a-kind work capturing the essence and purpose of staffs supporting commanders across the gamut—from squadron, fleet, and combatant commands to the enterprise level and echelon one. Rielage deftly outlines the skill and art of effectively supporting 'commander's intent' in an increasingly connected world."

> —**RADM Robert P. Girrier, USN (Ret.),** Senior Fellow, CNA; president emeritus, Pacific Forum International; co-author, *Fleet Tactics and Naval Operations, Third Edition*

NAVY STAFF OFFICER'S GUIDE

LEADING WITH IMPACT FROM SQUADRON TO OPNAV

CAPT DALE C. RIELAGE, USN (RET.)

Naval Institute Press
Annapolis, Maryland

Naval Institute Press
291 Wood Road
Annapolis, MD 21402

Library of Congress Cataloging-in-Publication Data
Names: Rielage, Dale C., author.
Title: Navy staff officer's guide : leading with impact from squadron to OPNAV / Capt. Dale C. Rielage, USN, (Ret.).
Description: Annapolis, Maryland : Naval Institute Press, [2022] | Series: Blue & gold professional library | Includes bibliographical references and index.
Identifiers: LCCN 2022019730 (print) | LCCN 2022019731 (ebook) | ISBN 9781682478264 (hardback) | ISBN 9781682478684 (ebook)
Subjects: LCSH: United States. Navy —Officer's handbooks. | BISAC: REFERENCE / Personal & Practical Guides | POLITICAL SCIENCE / Reference
Classification: LCC V133 .R54 2022 (print) | LCC V133 (ebook) | DDC 359.00973 —dc23/eng/20220831
LC record available at https://lccn.loc.gov/2022019730
LC ebook record available at https://lccn.loc.gov/2022019731

♾ Print editions meet the requirements of ANSI/NISO z39.48-1992 (Permanence of Paper).
Printed in the United States of America

30 29 28 27 26 25 24 23 22   9 8 7 6 5 4 3 2 1
First printing

CONTENTS

ILLUSTRATIONS

ACKNOWLEDGMENTS

Like a Navy career, a book is built on the support of shipmates. This one owes its existence first and foremost to the many senior officers who taught me by example what command should look like and how a staff could enable their leadership.

Across my eleven staff assignments, I have had the pleasure of working with and learning from some of the finest professionals in the Department of Defense. They modeled excellence in staff work, patiently teaching me how quality staff work ultimately makes victory possible. Some of the many to whom I owe thanks include VADM Tom Copeman, USN (Ret.); VADM Stuart B. Munsch, USN; VADM Phillip Sawyer, USN (Ret.); DISL David B. Dorman, PhD; SES Robert Giesler; DISL Zev Goldrich; DISES Cathy Johnston; SES Letitia A. Long; SES Margaret Palmieri; SES Bob Stephenson; RADM Jay Bynum, USN (Ret.); RADM Christopher C. French, JAGC, USN; RADM Vic Mercado, USN (Ret.); RADM Patrick Piercey, USN (Ret.); RADM Richard B. Porterfield, USN (Ret.); RADM Mike Studeman, USN; RDML Charles Brown, USN; RDML Thomas M. Henderschedt, USN; RDML Dave Welch, USN (Ret.); CAPT Albert A. Alarcon, USN; CAPT Jim Degree, USN (Ret.); CAPT Tom Dove, USN (Ret.); CAPT Jennifer Eaves, USN (Ret.); CAPT Bill Farawell, USN (Ret.); CAPT Maureen "Mo" Fox, USN (Ret.); CAPT Tom Halvorson, USN (Ret.); CAPT Greg Husmann, USN (Ret.); CAPT Vince Kapral, USN (Ret.); CAPT Rich LeBron, USN; CAPT Paul J. Lyons, USN (Ret.); CAPT Timothy McCandless, USN (Ret.); CAPT Kevin "Kmac" McHale, USN; CAPT Kevin E. Nelson, USN (Ret.); CAPT Santiago R. Neville, USN (Ret.); CAPT Fred Pfirrmann, USN (Ret.); CAPT Peter M. Swartz, USN (Ret.); CAPT Peter F. Smith, USN (Ret.); CAPT Harold "H. E." Williams, USN (Ret.); CAPT Andre Wilson, USN; CAPT Earle S. Yerger, USN (Ret.);

CAPT Dave Yoshihara, USN (Ret.); Special Agent Matthew Clement; CDR Leah Bray, USN (Ret.); CDR Peter A. Dutton, PhD, JAGC, USN (Ret.); CDR Kathleen G. Farris, USNR (Ret.); CDR David A. Radi, USN (Ret.); CDR Guy "Bus" Snodgrass, USN (Ret.); LCDR Purvis A. Broughton, USN (Ret.); LCDR Mike "General" Reed, USN (Ret.); and LCDR Jim Stobie, USN (Ret.). While I have lost contact with some of you over the years, your lessons remain fresh.

A number of friends and mentors generously reviewed this work, including ADM Scott H. Swift, USN (Ret.); DISES B. Lynn Wright; SES Todd L. Schafer; RADM Robert P. Girrier, USN (Ret.); CAPT Henry C. Adams, USN (Ret.); CAPT Jim Bock, USN (Ret.); CAPT Steve Deal, USN (Ret.); CAPT David P. Fields, USN; CAPT Patrick A. Molenda, USN (Ret.); CDR David Kohnen, PhD, USN (Ret.); and CDR Christopher Nelson, USN. They dissected my words like the experienced staff officers they are; their commentary was thoughtful and incisive. The errors that remain are mine, as are the views expressed in this publication, which do not reflect the official policy or position of the Department of the Navy, Department of Defense, or the U.S. government.

I owe thanks to the Scotch and Strategy group, who kept me going through the COVID pandemic and offered thoughtful encouragement along the way. Due to the nature of your work, I will acknowledge most of you silently. You know who you are and you know my esteem for you.

Readers will note that this volume benefits immensely from quotes and documents from ADM Arleigh Burke. These are entirely due to the generosity of CAPT David A. Rosenberg, PhD, USNR (Ret.), a dear friend, scholar, and practitioner who is the institutional memory of some of our Navy's most heroic episodes. Likewise, CDR B. J. Armstrong, PhD, USN, generously pointed me to RADM Alfred T. Mahan's writings on Navy staffs.

Most importantly, this work was built on the loving support of my bride, Lisa (USNA 1991), and the energy and motivation of my sons, two of whom are embarked on their own Navy adventures.

ACRONYMS AND ABBREVIATIONS

NOTE: Even by U.S. military standards, the U.S. Navy is remarkably ill disciplined with its acronyms and abbreviations. It is common for a command to be known by two or more abbreviations. For example, the commander, U.S. Fleet Forces Command is formally abbreviated as COMUSFLTFORCOM but is referred to in official sources as "USFLTFORCOM," "USFFC," and "FFC." Generally, "COM" or "C" is added to abbreviations to distinguish between the commander and the command they lead (though a leading "C" can also mean "combined" in joint context). Which abbreviation is used in a communication often has informal connotations about the formality of the message. Below is an effort to identify the formal abbreviations and some variations. How to use each is, unfortunately, often a matter of experience.

1MC	shipboard general announcing circuit
3M	maintenance and material management
9/11	11 September 2001
A/	acting (followed by abbreviation for official position)
AAR	after action review
ACMC	Assistant Commandant of the Marine Corps
ADA	Anti-Deficiency Act
ADC	authority, direction, and control
ADCON	administrative control (authority)
AEGIS	shipboard weapons system based on a SPY phased-array radar system
ALNAV	record message addressed to All Navy
AMD	Activity Manpower Document
AMDC	air and missile defense commander

AO	action officer
AOC	air operations center
AOR	area of responsibility
AQ	command and control warfare commander
AREC	air resource element coordinator
ARG	amphibious ready group
ASN	Assistant Secretary of the Navy
ASW	antisubmarine warfare; see AX
ASWC	antisubmarine warfare commander
AT/FP	anti-terrorism/force protection
ATF	Bureau of Alcohol, Tobacco, and Firearms
ATO	air tasking order
AUDGEN	auditor general
AV	audiovisual
AW	anti air warfare commander
AWC	air warfare commander
AX	air submarine warfare commander; see ASW
B2C2WG	boards, bureaus, centers, cells, and working groups
BA	budget authority
BCC	blind carbon copy
BCR	billet change request
BDA	battle damage assessment
Blue	Navy or friendly forces
BLUF	bottom line up front
BOGSAT	"bunch of guys sitting around talking" (informal)
BSO	budget submitting office
BUPERSINST	Bureau of Naval Personnel Instruction
BWC	battle watch captain
C2	command and control
C4	command, control, communications, computers
C5ISRT	command and control, communications, computers, cyber, intelligence, surveillance, reconnaissance, and targeting
CAC	common access card
CAG	Commander's Action Group or carrier air wing commander
CALENDARINT	calendar intelligence (informal)

CAP	crisis action planning
CARAT	Cooperation Afloat Readiness and Training
CASREP	casualty report
CC	carbon copy
C-C4ISR	counter command, control, communications, computers, intelligence, surveillance, and reconnaissance
CCDR	combatant commander (person)
CCIR	commander's critical information requirements
CCMD	combatant command (organization)
CDC	concept development conference or combat direction center or cleared defense contractor
CENTCOM	U.S. Central Command
CFT	cross-functional team
CHINFO	Chief of Naval Information
CHOP	change of operational control
CIC	combat information center
CICA	counterintelligence coordinating authority
CINCUS	Commander in Chief, U.S. Fleet
CIO	Chief Information Officer
CIP	critical intelligence parameter
CISC	Communications and Information Systems Center
C-ISRT	counterintelligence, surveillance, reconnaissance, and targeting
CLA	Chief of Legislative Affairs
CLO	chief learning officer
CMC	Commandant of the Marine Corps or Command Master Chief
CNFJ	commander, U.S. Naval Forces Japan
CNFK	commander, U.S. Naval Forces Korea
CNIC	Navy Installations Command
CNO	Chief of Naval Operations
CNO IP	CNO Intelligence Plot
CNR	Chief of Naval Research
CO	commanding officer
COA	course of action
COCOM	combatant command (authority)
COG	center of gravity
COMINCH	Commander in Chief, U.S. Fleet (obsolete)
COMMO	staff communications officer

COMNAVAIRFOR	commander, Naval Air Force
COMNAVAIRLANT	commander, Naval Air Force Atlantic
COMNAVAIRPAC	commander, Naval Air Force, U.S. Pacific Fleet
COMNAVAIRSYSCOM	commander, Naval Air Systems Command
COMNAVFORKOREA	commander, U.S. Naval Forces Korea
COMNAVRESFOR	commander, Naval Reserve Force
COMNAVRMC	commander, Naval Regional Maintenance Center
COMNAVSEASYSCOM	commander, Naval Sea Systems Command
COMNAVSO	commander, U.S. Naval Forces South
COMNAVSUPSYSCOM	commander, Naval Supply Systems Command
COMNAVSURFPAC	commander, Naval Surface Forces, U.S. Pacific Fleet
COMNAVSURLANT	commander, Naval Surface Force Atlantic
COMPACFLT	commander, U.S. Pacific Fleet
COMPLAN	communications plan
COMSEC	communications security
COMSPAWARSYSCOM	commander, Space and Naval Warfare Systems Command
COMSUBLANT	commander, Submarine Force, Atlantic
COMSUBPAC	commander, Submarine Force, U.S. Pacific Fleet
COMUSFLTFORCOM	commander, U.S. Fleet Forces Command
COMUSNAVAF	commander, U.S. Naval Forces Africa
COMUSNAVCENT	commander, U.S. Naval Forces Central Command
COMUSNAVEUR	commander, U.S. Naval Forces Europe
COMUSNAVSO	commander, U.S. Naval Forces Southern Command
COMUSPACFLT	commander, U.S. Pacific Fleet
CONPLAN	concept of operations plan
CONUS	contiguous United States
COOP	continuity of operations planning
COPS	current operations
CoS	chief of staff
CPF	commander, U.S. Pacific Fleet
CPX	command post exercise
CSG	carrier strike group
CSO	chief staff officer or combat systems officer
CVIC	carrier intelligence center
CVN	nuclear powered aircraft carrier
CVW	carrier air wing
CWC	composite warfare commander

DAO	defense attaché office
DAWIA	Defense Acquisition Workforce Improvement Act
DCNO	Deputy Chief of Naval Operations
DDG	guided missile destroyer
DESRON	destroyer squadron
DIM	daily intentions message
DIRLAUTH	direct liaison authorized
DISES	Defense Intelligence Senior Executive Service (SES-equivalent civilian grade)
DISL	Defense Intelligence Senior Level (SES-equivalent civilian grade)
DLA	Defense Logistics Agency
DLPT	Defense Language Proficiency Test
DMO	Director, Maritime Operations
DMOC	Director, Maritime Operations Center; see also MOC-D
DNI	Director of Naval Intelligence
DNS	Director, Navy staff
DoD	Department of Defense
DoDCAF	DoD Central Adjudication Facility
DoN TRACKER	DoN Tasking, Records and Consolidated Knowledge Enterprise Repository
DoN	Department of the Navy
DoN-SAPCO	DoN Special Access Program Central Office
DoN-SAPRO	DoN Sexual Assault Prevention and Response Office
DoS	Director of Staff
DoS	Department of State
DPG	defense planning guidance
DRRS	Defense Readiness Reporting System
DRRS-N	Defense Readiness Reporting System—Navy
DSD	Deputy Secretary of Defense
DTS	defense travel system
DUSN	Deputy Under Secretary of the Navy; see UNSECNAV
EA	executive assistant or executive agent
ECG	exercise control group
ED	executive director
EEFI	essential element of friendly information
EEI	essential element of information
EI&E	Assistant Secretary of the Navy (Energy, Installations and Environment)

ELOC	Executive Level Operational Level of Warfare Course
EW	electronic warfare
EXORD	execute order
FAO	foreign area officer
FAR	federal acquisition regulation
FBI	Federal Bureau of Investigation
FCC	Fleet Command Center
FDNF	forward-deployed naval force
FDO	foreign disclosure officer
FDR	foreign disclosure representative
FFC	U.S. Fleet Forces Command; see USFF
FITREP	fitness report
FLTCDR	fleet commander
FMB	Deputy Assistant Secretary of the Navy for Budget
FMC	Assistant Secretary of the Navy (Financial Management and Comptroller)
FMO	Fleet Marine Officer
FMS	foreign military sales
FMV	full motion video
FO	front office
FOIA	Freedom of Information Act
FOPS	future operations
FPA	foreign policy advisor
FPC	final planning conference
FRAGO	fragmentary order; see FRAORD
FRAORD	fragmentary order, secondary abbreviation; see FRAGO
FRTP	fleet readiness training plan
FSO	Foreign Service officer
FTC	fleet training continuum
FTX	field training exercise
FUOPS	future operations
FUPLANS	future plans
FYDP	Future Years Defense Program
GAL	global address list
GC	general counsel
GCC	geographic combatant command
GEM	ghost email

GFM	Global Force Management
GG	excepted service (civil service)
GOFO	general officer/flag officer
Green	Army or Marine Corps (informal)
GS	general schedule (civil service)
GTCC	government travel charge card
GWOT	global war on terrorism
HHQ	higher headquarters
HoN	head of Navy (to describe a foreign CNO-counterpart)
HQ	headquarters
HQMC	headquarters, Marine Corps
HRO	human resources office
HUMINT	human intelligence
HVA	high-value asset
HVU	high-value unit
IA	information assurance
IDP	individual development plan
IFR	international fleet review
IG	inspector general
INSURV	Board of Inspection and Survey
IO	information operations
IP	information professional
IPC	initial planning conference
IPOE	intelligence preparation of the operational environment
ISIC	immediate superior in command
ISR	intelligence, surveillance, and reconnaissance
ISS	International Seapower Symposium
ISSA	interservice support agreement
ISSM	information systems security manager
ISSO	information systems security officer
IT	information technology
IW	information warfare
IWC	information warfare commander
JAG	judge advocate general
JCC	joint command ship
JFACC	joint force air component commander

JFMCC	Joint Force Maritime component commander
JIC	joint intelligence center
JIOC	joint intelligence operations center
JMTC	Joint Maritime Tactics Course
JOPES	Joint Operations Planning and Execution System
JOPP	joint operation planning process
JOTS	Joint Operational Tactical System
JROC	Joint Requirements Oversight Council
JS	Joint Staff
JTF	Joint Task Force
JWICS	joint worldwide intelligence communications system
KLE	key leader engagement
KMO	knowledge management officer
LA	legislative affairs
LACM	land attack cruise missile
LCAC	air cushion landing craft
LCC	command ship
LCU	conventional landing craft
LDO	limited duty officer
LHA	amphibious assault ship; see LHD
LHD	amphibious assault ship; see LHA
LNO	liaison officer
LPD	amphibious transport dock ship
LRC	Logistics Readiness Center
LREC	language, regional expertise, and culture
LSD	amphibious dock landing ship
M&RA	Assistant Secretary of the Navy (Manpower and Reserve Affairs)
MAWS	Maritime Advanced Warfighting School
MCA	manning control authority
MCPON	Master Chief Petty Officer of the Navy
MCSC	Marine Corps Systems Command
MDA	maritime domain awareness
MDC	MSEL development conference
MET	mission essential task
MEU	Marine expeditionary unit

MFR	memorandum for the record
MFT	mission, functions, and tasks
MHA	major headquarters activity
MHQ	Maritime headquarters
MHQ w/MOC	Maritime headquarters with Maritime Operations Center
MilCon	military construction (funding)
MIOC	Maritime Intelligence Operations Center
MIP	Military Intelligence Program
MOA	memorandum of agreement
MOC	Maritime Operations Center
MOC-D	Director, Maritime Operations Center; see DMOC
MOE	measure of effectiveness
MOP	measure of performance
MOU	memorandum of understanding
MOVREP	movement report
MPC	mid-planning conference
MPG	maritime planning group
MSC	Military Sealift Command
MSEL	master scenario events list
MSOC	Maritime Staff Operators Course
MTE	man, train, equip (this term is obsolete); see OTE
MTT	mobile training team
N00	common staff code for commander
N1	common staff code for administration and personnel
N2	common staff code for intelligence
N3	common staff code for operations
N4	common staff code for logistics and maintenance
N5	common staff code for plans and policy
N6	common staff code for communications
N7	common staff code for training
NALE	naval and amphibious liaison element
NAVADMIN	Naval Administration record message
NAVAIR	Naval Air Systems Command
NAVCENT	U.S. Naval Forces Central Command
NAVEUR	U.S. Naval Forces Europe
NAVFAC	Naval Facilities Engineering Command
NAVIFOR	Naval Information Forces
NAVINSGEN	Naval Inspector General
NAVSEA	Naval Sea Systems Command

NAVSO	US. Naval Forces South
NAVSUP	Naval Supply Systems Command
NAVWAR	Naval Information Warfare Systems Command (known as SPAWAR until 2018)
NCAT	Navy Crisis Action Team
NCC	Navy Command Center or Navy Component Commander
NCCC	Navy Communications Systems Coordination Center
NCIS	Naval Criminal Investigative Service
N-code	a principal element within a staff designated with an "N" prefix office code or the director of such an element
NCR	National Capital Region
NDAA	National Defense Authorization Act
NDS	National Defense Strategy
NEC	Navy enlisted classification
NECC	Commander, Navy Expeditionary Combat Command
NETC	Naval Education and Training Command
NFC	numbered fleet commander
NFO	naval flight officer
NGO	nongovernmental organization
NIP	National Intelligence Program
NIPR	nonclassified internet protocol router network; see NIPRNet
NIPRNet	nonclassified internet protocol router network; see NIPR
NIS	Naval Investigative Service
NMCC	National Military Command Center
NMCI	Navy–Marine Corps Intranet
NNSA	National Nuclear Security Administration
NOC	Navy Operations Center
NR	Naval Reactors
NSS	National Security Strategy
NSW	naval special warfare
NTDS	Navy Tactical Data System
NTRP	Navy Tactical Reference Publication
NTTP	Navy Tactics, Techniques, and Procedures
NWP	Navy Warfare Publication
O&M	operations and maintenance (funding)
OASN/FMC	Office of the Assistant Secretary of the Navy for Financial Management and Comptroller
OCA	original classification authority

OCO	overseas contingency operations
OCONUS	outside contiguous United States
ODNI	Office of the Director of National Intelligence
OFRP	optimized fleet response plan
OGA	other government agency
OLA	Office of Legislative Affairs
ONE-Net	OCONUS Navy Enterprise Network
ONI	Office of Naval Intelligence
ONR	Office of Naval Research
OoP	order of precedence
OPCON	operational control
OPFOR	opposing force
OPINTEL	operational intelligence
OPLAN	operational plan
OPM	Office of Personnel Management
OPNAV	Office of the Chief of Naval Operations
OPNAVINST	OPNAV instruction
OPORD	operational order
ops	operations (informal)
OPSEC	operational security
OPT	operational planning team
OPTASK	operational task (order or record message)
OSBP	Office of Small Business Programs
OSD	Office of the Secretary of Defense
OTC	officer in tactical command
OTE	organize, train, equip; see MTE
PA	public affairs
PACFLT	U.S. Pacific Fleet
PAO	public affairs officer
PAS	presidentially appointed, Senate confirmed
PD	position description or principal deputy
PEO	program executive officer
PEP	professional exchange program
PFIF	Pacific Fleet Intelligence Federation
PII	personally identifiable information
PIR	priority intelligence requirement
PKI	public key infrastructure
PLAD	plain language address
PM	program manager

PMS	planned maintenance system
PNAT	Pacific Naval Aggressor Team
POC	point of contact
POL	petroleum, oil, and lubricants
POLAD	political advisor
POM	Program Objective Memorandum
PPBE(S)	planning, programming, budgeting, and execution (system)
PPR	preplanned response
PPT	PowerPoint
PRC	People's Republic of China
PSA	principal staff assistant
PTDO	performing the duties of
RAH	read ahead
RD&A	Assistant Secretary of the Navy (Research, Development, and Acquisition)
RF	radio frequency
RFI	request for information
RMT	religious ministry teams
RN	Royal Navy (UK)
ROC/POE	Required Operational Capability/Projected Operational Environment
ROE	rules of engagement
RSAC	Resource and Situational Awareness Center
RSOI	reception, staging, onward movement, and integration
SAG	surface action group
SAP	special access program
SAPR	Sexual Assault Prevention and Response program
SARC	sexual assault response coordinator
SATCOM	satellite communications
SCC	sea combat commander
SCI	sensitive compartmented information
SCIF	sensitive compartmented information facility
SCIO	staff counterintelligence officer
SD	Secretary of Defense; see SECDEF
SEA	senior enlisted advisor
SECDEF	Secretary of Defense; see SD
SECNAV	Secretary of the Navy; see SN

Secretariat	Office of the Secretary of the Navy
SEL	senior enlisted leader
SELRES	selected reserve
SES	Senior Executive Service
SIPR	secret internet protocol router network; see SIPRNet
SIPRNet	secret internet protocol router network; see SIPR
SL	senior level (SES-equivalent civilian grade)
SLBM	submarine-launched ballistic missile
SME	subject matter expert
SMEE	subject matter expert exchange
SMRD	Shore Manpower Requirements Determination
SN	Secretary of the Navy; see SECNAV
SNDL	Standard Navy Distribution List
SOE	schedule of events
SOFA	status-of-forces agreement
SOP	standard operating procedure
SORM	standard organization and regulations manual
SORTS	Status of Resources and Training System
SPAWAR	Naval Information Warfare Systems Command (known as NAVWAR as of 2018)
SSBN	ballistic missile submarine, nuclear powered
SSES	ship's signals exploitation space
SSIC	Standard Subject Identification Code
SSO	special security officer
ST	senior technical (SES-equivalent civilian grade)
STWC	strike warfare commander
SUBOPAUTH	submarine operating authority
SURFOR	surface forces
SUWC	surface warfare commander
SWO	surface warfare officer
SYSCOM	systems command
TACON	tactical control
TASW	theater antisubmarine warfare
TDY	temporary duty
TF	task force
TFCC	Tactical Flag Command Center
TG	task group
TIS	transfer in status
T-JFMCC	Theater Joint Force Maritime component commander

TOA	total obligation authority
TOW	training objectives workshop
TPFDD	time phased force deployment data
TTX	table-top exercise
TUSWC	theater undersea warfare commander
TYCOM	type commander
UCMJ	Uniform Code of Military Justice
UIC	unit identification code
UNODIR	unless otherwise directed
UNSECNAV	Under Secretary of the Navy; see DUSUN
U.S.C.	U.S. Code
USFF	U.S. Fleet Forces Command; see FFC
USG	U.S. government
USN	U.S. Navy
USNS	U.S. naval ship
USS	U.S. ship
USTRANSCOM	U.S. Transportation Command
UWE	Undersea Warfare Enterprise
VCNO	Vice Chief of Naval Operations
VTC	video teleconference
WESTPAC	Western Pacific
XO	executive officer
YN	yeoman

Introduction

So you have orders to a staff. Congratulations!

If you are like most U.S. Navy officers, you have an ambivalent view of staff duty. The culture of the U.S. Navy focuses on our operational forces. Sea duty is the touchstone of our professional identity. Our founding narrative centers on the six frigates commissioned in the 1790s. Led by captains such as Decatur, Bainbridge, and Preble, they sailed over the horizon, orders in hand, to represent and defend the new nation. Having defeated Barbary pirates and bested individual ships of the British Royal Navy—then the most powerful navy in the world—their names have been preserved and honored for more than two centuries. It is hard for us to imagine any of them answering to a staff.

Good Navy officers want to be at sea, and in as independent and responsible a role as possible.

Nonetheless, the way the U.S. Navy fights—the way it must fight to defend our nation—is impossible without the command and control provided by the naval staff structure. Military staffs are a relatively new invention, born of necessity in the face of the complexities of modern warfare. Our counterparts in the ground and air forces came to this realization generations ago and embraced both the need for and the requirements of staff work as an essential part of victory. Our Navy has had a more complicated relationship with its staffs. Even while advocating for more effective naval administration, RADM Alfred Thayer Mahan warned that "the habit of the arm-chair easily prevails over that of the quarter-deck; it is more comfortable."[1] The Navy has often dismissed the impact of its staffs even when they have gotten their challenging work nearly perfect.

In that light, this book has two purposes.

1

The first is simply to convince you that what Navy staffs do matters—often profoundly—to our service and to our success at sea. The law that creates the U.S. Navy states that it exists "primarily for prompt and sustained combat . . . at sea."[2] Staffs do not fight, but they set the stage for the fight. The Navy that sails forth tomorrow will be the product of decades-old staff work; it will be trained to a standard established by a staff to execute tactics designed by a host of other specialized staffs, all to execute a plan conceived and written by yet another staff. Staffs might not win the fight, but bad staff work can lose it before the first shot is fired. To understand how good staff work happens, this book will walk through how we got to where we are, the reasons that our staffs exist as they do, the impact they have on our Navy, and how you as a Navy leader can use a staff to make meaningful and enduring change.

The second purpose of this volume is to arm you to function effectively within a staff. No competent naval officer would go to operational command without careful preparation. Indeed, any operational assignment will usually include formal schooling on the platform and its weapons and sensors, along with a hundred ways to teach the informal norms and expectations of the operational environment, even down to what sea stories are considered worth telling in our wardrooms, clubs, and ready rooms. But when was the last time you had shipmates together swapping staff stories? Staff duty uses a different set of tools, has its own formal and informal expectations, and offers unique opportunities, challenges, and pitfalls. Many officers arrive on staff with no idea of the tools at hand, but the best officers work to understand those tools before they report on board.

Along the way, the path will be marked with vignettes, or sea stories. Like buoys (or wrecks) on a chart, they serve to mark our course. They also remind us that some of our greatest naval leaders have made an impact serving in and leading staffs.

One of the reasons that a Navy Staff Officer's Guide has not been attempted before is the complexity and diversity of Navy staffs. Consider the different experiences and needs of

- an unrestricted line lieutenant on a destroyer squadron (DESRON) staff, someone who is comparatively junior and learning to think beyond the needs of a single unit for the first time;

- a post-department-head lieutenant commander joining a numbered fleet staff and tasked with defining how the full range of maritime power fights at the operational level of war;

- the senior commander who has dodged staff duty, but who is now going to the Pentagon to join the Office of the Chief of Naval Operations (OPNAV) staff, and who is suddenly in the midst of shaping the Navy that will exist long after they have retired; and

- the captain arriving at a systems command, and who is expected to be the voice of the fleet to an audience of hundreds of systems developers and scientists.

While the mission of each of these staffs is different, there are common elements to how staff officers function and succeed. Effective coordination, clear communication, and an understanding of the commander and their mission remain central to the staff experience. That said, part of this volume will consider the unique elements of each type of Navy staff, which is an understanding that should be part of every officer's tool kit.

Readers familiar with the U.S. Naval Institute's Blue & Gold Professional Series, including such excellent works as *Watch Officer's Guide* and *Command at Sea*, will find this volume to be slightly different. This book is not intended as a reference. Staffs excel at generating paperwork, and there are plenty of directives, instructions, and doctrine that cover the official details of each staff. This volume will be less formal and will focus on the best practices and hard-won experience of Navy officers tasked with turning these instructions into action for the service.

It is worth noting that service on joint staffs is also an essential part of how our Navy works. Since the passage of the Goldwater-Nicholas Department of Defense Reorganization Act of 1986, service on joint staffs has gone from career-limiting anomaly to a routine and important part of a Navy officer's career progression. Much of this book should be useful to officers in joint assignments. That said, the joint world has a somewhat different culture and is already served by a number of staff guides, both formal and informal. Several of these are found in the Further Reading list at the end of this book.

Whether your assignment represents an eagerly sought opportunity or a necessary step in your career progression, duty on a Navy staff can have a profound and positive impact on both you and the Navy. There is opportunity in staff work: opportunity for impact, for growth, for learning, and for personal success. When you do go back to the fleet, you will have a better understanding of the guidance and process that makes it go. Embrace it and make a difference for our Navy.

Let's get under way.

CHAPTER 1

What Is a Navy Staff?

Grouping Navy staffs together is a bit like describing mammals as a group. The category describes a breathtaking diversity of life, but also a diversity bound together by common elements.

At the most fundamental level, a Navy staff is an administrative structure designed to help a commander carry out the responsibilities of command that extend beyond a single unit. A staff has only two purposes—to inform the commander, and to exercise some element of the commander's authority. Thus, the size and structure of any staff flows from the command responsibility entrusted to the commander.

While each staff was created and developed over years for a multitude of reasons, the structure of a staff should be guided by the basic principles stated in the "Standard Organization and Regulations of the U.S. Navy": "The requirements for battle shall be the primary basis for unit organization."[1]

The commander's role in battle, directly or indirectly, must be the foundation of any staff. That role will then drive the basic characteristics of the staff: focus, placement, size, time horizon, and permanence.

Focus

Some staffs have direct line authority over combat operations. For these staffs, clear lines of authority, speed of decision, and tight communications are essential. Other staffs have direct authority over support functions, such as maintenance or basing. These staffs will focus on integration between support elements and combat forces, producing partnerships and liaison elements. Other staffs have direct authority only in a highly specialized arena, such as the acquisition of a single complex weapons system. These staffs cultivate expert knowledge and apply it to decisions that will shape Navy forces for decades.

Sometimes, as will be discussed later, a staff will have a foot in several camps, directing both the operations and maintenance of a force. In these cases, the natural habit of naval commanders is to focus on current operations (COPS); their staff needs to ensure to the maximum extent possible that the commander addresses all aspects of their responsibilities.

Placement

Navy commanders love being at sea. The image of exercising command at sea is traditionally more glamorous and prized among seniors, and any exceptions, such as FADM Chester Nimitz, are rare. However, many Navy staff missions are best executed from shore, often in proximity to the other commanders and commands that share the mission or that impact the commander's success. Later in this book we will talk at length about the benefit and challenges of exercising command from both environments.

Size

Staffs come in all sizes, from the Navy staff in the Pentagon to the staff of the smallest destroyer squadron (DESRON). Each will have a significantly different feel based on size, and yet all believe they are undermanned for their tasks.

Staff Growth

It is an iron-clad rule that staffs are under pressure to grow. This dynamic creates a classic case where rational individual decisions cumulate in an irrational outcome. The operating environment grows more complex, new missions are added, and any rational staff officer will seek help in the form of more hands on the rope. Usually, that perceived need produces no results. Once in a blue moon, however, it produces a new billet, a new office, or a new staff code. Over years, these results accumulate, and staffs grow larger.

Afloat staffs have the constraint of fitting onboard an afloat platform. While the Navy has shoehorned more and more staff members on its flagships, there is usually recognition of some upper limit. Ashore, it is a different story.

Consider Third Fleet as an example. In World War II numbered fleets were created to plan and execute major combat operations. At the end of World War II, Third Fleet under ADM William "Bull" Halsey was, in the words of FADM Ernest J. King, "the greatest mass of sea power ever assembled."[2] Planning for the invasion of Japan contemplated more than three thousand vessels participating in the operation. At the time, the Third Fleet staff mustered fifty-six officers. Most of these were junior officers tasked with keeping the flag plot and manually coding and decoding the most sensitive messages, a task that naval regulations required be performed by a commissioned officer.

Today, Third Fleet operates from a complex of buildings on Point Loma, near San Diego, California. The staff supports the readiness and training of naval forces based on the West Coast, as well as commanding operations in the eastern Pacific and selected operations beyond. Its headquarters staff musters several hundred officers, Sailors, and civilians. Certainly, its scope of responsibility has changed, but the requirements of well less than two hundred ships in 2020 do not exceed by many times those of thousands of ships in combat in 1945.

Every staff officer should be familiar with Van Creveld's Law: "Confronted with a task and having less information available than is needed to perform that task, an organization may react in either of two ways. . . . [It may] increase its information-processing capability [or] design the organization . . . to enable it to operate on the basis of less information. These approaches are exhaustive; no others are conceivable."[3]

The challenge is that "the former approach will lead to a multiplication of communications channels (vertical, horizontal, or both) and to an increase in the size and complexity of the central directing organ [i.e.: the staff]."[4] These staffs of ever-increasing complexity eventually fail under the friction of their own processes. In combat, they are defeated by a more agile enemy who manages uncertainty better and who makes faster, timelier decisions. In peacetime, they become the staid bureaucracy that prevents adaptation and impedes the commanders they are supposed to enable.

Later in this book, we will discuss the mechanisms by which Navy staffs assess their personnel needs and control growth. The overarching rule, however, should be to assume that the cumulative impact of decisions made with good intent have made any staff too large until proven otherwise.

Time Horizon

The time horizon of their decisions is arguably the most critical element that distinguishes staffs from one another. It is easiest to understand when contrasted between a tactical-level staff, such as a DESRON focused on current operations, and the Navy staff, focused on multiple five-year budget cycles. Even within categories of staffs, time will be a significant discriminant. For example, a DESRON conducting underway operations may be focused on the present moment to the next day, with the next week being a distant consideration. The fleet staff, however, will properly focus on the next week to next month, aligning the pieces to support execution by subordinate commanders.

Permanence

Some staffs, by their nature, have permanent and largely unchanging relationships up and down the chain of command. For example, a staff overseeing shore installations is likely to have the same higher headquarters for decades. Similarly, changes in its subordinate relationships will be rare. However, a deploying staff may shift through several chains of command in a single deployment. A fleet staff permanently assigned to a region will have rotational forces moving in and out of its control. This variability places a staff emphasis on curating and deliberately transferring knowledge to units as they arrive.

Early Navy Staffs

When the U.S. Navy first began, there was little need of a staff. Most U.S. Navy officers were familiar with the command style of the Royal Navy, having either served with or fought them—and sometimes both—over their careers. During this era, the man, train, and equip (MTE) (now called organize, train, equip, or OTE) functions of the Royal Navy were vested in a group of commissioners called the Naval Board. The Naval Board was essentially a civilian institution. Operational issues were entrusted to a Lord High Admiral. For much of the seventeenth and eighteenth centuries, the role of Lord High Admiral was not given to a single person, but rather was held in commission, with the roles divided among a group of senior officers. As befit a monarchy, the entire apparatus existed by royal fiat, with Parliament weighing in only on financial topics and occasional issues of naval discipline.

Operational forces were placed under a series of flag officers, who often were assigned a geographic area. Within their area, they directed operations through written orders passed by smaller units used as couriers or left in port for units arriving. At close range, visual signals were used. Commanders in Chief of some stations were ashore, as evidenced by the number of former British colonies having an Admiralty House in their historic districts. When afloat, flag officers usually did not have a formal staff. At best, they would have the assistance of a small number of directly assigned personnel. These would include a flag lieutenant, whose primary job was literally managing the signal flags that were so essential to command and control (C2) in combat; and a flag captain. The flag captain commanded the flagship, relieving the admiral of the need to manage a large combatant as well as a fleet.

The new U.S. Navy, at a fraction of the size of the Royal Navy, saw little need for such complexity. In 1802 CAPT Thomas Truxton was proposed to command U.S. Navy forces ordered to the Mediterranean to fight the Barbary pirates. A privateer during the Revolutionary War and accomplished merchant captain, Truxton had distinguished himself in command of USS *Constitution* during the Quasi-War with France. Faced with the challenge of fitting out and commanding USS *Chesapeake* as well as commanding a squadron, the prickly Truxton made it clear he would resign if not provided with a flag captain. The Navy Department denied his request for a flag captain, accepted his resignation, and sent a less qualified officer in his place.

Ashore, naval administration consisted of the Secretary of the Navy (SECNAV) and a handful of civilian clerks. It was not until the closing days of the War of 1812 that Congress created a Board of Navy Commissioners consisting of three senior captains. The board was immediately thrown into controversy, as the law stated the board would handle the "construction, armament, equipment, and employment, of vessels of war."[5] The SECNAV and President James Madison saw the board's control over naval operations as an infringement on their constitutional responsibilities and restricted the board to administrative issues. Today the board is largely remembered for its support (or lack of support) for what were then cutting-edge emerging technologies, such as rifled cannon and steam propulsion.

In 1842 this ossified and heavily politicized structure was replaced with five bureaus; (1) shipyards and docks; (2) ordnance; (3) construction, equipment, and repair; (4) medicine; and (5) supply. Each was to be headed by a professional expert who was appointed by the President, confirmed by the Senate, and answerable to the SECNAV. The creation of the bureaus ushered in a generational change and the beginning of the professionalization of the naval service. The establishment of the U.S. Naval Academy also dates from this era. The fleet, of course, viewed these changes through a critical eye, often referring to the Department of Construction, Equipment, and Repair as the Bureau of Destruction and Despair.[6]

Today, the bureaus are remembered as the hidebound elements that were replaced by the forerunner of today's modern staff structure. Nonetheless, in 1842 the bureaus represented a significant reform. What they lacked, however, was a mechanism for planning and coordination across the entire service. Each bureau chief was empowered to act independently within their area of responsibility, with only the SECNAV in a position to enforce unity of effort.

The demands of the Civil War increased the number of bureaus from five to eight. The bureaus focused on the herculean task of shifting a small constabulary navy to a major force capable of both a sustained blockade of Southern ports and extensive littoral combat operations. Meanwhile, combat operations functioned much as they had half a century before, with the SECNAV creating flotillas and squadrons and assigning them to conduct operations in specific geographic areas. Anticipation of the epic battle between the ironclads USS *Monitor* and the captured USS *Merrimack* saw Assistant Secretary Gustavus Fox launch himself from Washington to Hampton in an effort to exercise on-scene command.

After the Civil War, the Navy returned to the familiar pattern of single ships conducting operations on distant stations, while the bureau structure struggled to make the best of limited budgets and rapid technological change. Nonetheless, innovators in the ranks saw that the future lay less in protection of trade and more in sea control. That change meant large naval formations cruising, maneuvering, and fighting as a unit against other naval forces. These progressive elements ultimately founded the Naval War College and the Office of Naval Intelligence (ONI), and introduced new technologies into the fleet. When the nation decided to build a new steel navy, the Navy was ready to use it in every way, except in its staff structures.

The new steel navy emerged from the Spanish-American War (1898) acclaimed for brilliant victories at Santiago and Manila Bay. Professionals, however, knew these victories were won despite shortcomings in C2. During the war, Secretary of the Navy John Davis Long established a Naval War Board. The board was something of a dream team, including as it did both Alfred Thayer Mahan and Assistant Secretary of the Navy Theodore Roosevelt. Providing recommendations to the secretary for the movement of naval forces during the conflict, it was acknowledged as answering a key deficiency in U.S. naval organization. In 1900 Secretary Long established the General Board of the Navy, making the arrangement permanent. With no standing in law, the General Board was a creature of the secretary, its scope and authority deriving from the secretary's mandate.

While recent historians have argued that the General Board functioned in practice as a strategic planning staff, it could not fulfill the need for control of operations.[7] In this realm, the need for a naval staff was clear.

The Emergence of a Professional Staff

It is difficult at the distance of more than a century to understand the profound resistance in the United States and in the U.S. Navy to the adoption of a modern staff structure. The word "staff" in the sense of a dedicated element to assist the commander in the exercise of authority has its roots deep in military history. Standard works on the subject suggest that precursors to the modern military staff could be found in ancient Assyria, Egypt, and Greece. The dramatic victories of King Gustavus Adolphus of Sweden in the Thirty Years War (1618–48) were enabled in part by a rudimentary staff structure. The modern staff system, however, grows from two intertwined branches: France and Prussia.

The mass armies Napoleon created and led in his multidecade campaign to subjugate Europe were guided by the *état-major*. This great general headquarters served both as Napoleon's strategic command for the French nation and as the senior operational staff during his campaigns. It is in this operational staff element that we first see the division of command functions by section, with distinct elements for operations, intelligence, fires, supply, and so on. Indeed, this innovation is so closely associated with the French army in this period that U.S. Navy officers today routinely call the traditional staff structure "Napoleonic."

The Prussian army fared badly during the Napoleonic wars. In defeat, they and the later German militaries adopted the Napoleonic structure with the passion of the underdog, turned it into a deliberate and professional process, and then adapted it to the emerging demands of modern industrial warfare. By 1828 the Prussian staff had put in place all the elements of the modern staff system:

> A formal professional education system for command and staff duty;
> Delegated authority to the staff to issue orders in the name of the commander;
> Set processes for issues to be handled by a designated staff element depending on their nature;
> Authority to observe and review how subordinate commands execute the orders of the higher headquarters.[8]

By the Franco-Prussian War of 1870–71, the Prussian army that defeated France in mere days had added a dedicated deliberate planning element. Effectively exploiting telegraph communication and the mobility of the new railroads, that army established a tempo of mobilization and operations that the French army could not match.

U.S. Navy reformers of the late nineteenth century knew of these developments and had thought about how changes in the tempo of naval warfare and the impact of modern communications paralleled those on land. The idea of a general staff–like structure, however, conflicted with deeply held American views about civilian control of the military and faith in the effectiveness of patriotic amateur improvisation.

The U.S. Army had experienced similar dysfunctions during the Spanish-American War, when it tried to command operations in two hemispheres using a system designed for military operations inside the continental United States. Under the visionary Secretary of War Elihu Root, the Army adopted a staff structure in 1903. The commanding general of the Army became the Army Chief of Staff (CoS), the title he bears today, at the head of a dedicated staff of forty-four officers.

The establishment of the position of Chief of Naval Operations (CNO) in 1915 was largely a tactical measure taken by Secretary of the Navy Josephus Daniels to forestall more sweeping reforms. As calls from naval reformers for a staff system grew more strident, Daniels crafted congressional language that created a rear admiral as CNO. The CNO would control fleet operations and create war plans, but could not issue orders except through the SECNAV. Daniels then chose as the first CNO not a reformer, but ADM William S. Benson, a well-regarded but moderate officer.

Benson's approach to the new office remains a lesson in how to achieve effective long-term institutional change in difficult circumstances. He realized that his job was a compromise position, created without a staff and unable to provide the forceful expert direction to naval operations that his reform-minded colleagues advocated. For him, the path to success lay in serving his boss, a SECNAV jealous of his right to control naval operations. In the face of sometimes personal attacks from other officers, Benson remained scrupulously loyal to Daniels in public. In private, Benson sought to create trust with Daniels, bridging between the secretary and the bureau chiefs and acting to align their efforts.

As a result of Benson's bridge building, he was in a position of trust when war in Europe pushed America into preparing for war. By 1916 Congress had made the CNO a four-star admiral, authorized a dedicated CNO staff, and allowed the CNO to issue orders on behalf of, rather than via, the SECNAV. Daniels offered no objections.

American entry into World War I offered a new challenge to the command of naval forces: fighting as part of a coalition. The U.S. Navy ultimately deployed almost four hundred ships to the European war zone, along with

When it was not yet three years old, the Navy staff confronted the challenges of World War I. Here, civilians work alongside male and female Sailors around 1919. *Naval History and Heritage Command*

shore-based patrol and bombing aircraft and the material for the largest mining operation ever conducted to that time. How to C2 these forces was a matter of controversy early in the war. The existing Atlantic Fleet staff presumed that they would be deployed to Europe as the command staff running operations. However, shortly before the U.S. declaration of war, RADM William S. Sims was dispatched to London on a special mission to investigate Allied needs and to report how U.S. Navy forces could best support the war. Sims, a reform-minded officer with long experience working with the Royal Navy, advocated integrating U.S. Navy forces into the Royal Navy command structure to the maximum extent possible. Sims's recommendations had both practical and political advantages. Upon declaration of war, Sims found himself unexpectedly designated as commander, U.S. Naval Forces in Europe. Rather than use an existing staff, Sims of necessity created a staff from whole cloth in London. As major elements of the U.S. Navy arrived in European waters, they were integrated into the British command structure as organic elements. Thus, the Battleship Division of the Atlantic Fleet under ADM Hugh Rodman served as the Sixth Battleship Division of the Royal Navy's Grand Fleet in the last year of the war.

The end of the war pushed the U.S. Navy into a period of downsizing and economy. The experience of war, however, had changed the mindset of the fleet, removing all doubt that the United States would both protect global interests and maintain a battle force charged with engaging enemy naval forces at sea. The war had illustrated the importance of concentrating naval power, and in 1922 the Navy created a single unified fleet structure. Commander in Chief, U.S. Fleet, or CINCUS, replaced both the Atlantic Fleet and the Pacific Fleet as the sole commander with both operational and administrative control (authority) (ADCON) over the bulk of the Navy. Maneuver elements were organized by major mission—for example, the Battle Fleet and the Scouting Fleet—and were placed directly under CINCUS.[9]

Despite the new arrangement, CNO retained an operational focus. CINCUS was subordinate to the CNO, and the Navy staff continued to conduct administration and strategic planning. CNO also retained direct control of logistics forces and the Asiatic Squadron, an arrangement that reflected the squadron's mission of providing presence in a politically charged region rather than combat power integrated with the wider fleet.

In 1923 the Navy began the Fleet Problem exercise series, which continued through 1940. These major fleet exercises allowed the bulk of the Navy to train and maneuver as a single force in a unique and innovative free-play environment. The CNO remained the ultimate operational authority for these operations, selecting which operational challenges the fleet would address.

In 1940 the Fleet Problem concluded with the Battle Force in Pearl Harbor, Hawaii. Concerned by the growing Japanese threat, President Roosevelt ordered the fleet, and thus CINCUS and staff, to remain in Hawaii indefinitely. The decision was made piecemeal over several months, with the fleet being told it would remain in Hawaii for a short period, then told it would remain until further notice. Since the movement was not a planned permanent change of home port, the disruption to the fleet was considerable. Fleet commander ADM James O. Richardson disagreed with the decision, concerned about both the fleet's vulnerability in a forward position and the lack of infrastructure in Hawaii to support his many units. His pointed objections ultimately led President Roosevelt to remove him from command in early 1941. The fleet remained in Pearl Harbor until the start of World War II. With the bulk of fleet permanently in the Pacific, it made sense to again bifurcate the Atlantic and Pacific command structures, and the Atlantic Fleet was reestablished under ADM King in February 1941.

A Staff for a Global Navy

By 7 December 1941, the U.S. Navy comprised three fleets—the Asiatic Fleet, Pacific Fleet, and Atlantic Fleet—with ADM Husband Kimmel in Pearl Harbor, Hawaii, designated as CINCUS.[10] Thrust into a global war, the Navy needed a command structure that also had a global view. Thus, in the opening months of the war ADM King was detached from Atlantic Fleet and moved to Washington, DC, to act as a single operational commander for global fleet operations. Historians often note that the standard Navy abbreviation of his new position was pronounced "sink us," making it one of the more ironic titles in U.S. Navy history. ADM King wasted no time changing the official abbreviation of his title to COMINCH (Commander in Chief).

In March 1942 ADM King was appointed as CNO while retaining his role as COMINCH. Throughout the war, ADM King maintained two separate staffs, one for each of his major command roles. Where some would have seen combining the two staffs as a sensible economy measure, King saw the two roles as requiring different processes and mindset. The CNO staff was required to administer the construction, training, and organization of the massive naval forces needed to win the war. In contrast, the COMINCH staff was officially sea duty, tied to the tempo of ongoing combat operations.

Despite his sweeping authority, ADM King was a passionate advocate of decentralized C2. His approach as COMINCH was to provide his fleet commanders with intent and campaign priorities, leaving them latitude in operational design, detailed planning, and execution. The exception to this rule was found in the strategic antisubmarine warfare (ASW) campaign in the Atlantic. The COMINCH Combat Intelligence Division had access to sensitive intelligence gained from breaking the German Enigma cipher machine. The decision to act on this information carried the risk of revealing this critical intelligence source, making each tactical engagement potentially a strategic decision. In response, King created the Tenth Fleet as an operational element of COMINCH. Tenth Fleet routed convoys, taking care to avoid areas of German submarine operations where possible. However, Tenth Fleet had no permanently assigned forces. When offensive ASW action was ordered, Tenth Fleet would take control of forces and conduct the operation. Once the operation concluded, the task force would be dissolved.[11]

Meanwhile, in the Pacific, ADM Nimitz assumed command from the ill-fated Admiral Kimmel. With the duty of CINCUS moved to Washington, Nimitz could focus on the war against Japan.

Interestingly, both King and Nimitz wanted to retain the option for their staffs to embark a flagship. This desire created a conflict between the size constraints of a flagship and the need for larger staffs to control forces of enormous complexity. In the case of COMINCH, the staff was divided between personnel on the staff and personnel attached to the headquarters. The official staff remained under the flagship limit even while the total size of the team grew to more than five hundred personnel. This distinction also allowed female Sailors, who were at the time not permitted on sea duty, to serve in these staffs. Neither staff would go afloat during the war, though Nimitz did take a large part of his core staff to Guam as a forward headquarters later in the conflict.

The Confidence of the Commander: Nimitz and His Staff

When the flying boat carrying Admiral Nimitz landed in Pearl Harbor, Hawaii, on Christmas Day, 1941, the normally clear blue Hawaiian waters were littered with debris. "A miasma of black oil, charred wood, blistered paint, and burned and rotting bodies" hung in the air.[12] Ashore, Nimitz found a staff that was similarly in shambles. The Pacific Fleet staff had been hastily formed after the move of the fleet to Hawaii in 1940. Built as an afloat staff, they had been operating in temporary spaces ashore on 7 December. USS *Pennsylvania*, their flagship, had been in drydock maintenance at Pearl Harbor Naval Shipyard during the attack. When the commander, Admiral Kimmel, was removed from command, deputy commander VADM William S. Pye had become acting fleet commander. In the dark days after the attack, he struggled to find the line between risk and prudence. Concerned about potential losses, he recalled ships that had been sent to assist Wake Island, dooming its heroic garrison to fall before a larger Japanese force. With the arrival of the new commander, most of the staff expected to be fired.

Hours after his change of command, Nimitz called together his staff ... and fired no one.

Nimitz had served as chief of the Bureau of Navigation before the war. There, he had controlled detailing in a role analogous to today's Naval Personnel Command. Forming a new fleet staff had been a high-profile effort, and he had monitored the assignment of officers to the newly established Pacific Fleet staff. He knew they represented some of the best available talent in the Navy. He also realized that they had an awareness of the situation that would take weeks or months for new personnel to learn.

Instead of firing them, Nimitz set out to restore their confidence, telling them that he knew their professional reputations and trusted them to help him through the coming years of war.

As a result, the Pacific Fleet staff that enabled the critical U.S. victory at Midway was largely the same staff that had watched its fleet burn less than six months before, able to do so because a new commander made clear his confidence in the staff and its work.

It is difficult to comprehend the massive explosion in the size of the U.S. Navy in these years. Using commissioned officers as an indicator, the U.S. Navy increased from 13,162 officers in July 1940, to 38,601 on 7 December 1941, at the time of the attack on Pearl Harbor. Within a year, that number had spiked to 118,038. By the end of the war, the U.S. Navy had more than 325,000 officers.[13]

By late 1942, it was apparent to ADM King that the scope of naval operations, especially in the Pacific, would require dedicated staffs capable of focusing for a time on a specific operation or campaign. On 19 February 1943, King issued COMINCH order 192200, directing that, "EFFECTIVE NOON GCT [Greenwich Civil Time] MARCH 15 US

FLEET WILL COMPRISE NUMBERED FLEETS WITH TASK FORCE ORGANIZATION." King's order established the convention that even-numbered fleets served in the Atlantic, while odd numbered fleets serve in the Pacific.[14] With the exception of ADM King's Tenth Fleet, these were afloat commands, sized to embark a battleship or heavy cruiser as their flagship. The most distinctive numbered fleet command arrangement was found in the Pacific, where Third Fleet under ADM Halsey and Fifth Fleet under ADM Raymond Spruance alternated command of the central Pacific island-hopping campaign. Commanding the same set of forces, one staff would conduct an operation while the other staff planned the next move in the campaign. Seventh Fleet was dedicated to support GEN Douglas MacArthur's operations, particularly landing in the Solomons and Philippines.

After World War II, the most senior levels of the Navy were impacted by the creation of the Department of Defense (DoD) in 1947. The position of SECNAV, previously a cabinet position, became a senior civilian under the new cabinet-level Secretary of Defense. Navy operational forces, while drastically reduced from their World War II numbers, remained larger than ever before in peacetime. As a result, the numbered fleet structure, intended as a wartime expedient, became permanent, while the CNO retained operational authority over the entire fleet structure.

Two of the most significant post–World War II Navy staff creations were themselves efforts to cut through the existing staff structure to deliver urgent results.

In 1947, less than two years after the first use of atomic weapons in warfare, CAPT Hyman Rickover convinced FADM Nimitz of the potential of submarine nuclear propulsion. Rickover was made head of a new branch of the Bureau of Ships. He shortly combined that Navy role with the civilian title of Naval Reactors Branch of the Atomic Energy Commission. Under Rickover's leadership, USS *Nautilus* went under way on nuclear power in 1954. Naval Reactors' dual reporting responsibility to both the Navy and the Department of Energy remains a unique feature of the Navy nuclear power program today.

In 1955 it appeared that Soviet nuclear forces threatened to overwhelm the United States. As a result, the Navy received a presidential task to create a practical fleet ballistic missile as rapidly as possible. ADM Arleigh Burke selected RADM Bill Raborn to head the new Special Program Office and empowered him with what was essentially a bureaucratic letter of marque. Secretary of the Navy Thomas S. Gates added his authority to the effort, stating officially that the importance of the program justified violating the normal chain of command. ADM Raborn made good use of his authority, delivering the first Polaris submarine-launched ballistic missile (SLBM) only four years after the program began.

The operational history of the U.S. Navy after 1947 is largely a tale of Navy staffs interacting with the joint command structure. Officers with short memories date the Navy's experience with joint command to 1986. In fact, joint command structures were the main area of contention between the Army and the Navy during World War II, and continued as an issue in the Korean, Vietnam, and Cold War eras.

Joint Duty

Today, Navy officers know that time in joint assignments is a requirement for professional development and advancement to flag rank. The requirement for joint duty as part of an officer's professional development originated with the Goldwater-Nichols Act of 1986. Goldwater-Nichols was itself a reaction to multiple perceived failures in the joint command process between 1980 and 1983:

- Operation Eagle Claw, 1980. A joint force operating from U.S. Navy platforms attempted to move more than five hundred miles inland to rescue fifty-two American hostages being held at the U.S. Embassy in Tehran, Iran. The operation failed in part because of confusion between what were essentially four independent on-scene commanders.

- Operation Urgent Fury, 1983. A joint force invaded the Caribbean island nation of Grenada to rescue U.S. medical students threatened by a Cuban-backed Marxist coup. While successful, the operation was hampered by the inability of individual units to communicate and coordinate across service boundaries. In one notorious incident, an Army officer used his civilian AT&T calling card to place an international phone call back to his home base in the continental

United States, trying to get them to reach nearby Navy elements. Such failures could easily have been fatal in a more challenging operation.

- Beirut Marine Barracks Bombing, 1983. Sent as peacekeepers in the midst of a Lebanese civil war, a U.S. Marine base was attacked by a suicide truck bomb that killed 241 U.S. service members. Subsequent investigations revealed that the chain of command, both formally and in practice, made it unclear who was responsible for the force protection of the Marines ashore.

Different service cultures and the natural friction of operations mean that the U.S. military's joint approach to warfare continues to be a source of lively debate. What cannot be disputed, however, is the fundamental need to be able to understand and integrate all the military tools at our disposal within a clear chain of command in combat; these are the roots of today's joint duty requirements.

The wars fought by the United States after the 1986 Goldwater-Nichols reforms have been land wars, with naval forces enjoying overwhelming overmatch of any adversary at sea. In almost every case, the sea has been a secure sanctuary for projecting power ashore. As a result, the command structures that have grown up in the past thirty years—and the Navy staffs that have integrated with them—have been optimized for this style of joint warfare.

With the return of Great Power competitors such as the People's Republic of China and Russia, the sea is no longer a sanctuary, and high-end naval combat at sea is no longer merely a historic topic. U.S. Navy staffs face the challenge of commanding naval power in a new and more complex environment, normally while integrating effectively into complex joint command structures. In 2016, CNO ADM Richardson wrote that these new challenges could not be answered by individual carrier strike groups (CSGs) or formations. Rather, they require the coordinated operation of the full range of naval power—a change that requires the Navy to think of the fleet as its combat maneuver element. Commanding and controlling this range of forces across half the earth is a challenge of daunting complexity.

It is the job of a Navy staff.

CHAPTER 2

The Commander

The staff is a creature of its commander.

Every staff exists to inform a commander and to execute some part of that commander's authorities and responsibilities on their behalf. There is no other purpose for its existence, whether it is a DESRON staff that will fit comfortably around a table, or the staff of the sprawling Office of the Chief of Naval Operations (OPNAV).

Mariners since the days of the first sailing ships have known that a ship and its master are intertwined in a way that few landsmen can understand. The captain's style of command, the ship's identity, and the smartness and professional personality of the crew all become a single organic identity, the lens through which the ship faces the dangers of the sea and the challenges of its mission. It would never occur to a naval officer to suggest that a ship had an identity apart from its commander, or that a competent commanding officer would not inherently impress their style, personality, and way of doing business on their ship.

Send the same hard-charging officers to staff duty, however, and they suddenly doubt that the officer at the top of the command has the tools to drive the establishment in the directions it should go. Nonsense.

Every competent naval officer prepares thoughtfully before assuming command. As part of their pre-command training, they articulate their command philosophy and set specific personal and professional goals for their time in command.

A much smaller number make that same investment before assuming command of a staff, where arguably such focus and clarity often has a broader and more lasting impact on the Navy. The commander of a staff must define not only what they want their command to do—the directing role of every commanding officer—but also to a large extent how they want their command to do it.

The reality is that a staff will assume the personality of the commander. Are they imperial, conspicuously conscious of their seniority, and prone to avoid discussion? Odds are that their staff officers will also become known for their lack of collegiality or collaboration. Are they fascinated by the formal process for moving money, people, and resources within the Department of the Navy (DoN)? In short order, their team will be hotly engaged in budget discussions where earlier they were content to simply be present.

Getting the best out of a staff is an art, no different from leading and using a team for an operational mission. This is not a book about command nor is it a book about how to command a staff, but if the staff is going to effectively serve the commander and the commander's intent, there are a number of things each staff officer needs to understand about their boss.

Who Are Their Bosses, and How Do They Manage Them?

Everyone has a boss, and all authority exercised in the Navy is delegated or derived from a senior authority. Like any naval officer, the commander will be mindful of those who are senior to themselves. They will find mechanisms to communicate their actions and concerns, to take guidance, and inform decisions up echelon. These will be formal (operational reports) and informal (phone calls and point-to-point emails). How they do so will vary depending on how they perceive their bosses need to be informed and served.

Counterintuitively, the more senior the staff, the more bosses the commander has. Having an operational and administrative chain of command is a normal arrangement for most Navy commands. Despite the potential conflicts inherent in these relationships, at the lower levels most commanders are familiar with this dynamic and understand the formal and informal distinctions as to which chain has authority in any situation. Wise commanders also default to ensuring each higher-level commander is aware of issues that they would consider significant. A major accident, for example, has immediate impact on the unit's ability to conduct operations. It will also be of interest to the administrative commander, who may have responsibility to support repairs, consider impacts to the unit's long-term schedule, or support an investigation. "No surprises" is a good rule regardless of the formal lines.

Moving up the chain of command, this simple arrangement grows more complex. Most senior Navy commands wear multiple hats. They may be tasked as a Joint Task Force (JTF) headquarters for certain operational contingencies. On a day-to-day basis, these command relationships may be inactive, but they are often exercised on a regular basis, and create another senior with an interest in the staff's actions. If designated as a naval component commander, they will report to both a joint combatant commander (CCDR) and the CNO or a senior fleet commander. Traditionally, the former has operational control (authority) (OPCON), while the Navy has ADCON. However, it must always be remembered that the CNO is also a member of the Joint Chiefs of Staff and needs to be able to speak with authority on ongoing operations in order to provide the best military advice to the Secretary of Defense and the President and, practically, the commander's Navy chain of command will normally determine their future promotion and assignment.

Type commanders (TYCOMs) become a unique and variable part of this equation that will be considered in more detail later. Regardless of whether they have a formal command relationship with the commander, TYCOMs act as leads for platforms and forces within major warfare areas. The TYCOM will invariably have a relationship with other senior officers from that warfare community.

Even where there is not a formal controlling relationship, seniors may be part of what is called an enterprise. A good example is the Naval Aviation Enterprise. The Naval Aviation Enterprise comprises the commands (and commanders) who have responsibility for creating ready naval aviation forces—everything from the budgeting and procurement of aircraft to the management of spare parts and the training of new and fleet aviators. These commands generally do not have formal command relationships, but, under the right conditions, produce a unified community voice and coordinated approach to problems. Unless these enterprises are clearly failing, senior Navy leaders outside that particular community tend to defer to them in addressing systemic issues in their area.

An astute staff officer will also learn the commander's informal bosses. A mentor once defined these as "people you don't work for who can get you fired." While that is a negative way of thinking about it, it is a neat rule-of-thumb for a category that covers a multitude of folks. For example, with the centralization of naval facilities, most bases and naval regions report to the commander of Navy Installations Command (CNIC). Nonetheless, the commander of a naval region will keep a close relationship with the fleet commander whose needs they serve, perhaps even to the point of attending their staff meetings. Informal bosses may not even be inside the DoD. In some cases, ambassadors, members of Congress, and seniors from other agencies will have a deciding vote on a commander's work—or even the commander's continued service—a reality that their staff must understand.

The point is not that the staff needs to create and manage these relationships—that is the commander's affair. In understanding them, however, the astute staff officer will discern how information needs to flow (which will influence things that matter to their commander), and how to ensure their commander can accomplish their mission.

What Does the "Commander Control"?

New staff officers will quickly learn that Navy commanders have an acute focus on C2. They know that what appear to be arcane doctrinal nuances determine who is inside and who is outside the lifelines, how assets can be tasked, and where responsibility for mission lies. Thus, a staff officer must know what entities and activities are under their commander's formal control. They must also know the vocabulary of command. There are only four types of operational command relationships: combatant command (authority) (COCOM), OPCON, tactical control (TACON), and support. ADCON is derived from the military services' responsibilities under Title 10 to organize, train, and equip (OTE) their forces. These will be discussed more in chapter 13.

What Is "Commander's Business"?

The term "commander's business" has developed in recent decades to mean whatever initiatives, efforts, and actions are considered too significant for decisions to be delegated below the commander. Some of these issues are formally articulated. For example, commanders are required to brief the results of a defense organizational climate (also called command climate) survey of their staff to their immediate superior. This requirement forces each commander to engage personally with the results of this process. In other cases, a superior can make something commander's business by insisting that subordinate commanders be present in a discussion or that they provide a personal response to their inquiry. Beyond these formal requirements, commanders signal what they consider to be commander's business by expressing what information must be brought to their attention and where commanders invest their time and attention. This process can be formalized through a deliberate list, such as commander's critical information requirements (CCIRs), but the informal cues that the commander expects to be apprised of certain information are even more important. A good staff officer needs to understand both what must be in their commander's field of view and what is not worth their commander's time.

How Much Latitude Do They Give Their Staff?

To serve the commander effectively, the staff must be able to speak on behalf of the commander. In many cases, the authority to do so is clear—for example, when delegated as part of the composite warfare commander (CWC) watch system or in operational standing orders. Leaders of major staff elements are often delegated significant authority over the operations of their specialized functions. For example, a fleet intelligence officer is often given formal authority to direct and synchronize the intelligence functions of all subordinate staffs. It is that officer's responsibility to align their direction to their commander's priorities and to advise the commander when an action or event reaches the commander's threshold of interest.

In other cases, however, the staff's latitude is less clear. In a large staff, it is neither possible nor helpful for the commander to try to stay abreast of every effort that the staff is making. A commander whose staff understands their intent can act confidently consistent with their vision and values, taking advantage of opportunities where there is neither time nor bandwidth to "phone home." This approach ensures that subordinates' speed of decision can match the speed of opportunity—or warfare. However, the reality is that, bureaucratically, inaction is almost always safer than action. Empowering a staff to act requires clear communication and deliberate trust-building by the commander. While there is risk in giving subordinates latitude, the staffs that enjoy this trust are almost always more effective and able to move their commander's vision into reality. As ADM Scott Swift noted in his guidance to the Pacific Fleet, risk properly embraced is a resource, and should be understood as such.

Good Commanders Communicate Empowerment

A four-star fleet staff once tasked a lieutenant as lead action officer for a complex and contentious multicommand project. While the fleet lead would usually be more senior, the officer assigned was technically brilliant and operationally experienced—exactly the right choice. Conducting a field visit to another command, she was unexpectedly invited to a project briefing to the hosting command's three-star commander. There, her hosts indicated to the three-star that the fleet supported their work, then pointed to the lieutenant's presence as evidence of that fact. Poor staff work on their part. The three-star staff knew that the fleet had major concerns, but thought they could put a junior officer on the spot and bully her into acquiescence. She had none of it, respectfully telling the three-star commander why the fleet had not bought into their project yet. The three-star received her input badly, at one point asking derisively, "Does your commander even know who you are?"

Fast forward a month—the four-star fleet commander visits the same command. Listening carefully to his three-star host, he affirmed the fleet's interest in partnership while outlining his continuing concerns about their program. Then, as the meeting wound to a close, he politely asked his hosts to give him the room for ten minutes to talk to his expert on the topic—specifically, the lieutenant.

The commander's deliberate empowerment of his officer resonated not only in that interaction, but also throughout his staff.

How Do They Use Their Time?

Time is the one element that constrains commanders and subordinates alike. A wise fleet commander once commented, "We vote with our time." That is why a good staff officer pays attention to how the commander is investing their time as much (or more) than what the commander says.

Understanding time starts with understanding the commander's battle rhythm. The commander's battle rhythm is separate from the staff's battle rhythm, to be discussed in chapter 19. Rather, the question is what staff events the commander attends regularly. These are important as both indicators of what the commander values and as venues where the staff can provide information.

Beyond the recurring schedule, it is worth understanding what one-off events are consuming the commander on any given day. In most large staffs, the commander and principal staff officers maintain an online calendar. Sharing access to these schedules across key staff elements has become an important if informal way of communicating priorities. Wags have dubbed this process calendar intelligence, or CALENDARINT. The presence of a visit by an air program office, for example, can cue the responsible staff element to update their understanding of the program and find an effective means or venue to arm the commander for the discussion.

It is also worth learning how the commander manages their schedule. While most commanders have someone (or a host of folks) who help manage their agenda throughout the day, in the end the commander chooses how to use their time. Are they punctual? Do meetings end on time? Do meetings always expand, creating a compounding series of changes that cascade through the day and create a permanent sense of crisis? How does the commander manage personal time? Do they carefully fence time for physical exercise? Do they take leave? When on leave, do they really detach from the workflow, or do they just respond to emails with the door closed?

With the spread of connectivity, both unclassified and classified, a number of commanders prefer to work remotely, either prizing the relative freedom from distractions or knowing that their staffs will remain at work as long as the commander is in the office. More than one fleet commander will depart their office to "go home" for the sake of their staff, only to attack their inbox from a different venue.

Who Do They Listen To?

Influence and trust are not always found in formal titles. Every staff, whatever its size, brings a team of different skills and styles. Invariably, every commander develops a relationship with parts of their team based on respect for their experience and insights and comfort with their competence. It is important to understand who these influencers are. They are, in many cases, the avenue for the commander to see and hear new ideas in an informal setting. When they are in other parts of the staff, they form a key path to reinforce and carry ideas into action.

Halsey and His Dirty Tricks Department: The Weakness of Small Groups

In command of Third Fleet, ADM Bull Halsey developed a small, informal group his CoS dubbed the "dirty tricks department." Comprised of no more than half a dozen staff officers, they became Halsey's sounding board when opportunities arose in the course of the drive across the Pacific in 1944 and 1945. The dirty tricks department notably did not include a number of senior staff members, particularly CAPT Marion Cheek, the fleet intelligence officer.

During the Battle of Leyte Gulf, the members of the dirty tricks department were key in Halsey's decision to go north after the Japanese carrier force—a decision that left ongoing amphibious landing to the south in a vulnerable position. A number of senior staff found out about the decision after it had been made and placed in motion. Their concerns, which were in retrospect well-founded, never found their way into Halsey's ear. Halsey might have made the same decision even after a wider discussion, but his decision did not exploit the full capabilities of the staff.[1]

How Do They Take Information?

Each person has different ways of taking and assimilating information. Since one of the key missions of the staff is to inform the commander, how they take information most effectively is an essential question for the staff.

When interacting with a new senior leader, the most experienced operational planner in the U.S. Navy, CAPT Dave Fields, would "try to sit in the room while new leaders are being briefed by other people before we do our first brief. As a disinterested observer it's easier to see the commander interact with the briefer and how he receives information."[2]

In operational staffs, there will be a strong focus on standardization of reporting. It is worth remembering why this seemingly petty focus is important. First, standardization ensures completeness; it is readily apparent when an element of information is missing. Second and equally critical, standardization allows seniors to monitor an enormous amount of information and, by fitting it into a pattern, rapidly discern when there is a break in the pattern—an anomaly that suggests that something is not right. That anomaly is usually a cue for the commander to dive deeper into the information. CAPT Fields again notes that the staff "may not like a particular template, but deviating wastes time and distracts from the message. I've had a commander who prefers a template for presenting concepts of operations that doesn't match the planning process. To us the information seemed out of order, but for him it made perfect sense."[3]

How Do They Learn?

This question sounds like how they take information, but there is a subtle and significant difference. Commanders take information to inform decisions, often focusing the process on speed and efficiency. Good naval professionals, however, continue deliberate learning throughout their careers. Knowing that, the best commanders make learning opportunities. They may request briefings from outside experts, travel to centers of excellence, or look for informal venues where they can dialogue with thought-leaders from inside and outside the Navy. Knowing the commander's interests and appetites, the staff can identify worthwhile opportunities to invest the commander's limited time.

How Do They Communicate?

Commanders give orders, convey their priorities, and establish policy. In operational settings, this communication is often formal—written orders, formal verbal orders, signed instructions. These are, however, only a small part of what the commander communicates. How they communicate becomes a key question for the staff. Do they send emails or memos, valuing the thoughtful deliberation of the written word? Are they a showman, always comfortable with being the briefer—or does the requirement for the commander to deliver a briefing entail days of careful preparation and rehearsal? Do they give verbal guidance during meetings? Or do they prefer to dialogue, using the assembled staff as a sounding board to inform a decision they will make later?

How to Waste Staff Time

A major staff had just had a change of command. The outgoing senior was methodical, giving deliberate verbal guidance that would be captured into staff actions. The new commander was an interactive, stream-of-consciousness thinker. In his first weeks in command, his new staff wrote down his every idea, and then turned them into formal tasks to the command. The staff reeled under the workload. Eventually, during one of his roundtables, the commander noticed his executive assistant (EA) furiously writing. "You aren't tasking that, are you?" the commander asked, adding, "I am just thinking." A little clarity on both sides would have saved much staff time and effort.

A Word on Personalities

The questions above in many cases go to the interplay of the commander's personality and their professional persona. The first is a natural development, and the second is a learned response to the demands of the service. Many good but less-experienced officers underestimate the extent to which good leaders mold their professional persona in order to accomplish their mission. Simply, they present themselves in a way that is most effective in leading their teams while at the same time exploiting the unique strengths of their own personality. Some large part of the Navy's advanced leadership classes at the pre- and post-command level focuses on identifying these elements and helping senior leaders to be aware of and to leverage their leadership style.

Introverts in Action: A Tale of Two Four-Stars

At one point, the two most senior officers on the OPNAV staff were hardcore introverts. The trick was that both had disciplined themselves over the years to present forcefully and engagingly in public settings. Anyone who saw them in an all-hands call or major meeting would have taken them for extroverts. As a result, few outside their immediate staffs understood how these seniors' personalities shaped their style of work. The key was that the commanders' personal staffs knew and handled each of their schedules to allow time to recharge after public events. Each senior took a different approach to this quiet time, with one allowing desk time for reading and reflection, and another preferring routine administrative tasks. Both staffs deliberately enabled their bosses' strengths—in this case, a fearsome introvert ability to focus on understanding difficult issues.

Communicating expectations clearly and early in a relationship allows all involved to move quickly past the introductions and into tackling the problems at hand. In recent years, two key tools have become popular.

A number of commanders have produced a Day One brief. Usually delivered personally to the entire staff shortly after a change of command, these briefs commonly include insight on the new commander's priorities, as well as a discussion of how they intend to do staff business. Similarly, some major staffs have taken to providing Day One letters to newly arriving senior staff officers. These formal letters from the commander provide new senior staff with the commander's specific concerns and tasking within the new senior staff's area of responsibility.

For Commanders

The paragraphs above suggest the kind of questions an astute officer on your staff should ask as they seek to support your vision. They might never voice these questions to you directly, but they will arrive at answers. Their answers will shape their actions—and your success. There are three key elements of the staff culture that the commander establishes by word and example: information flow, time, tone. While they parallel the commander's role in any command, using a staff to its full potential will require a level of deliberateness about each.

Information Flow

The classic World War II–era volume *Sound Military Decision* noted "a competent staff brings to the commander's attention *all* the items necessary—but *only* those necessary."[4] Your staff should be an extended sensor network, able to feed critical information to you in time for you to be able to make correct, thoughtful decisions. Like any sensor, what they detect and report will be determined by how they are configured and tasked. Thoughtful attention to formal statements of your information needs (such as CCIRs) will set the sensor to the right zone and search patterns. Equally critical is your handling of the input. If you immediately focus on detail, you will likely not receive reports until details are available. If your focus is always knowing more than the next level of command, you will train your teams to flood you with information—but not necessarily insight—in an effort to ensure you are never caught flatfooted.

Time

Your staff will read your calendar, and they will respond to your actual priorities over whatever you say. Today, the core Navy value of commitment to the mission is being shaped by a society of constant connectedness. Your peers at the most senior levels of the civilian world are working more hours, demonstrating their professional commitment by being constantly available to seniors and customers. The technological ability to be always on has paired badly with the Navy culture. Our Navy is by its nature a greedy institution—an organization that "demands an especially fervent and total commitment" in the service of a higher cause.[5] The temptation for seniors is to take advantage of this ability, to plug into more information each day and to maintain that connection twenty-four hours a day, seven days a week (24/7).

Technology has made it easier than ever to crush a staff under the weight of your demands. If you fall into this trap,

- You will fail to make the most of your position. At every level of command, the commander is tasked to articulate a vision for the future, whether the future is the operation after next or the structure of the service in twenty years. Strategic thought takes time. Commanders who do not protect time to think find themselves responding to events rather than driving them. Your staff can make your thinking more effective, but they cannot think for you.

- You will fail to develop your subordinates. Someday, someone on your staff will be in your seat. We develop leaders at sea by allowing them to conduct and lead evolutions of increasing complexity. If you are always plugged in, those opportunities will not exist for our next generation.

- You will crush some of the best of your team. Low-performing staffs usually have a staff hero. These tough guys come to be seen as essential and so are driven to heroic work hours and routine episodes of all-night work. Having exhausted themselves in support of the command, they are often celebrated for their dedication and rewarded with praise, prestige, and glowing fitness reports (FITREPs). The best staffs have teams of heroes, however, with no one officer being seen as—or making themselves into—the essential player.

- You will discourage the rest of your team. Not all of your best and brightest want to be the staff tough guy. They are astute enough to recognize when the staff investment of time and effort has exceeded the payoff for the Navy. They know when their leaders see them as a long-term investment and when they are transactional tools for advancing a short-term cause. Remember, our future Navy is not always led by the best qualified—it is led by the best qualified who stay in the Navy.

- You will remove any margin for surge operations. Every staff faces storms and shoals along its course. For an afloat staff, it may be a real-world conflict, a hostile action, or a humanitarian crisis. For a TYCOM, it may be responding to an emergent change in readiness requirements or a shipyard strike that impacts maintenance. While unexpected in their specifics, the fact that some crisis will hit every staff is completely foreseeable. Like a ship operating with no redundancy in its engineering plant, the staff that is sprinting all the time has no margin to respond.

- Your external relations will suffer. You set the tone for your staff's dealings—internally and externally. If you treat information as a guarded commodity, your staff will quickly gain a reputation for hoarding information, and will receive less in response. If you tolerate senior staff who do not measure up to the requirements of the job, your staff will assume you are unwilling to make difficult choices.

Tone

FADM King, the architect of the U.S. Navy in World War II, recalled that his image of a successful staff was formed on the staff of ADM Henry T. Mayo in the early days of World War I. Mayo, King recalled, "had a gift for using his staff to work for him, and that was largely because they were made truly to feel that they were working with him."[6] A commander who sets such a tone will always benefit from the best efforts their staff can offer.

Commander's Business: How the Fleet Fights

A staff, even a fleet or afloat staff, does not fight . . . at least, not directly. Commanders, however, define the fight, and commanders who share a vision for how to fight can transform the Navy and shape the future of naval warfare.

In World War II, Arleigh Burke became known not only for leading DESRON 23 to victory in combat, but also for capturing his insights in clear, thoughtful written orders. These instructions became the basis for destroyer tactics for the remainder of the war.

In the 1980s VADM Hank Mustin, the commander of U.S. Second Fleet, faced the challenge of Soviet long-range aviation and submarines. The Navy had new tools—F-14s with long-range air-to-air missiles, *Los Angeles*–class nuclear-powered general-purpose attack submarines, or SSNs—but no concept of how to integrate them in a fight across an entire ocean. To answer the need, Mustin consciously emulated Burke, even to the point of seeking the aging warrior's advice on his concepts. Mustin's "Fighting Instructions" provided the basic outline for how NATO Striking Fleet Atlantic and U.S. Second Fleet would fight the Soviet Navy. They also established the outline of modern naval warfare for decades.[7]

Forty years later, and in a different ocean, another fleet commander faced the challenge of an expanding oceangoing Navy. ADM Scott "Notso" Swift took inspiration from ADM Mustin's work, creating Pacific Fleet Fighting Instructions to capture his overall design and intent for operations in the Pacific. His design has become the foundation for the advanced operational naval warfare concepts being used today.[8]

Creating meaningful and enduring guidance requires a fleet commander who has thought rigorously and broadly about naval warfare, usually well before they assume command. It also requires an extraordinary level of support from the staff, who will provide ideas, analysis, critique, and writing throughout the process.

Few moments in history require a fundamental reassessment of how the Navy should fight. When those moments come, however, creating enduring guidance is one of the most important and impactful investments a commander can make during their time in command.

CHAPTER 3

The Staff Command Triad

Deputies, Chiefs of Staff, Executive Directors, and Senior Enlisted

U.S. Navy Sailors of all ranks understand the command triad: commanding officer, executive officer, and the command master chief or chief of the boat. They instinctively understand that every triad is built on a unique balance of formal roles and authority, personal and professional trust, and individual strengths and weaknesses. They also understand that this team approach does not diminish the absolute responsibility of command, a responsibility that is vested in one leader and one leader only.

Even though triads are essential to almost every Navy command, it nonetheless sometimes surprises new staff officers to discover a triad on their staff. We have said earlier that the staff exists to inform the commander and to execute some part of the commander's authorities—it acts, in essence, like a very large command triad. However, to lead the staff and subordinate commanders, a senior leader will build something like a command triad within the staff. In the case of a fleet staff, the triad will usually consist of the commander, deputy commander or CoS, and the fleet master chief. It is also possible to have essentially two interlocking triads within a large staff—one focused on outside the staff, and one focused on internal staff functions. This latter case is less confusing than it may sound and will be discussed at the end of the chapter.

The Deputy Commander

It is most important that every commander choose as his principal subordinate an officer who will complement his own shortcomings. If an officer is audacious and perhaps inclined to be reckless, it is incumbent upon him to choose as his chief of staff a cautious, careful officer who will balance the commander. On the other hand, a commander who is apt to feel himself overcautious should choose an audacious extrovert. The family life of the staff under these conditions are not as pleasant as they would be if the admiral and all members of the staff had approximately the same temperament, but the effectiveness of the staff is increased immeasurably. It takes a big man, an admiral of great experience, to operate with and tolerate a chief of staff who balances the admiral's own shortcomings.

Arleigh Burke[1]

First and foremost, the deputy commander exists as the commander's second, acting for and in the name of the commander when required. With the advent of modern portable communications, the role of the deputy commander has diminished in the past two decades. Deputy commanders used to make consequential operational decisions, especially in response to unexpected events, when the commander was absent from the headquarters or flagship. Now, it is the rare senior leader who allows their deputy the latitude that was routinely theirs in earlier generations.

Despite this erosion, deputy commanders still fill two essential roles. Like an executive officer, the deputy should act as counselor, sounding board, and trusted agent to the commander. As Arleigh Burke appreciated, the right deputy or CoS will ideally bring a diversity of thought, experience, and approach to the relationship, complementing the commander's strengths.

The deputy should also lead specific issues and functions delegated by the commander. These can be delegated formally by letter or instruction, or, more commonly, by the simple function of which senior officer chairs a meeting or event. No commander has enough time; intelligent use of a senior and capable deputy is a key tool for enabling the commander.

The Chief of Staff or Chief Staff Officer

Generally, a CoS or chief staff officer is found on Navy staffs that do not have a full-time deputy commander. There is a fine distinction between the two. A CoS serves a flag officer; a chief staff officer performs the same functions for a commodore and are usually found on smaller afloat staffs. The CoS or chief staff officer is not a deputy commander, but rather serves to direct and administer the staff. Nonetheless, a good CoS will have a similar role as the commander's second and trusted advisor.

Blurring the Lines

In every staff, the roles of the senior officers assigned will vary based on structure and conditions. In most numbered fleets, the position of deputy commander is filled by a reserve flag officer. These officers will generally only be with the staff for a short period each year. They often are used for exercise events that place high demands on the staff. In many cases, the commander will not commit their full attention to an exercise, but appearances require a flag officer's presence. In very few cases is a reserve deputy equipped to take the place of the commander, nor is it commonly expected.

Absent a full-time deputy commander, it is common for the CoS to function essentially as a deputy commander. A numbered fleet CoS is generally a Navy captain, while direct numbered fleet subordinate commanders are often flag officers. The resulting relationship obviously requires extraordinary diplomacy and a keen sense of the commander's direction on the part of the O6-grade CoS. This dynamic is but one of the many reasons that the position of numbered fleet CoS is considered one of the toughest O6 jobs in the Navy.

ADM John C. "Lung" Aquilino, Pacific Fleet commander, and Fleet Master Chief James Honea hold an all-hands call on the aircraft carrier USS *Abraham Lincoln* (CVN 72). *U.S. Navy*

Fleet Master Chief, Force Master Chief, and Command Master Chief

Major commands usually have a senior enlisted advisor to the commander. While most officers will have worked closely with a command master chief in previous assignments, they are sometimes surprised by the scope of the master chief in a large organization. A fleet master chief, for example, will be concerned about issues across the entire fleet rather than in the staff itself. They will connect with the network of other fleet, force, and commander master chiefs to provide mentorship and advice, and will engage Sailors and family members to listen to concerns. They will often travel individually or with the commander, joining the commander for all hands calls and other public events and will sit in most senior staff discussions.

Large staffs will sometimes have a command master chief or senior enlisted advisor separate from the fleet or force master chief. This senior enlisted leader will act as the senior enlisted mentor for the enlisted personnel assigned the headquarters itself. They often report to the CoS or to the commander of troops, if such a construct is used.

A good staff officer will know the distinction and will leverage these experienced leaders appropriately. The staff Command Master Chief (CMC) of the Marine Corps or SEL (senior enlisted leader) is the expert on taking care of the Sailor assigned to the staff and solving local issues. The fleet or force master chief can be a source of insight on issues involving the entire force. For example, when contemplating significant changes to fleetwide training routines, the fleet master chief could provide feedback on how the current training regiment is working at the deck plates and the potential unforeseen impacts of changes to the status quo.

Executive Director

The executive director (ED) is a senior civilian leader who manages administrative, business, and support functions with the staff. Closely akin to a chief management officer in a civilian corporation, an ED is usually found only in large Navy staffs and is a relatively new position. Establishing an ED offers the headquarters the advantage of experience and long-term continuity for complex business functions, such as budgeting and civilian personnel administration. For example, at U.S. Pacific Fleet (PACFLT), the ED is responsible for the following:

- Enlisted staff, to include the commanding officer of enlisted staff and command master chief
- Security
- Comptroller and financial management functions
- Contract management
- Knowledge management
- Sexual assault prevention and response
- Equal employment opportunity

The ED will also normally oversee the education, training, and development of all civilian employees across their staff's span of control.

As a senior civilian leader, EDs also have the advantage of a network of other senior civilian leaders across the Navy and DoD. This informal network is as real in senior civilian circles as in any uniformed warfare community, and potentially is a useful tool for the commander.

As mentioned at the beginning of the chapter, large Navy staffs sometimes function as if they have two command triads. The first, or outside, triad will consist of the commander, deputy commander, and fleet master chief. It will address the major issues facing the entire force. The second triad is often more internally focused, and may consist of the commander, ED, and the staff command master chief. This team will focus on internal staffing and resource issues. While less prominent and arguably less critical, this second team can be a significant help to a staff officer addressing issues of internal staff administration.

CHAPTER 4

The Personal Staff

Any flag-level staff has a cadre of professionals whose primary job is what is known as "the care and feeding" of the commander. They are often called personal staff because their focus is on the personal side of the commander rather than on the operational side of the command's mission.

America has always prided itself on its democratic principles, rejecting many of the trappings of office that older European nations considered self-evidently part of command. The result is that many naval officers, and not a few commanders, harbor a slight if unspoken discomfort with the idea of a personal staff. Get over it. The reality is that the personal staff is integral to the commander's effectiveness and with it, the effectiveness of the entire staff.

Because officers in specific flag-support billets wear aiguillettes, officers assigned to personal staff are often referred to as loops. Note that who can wear an aiguillette is very specifically outlined in regulations. To wear a loop, the officer must have been specifically ordered into a billet titled CoS, flag lieutenant, flag secretary, EA, or aide. Nonetheless, it is not uncommon for officers drafted into or acting in such a role to wear the loop anyway. Deputy EAs and protocol officers sometimes wear a loop as well. Often the flag officer will expect it, and the loop serves as a useful signal to help others to quickly identify who is handling the admiral's arrangements.

The Executive Assistants

Depending on the size of the staff, there may be one EA, or an EA and a deputy. The EA is usually the staff member with the most exposure to the commander and the officer with the best insight into the commander's thinking. Their responsibilities may include

- attending meetings and sitting in on phone calls, usually to take notes and capture tasks for the staff as required;
- reviewing high-interest correspondence and emails;
- ensuring the commander's broad priorities are reflected in their travel and engagement schedules; and
- supervising the personal staff.

While focused on the commander, an EA also serves the commander by enabling their staff, and by building bridges to senior staff and director-ate leads. The EA often becomes the commander's sounding board and is privy to their frustrations, concerns, and personal assessments. Good EAs learn to use their insight to help the staff understand the command-er's needs. Effective staff principals ensure the EA is well-informed, often passing them insights and background information before issues become commander's business. This push/pull process enables both sides to antici-pate the commander's interests before they are articulated. This process is normal and expected, but requires judgment on the part of the EA as to where the line is between offering helpful insight and assuming part of the commander's authority.

What is clear is that an EA must never cross the line into gossip. The first requirement of all personal staff is discretion. Greeting each new EA, one senior officer usually stated bluntly, "You are furniture." Like most senior officers, they had also once held the job, and the remark was not meant to be denigrating. It simply meant that they needed to be able to forget the EA was in the room, talking freely and candidly to peers and seniors without concern. Most personal staff have a similar understanding with their boss and they honor that trust even years later. The reward is usually a candid and intimate view of a senior leader in action.

Across major staffs and within the Pentagon, the EAs form a signifi-cant information network. In some cases, this network is formalized. For example, the Vice Chief of Naval Operations' (VCNO) EA historically hosts scheduled meetings of all the EAs on the OPNAV staff. This forum handles minor issues (e.g., the need to replace fraying door mats in the

Navy Pentagon passageways) to major staff moves (e.g., the schedule for Navy budget submissions and the work plan for bringing these issues to the CNO).

Senior EA jobs are viewed as training grounds for future flag officers. While, in most cases, assignment as an EA does not offer an automatic golden halo, it does offer an extraordinary learning opportunity at the cost of a fearsome amount of work and a subordination of personal autonomy to a senior officer. As a result, most flag officers have served as an EA at some point in their careers.

The Deputy Executive Assistant

If a staff is large enough to require a deputy EA, the deputy normally plays an inside to the EA's outside role. Where the EA accompanies the commander to meetings and on travel, the deputy will remain in the office, focused on the daily business of the command. The deputy EA is usually one grade junior to the EA

Under the watchful eye of his flag aide, LCDR Colleen Moore, Pacific Fleet commander ADM Scott H. Swift speaks with Warfare Tactics Instructors (WTI) from the Naval Surface and Mine Warfighting Development Center (SMWDC). *U.S. Navy*

Flag Aides

The aide is the commander's personal assistant. In staff vernacular, the flag aide is often called "the loop." Fundamentally, the flag aide is an extension of the flag officer, performing officially actions that the senior would otherwise do for themselves. The scope of duties depends on the seniority of the flag officer and the size of the personal staff. On a small staff, the flag aide will perform duties that, on a larger staff, will be divided across a team. An aide may

- schedule official appointments;
- schedule unofficial appointments in order to ensure they are coordinated with the official schedule;
- set up and manage the flag officer's travel;
- assist with writing official correspondence;
- coordinate with the flag officer's family members to avoid conflicts between personal and professional events;
- schedule medical appointments for the flag officer;
- pick up meals from an official mess (but emphatically not from a restaurant or non-DoD messes);
- handle and account for official challenge coins;
- account for official gifts to and from foreign partners; and
- supervise the enlisted aides and the maintenance of the admiral's personal quarters, if assigned.

It is not uncommon for flag aides to handle a fund for their senior's incidental expenses. Even though the amounts are generally small, a flag aide must account for this money penny for penny and should never cover the senior's expenses, or mingle their money, even for a brief time.

The CNO will be distinctive in having two assigned aides. This arrangement is essential due to the enormous volume of meetings and engagements that these officers support. The aides typically alternate days, with one aide preparing for tomorrow while the second executes the plan of the day. They similarly alternate travel, with one or the other responsible for a given trip. It is also traditional that both the CNO and the CMC have an aide drawn from the other service.

Enlisted Aides

Until recently known as "personal quarters culinary specialists," enlisted aides are Navy culinary specialists who serve on the personal staff of flag officers who are assigned to official government quarters and whose duties meet certain specific thresholds. These usually include significant social responsibilities, both within the Navy and representing the Navy to senior military, civilian, and international audiences.

Enlisted aides exist to make time for senior officers by relieving them of tasks that would come at the expense of their military duties. These tasks can include maintaining the flag officer's uniforms, cleaning and upkeep of official quarters, and, of course, cooking for official events. They must never be used for personal needs such as child care, taking care of pets, or maintaining private vehicles. They must also never be used to do errands or laundry for dependents or unofficial guests.

Like all enlisted personal staff, enlisted aides are volunteers who have chosen a unique path of service. Often trained at some of the best culinary schools in the nation, their mastery of the arts of hospitality can set the stage for delightful command events or critical international engagements.

Ethics and the Personal Staff

Every good officer establishes and maintains the highest standards of personal and professional ethics. Commanders and flag officers are held to an even higher standard, where both reality and appearances are critical to their effectiveness. Across multiple staff tours, most staff officers will learn that our senior officers sincerely endeavor to meet this exacting standard. However, they will also learn that limited information, the pace of events, and the desire of others to please a senior officer can create a slippery slope. Good intent is not enough. A good personal staff, serving a commander who has set clear ethical expectations, will serve as a rudder check on the commander's personal ethical compass.

Having flag or enlisted aides requires that the flag officer and their personal staff need to be familiar with the rules concerning their employment. For enlisted aides, the rules are covered in detail in naval regulations. For flag aides, the rules are less explicitly defined, but no less consequential. Simply, aides are provided by the Navy to facilitate the senior officer in performance of their duties. They may not be used for personal services even if the intent and result of the personal services is to free more time for the flag officer's official duties.

The topic of proper use of personal aides is covered in the ethics training required of all senior officers. Within the staff, the judge advocate general (JAG) will also provide training and counsel, and should be called on in any case of doubt. However, Navy instructions are clear: "The flag officer is solely responsible for determining whether duties assigned to enlisted aides are reasonably connected to the officer's military and official responsibilities. This responsibility may not be delegated."[1] As part of taking care of their assigned senior officer, personal aides need to understand where the lines are. Breaching those lines, even voluntarily and *without the express request of the senior*, will get the senior officer in trouble. The enthusiastic staff who makes it happen without regard to the rules will, in the end, harm their boss. Compromising the commander's ethical bedrock is a poor service, however well-intentioned.

Flag Secretary

The flag secretary runs the paperwork behind the commander, supervising the office staff that handles incoming and outgoing correspondence and instructions.

Flag secretaries are found only in large staffs. They are almost always administrative specialty limited duty officers who started their careers as high-performing enlisted administrative specialists before moving into the officer ranks. By the time they arrive at a flag staff, they will typically have well over a decade of experience in administration, regulations and policy, personnel, and labor force planning and requirements, as well as ties to every other administrative limited duty officer (LDO) in the service. A good flag secretary is a ninja in the world of making the paperwork side of the service do what the command needs—and a good staff officer will learn from them.

Flag Writer

A flag writer is a senior yeoman who has been specially screened and trained to support the administrative requirements of senior officers. The flag writer will draft outgoing correspondence for the commander, screen incoming correspondence, process travel orders and claims, and coordinate the daily care of the front office spaces. If you have ever received a recommendation or Bravo Zulu message of congratulations from a senior officer, the odds are high it was first drafted by the flag writer. Depending on its size, the staff might also manage the commander's schedule.

Flag writers are required to be volunteers, petty officer first class or senior, warfare qualified, and be recommended by their command for outstanding communications skills. Sent to a five-week C school, they earn a specialized Navy enlisted classification (NEC) and will generally serve in flag officer support billets for most of their remaining career.

The flag writer is almost always the most visible enlisted Sailor in the commander's front office. They are often at once the most junior permanent member of the team and the member with the most experience in a flag front office environment. Where an EA or flag aide is serving for a tour and expects to return to their warfare community once done, the flag writer may have served in three or more flag officers of various grades, both afloat and ashore. A savvy officer serving in a personal staff capacity will tap this experience in the same way they would rely on the technical expertise of an experienced chief petty officer in an afloat environment.

By mutual agreement, a flag writer may often stay with a specific senior officer as they are transferred or promoted. If that is the case on your staff, you can be confident that the flag writer has developed a rapport with the commander.

Protocol Officer

The protocol officer handles ceremonies, special events, and distinguished visitors to the staff. These can range from simple awards ceremonies or promotions for members of the staff to major international conferences entailing dozens of events and hundreds of senior-level dignitaries. Such events can require arranging VIP lodging, vehicles, security, meeting venues, photographers, official gifts, all the way down to ensuring the menu for an official lunch meets the visitors' dietary requirements. Inexperienced staff officers may write this job off as party planning, but experienced staff officers know that getting such details right sets the stage for critical discussions, smooths relationships, and builds teamwork.

Protocol officers come in two flavors. First, there are civilian protocol officers. These professionals usually have significant experience and have seen most recurring events before. Where assigned, they are invariably an essential reservoir of corporate knowledge. There are also military officers, usually lieutenants or lieutenant commanders, who are assigned as protocol officers. Where the flag secretary and flag writer are specially screened and trained for their billet, the protocol officer is simply a junior officer who has volunteered or been recruited for front office duty. They come from every warfare community and go to no special school before assuming their role. In finest Navy fashion, they make it work.

CHAPTER 5

Special Staff

Separate from the personal staff is a cadre of professionals often referred to as the special staff. Exactly who falls in this category may be formal or informal depending on the staff and its level of seniority. Where the personal staff is focused on the general care and feeding of the commander, the special staff typically has a specific and limited function that is a particular concern to the commander. Understanding the roles of each staff is important to the general staff officer. In many cases, these specialists are a key source of expert advice within their areas of responsibility.

The Commander's Action Group

The most protean of special staff elements goes by many names—the Commander's Action Group (CAG), commander's initiative group, special activities group, or the strategic actions group, to name a few. CAGs first started in the joint world but have become a regular feature of Navy staffs at the three-star-and-above levels. Their composition is highly variable, ranging from a single O5 to a cadre of contractors headed by a senior O5 to a mixed team of as many as a dozen military and civilians. With the Navy staff, the staff code OPNAV N00Z has traditionally served as the equivalent of a CAG for the CNO, though the size and tasking has varied significantly from one CNO to another.

CAGs exist to carry out staff actions that the commander does not want to delegate to the broader staff. Examples include

- writing strategy and policy documents;
- drafting "personal for" messages;
- creating command-level briefings to capture the commander's vision;

- critiquing or murder boarding analyses from other elements of the staff; and
- planning and coordinating conferences between the commander and subordinate commanders.

A number of commanders allow these teams relatively free range, expecting them to interact widely across different internal and external lanes to identify emerging issues that should have the commander's awareness, as if each day the commander asked, "What should I be thinking about that I am not?"

In almost every case, these teams are created by name from officers and civilians of known insight and expertise. More than one has advertised "brilliance on demand," and some have delivered. Work in such teams is usually fast paced, intellectually diverse, and professionally rewarding. There is much potential for friction with other elements of the staff, especially when the CAG is tasked with grading the work of other staff elements. A bit of openness and humility on both sides can mitigate this dynamic. Skilled staff officers partner with the CAGs as an avenue to influence and inform their commander. Competent CAGs at a minimum ensure the senior staff is not surprised by a CAG recommendation that touches on their expertise. The best CAGs know that they are often working outside their immediate area of professional expertise, and understand that the staff will also be asked to critique their work. Using appropriate insight from the experts on the staff improves the CAG's work and avoids potential embarrassment.

Special Staff as Band-Aid

When a large staff is not functioning well, there is a strong temptation to have major staff elements directly under the commander to assume some critical staff functions. At one point, the special staff of the CNO grew to more than 120, with basic staff integration functions happening at the CNO level. The next CNO shifted more than eighty billets back into the OPNAV directorates, commenting, "You have a job insofar as the rest of the staff does not do theirs." The better answer in the CNO's mind was to empower (and hold accountable) the senior officers entrusted to run staff directorates.

Well prepared by his PAO, CAPT Dave Welch is interviewed by international media during a port call in the Philippines. *U.S. Navy*

Public Affairs Officer

Public affairs officers (PAOs) are professionals specializing in the presentation of Navy activities to the public through the press and other media. In operational staffs, they are usually drawn from the Navy's small cadre of restricted line PAOs, though other staffs sometimes employ government civilians in this role.

In order to function effectively, the PAO must be in the commander's inner circle. This connection allows the PAO to accurately represent the commander's thinking, to identify where a course of action (COA) may create public interest, and to be prepared for potential press inquiries. There is nothing less effective than a PAO who first learns of something the command is doing when called by a reporter. In representing the commander, the PAO needs to be tightly synchronized with other official avenues of outside engagement such as the speechwriter or congressional liaison.

The PAO's value to the commander is heavily based on their relationship with their colleagues in the media. PAOs attached to a regional staff will know the local media outlets that cover their market.

Most senior PAOs are well-known among the media who cover defense and security issues.

At any level, these professionals guard their reputation carefully. First and foremost, a PAO will never lie to the media. They are under no obligation to answer any question, and the good ones make turning aside a question into an art form. However, their statements to the press, whether on or off the record, reflect the integrity the public rightly expects of the Navy and its officers.

The best PAOs go beyond honesty, however. They understand the obligation the Navy has to share its actions with the public it serves and how the media are essential partners in that effort. They know that critical press coverage can ultimately serve and shape the Navy. Their press colleagues know that good PAOs will lean forward to share what information they can, and will enable the media's work even when it is difficult or inconvenient. When it works, the commander has an advisor on staff who can call Pulitzer Prize–winning reporters to share their message—or one who those reporters will call when news breaks.

ADM Burke's Guidance to His Public Affairs Officer

19 August 1959

Subj: Advice on what to say

It is understood that a great many Naval officers ask you for advice on what they can say in various speeches and that they also ask what I have said so that they can do likewise.

It is requested that you advise all such inquirers that they should not say what I say but they should say what I should have said.

ARLEIGH BURKE[1]

Public affairs posture on an event or issue can be active or passive. In an active posture, the PAO works to place the Navy message in the hands of the public. The PAO issues press releases, places posts on social media, and offers the press access to interviews and Navy locations. In a passive posture, the PAO will initiate no action. A passive posture may include response to query, where the public affairs team has planned answers to questions that members of the media are likely to ask. These answers will only be used if and when a query is made of the PAO.

In any event, the public affairs posture for major events, as well as the key messages, is commander's business, informed by the best advice of the PAO.

If a commander decides on an active public affairs posture, the PAO will plan to get the desired message into the right venues. That plan may be simple and involve a single action, or a complex, multi-month campaign involving multiple offices and public affairs teams.

Press availabilities and interviews are a key element of an active public affairs posture. These can range from formal press conferences to one-on-one off-the-record conversations. Most experienced PAOs will hold these discussions to thirty minutes, which is enough time to get the message out without the conversation wandering.

PAO teams often manage the social media profile of the command and the commander. The use of social media is a great way to make truthful, relevant Navy content available to the general public. It requires an ongoing effort, however, with the best PAO teams at large operational commands placing news of routine Navy operations, paired with compelling, high-quality photos, online every day. This regular feed is a mission enabler. Building a social media readership over months and years creates a venue to launch critical information into widespread discussion during a crisis. In several cases, U.S. Navy commands responding to disasters have used social media to provide excellent coverage of their efforts to alleviate suffering—to no avail, because their accounts were new and had essentially no readership.

PAOs are often involved in responding to leaks of sensitive or classified information into the public domain. It is a commonly accepted belief that most leaks originate in Washington, DC, and not within Navy operational elements. However they happen, they are a pernicious reality of the current media and social environment. Experienced reporters who learn of high-interest operations before they are scheduled know the commands involved and often reach out to a trusted PAO before the event. It is not uncommon for them to hold publication of an operational event until after it has occurred, with the understanding that they will receive a rapid and substantial response to their query just after the event. This is a clear case where the PAO's credibility potentially directly protects operational forces.

Getting Caught by the Media—Learning to COPE

Most senior officers will have the opportunity to interact with the media. The PAO is the expert in these engagements, and every officer should dedicate appropriate time to preparing for any deliberate press availability. However, sometimes rapidly moving events—an operational accident, for example—place an officer in the hot seat without being fully prepared. In most cases, the senior officer knows the substantive information. The challenge is organizing and expressing that insight clearly and cogently when the cameras are running without inadvertently becoming a news story yourself. One tool is the mnemonic COPE.

- Challenge. First, acknowledge the challenge posed by the event. Provide a brief and honest summary of the event and its implications.

- Opportunity. Second, note that there is opportunity in this situation. Even a tragic accident presents an opportunity to learn, and to improve training and equipment. Misconduct offers a chance to refocus on core values.

- Professionalism. Note your confidence in the professionalism of the Sailors involved or across the fleet.

- Education. Finally, note how education and training have prepared Sailors for this kind of crisis, event, or challenge.

Using a mnemonic like COPE is unlikely to lead to an award for best press engagement ever. It will, however, get you in and out of the discussion without an embarrassing misstep.

Speechwriter

Most flag officers are called on to speak in public venues ranging from retirement ceremonies to major Washington, DC, think-tanks. On smaller staffs, preparing remarks for the commander is a collateral duty that lands wherever there is a competent writer. Four-star staffs often have an assigned speechwriter, usually an O4 or O5 selected for their skills with the written word.

The highest goal for a speechwriter is to not only craft the substance of a senior's remarks, but also to do so in the unique voice of the commander. Speechwriters at the most senior levels often have the advantage of serving a commander who has made dozens, even hundreds, of public statements that can be used to gain a sense of how the senior uses the spoken word.

The golden rule of the speechwriter is that whatever they write, once the boss says it, it is the boss who owns it. Speechwriters craft their products to fit the commander. What the commander needs will vary with the topic and audience. In a friendly, informal setting speaking on familiar topics, many commanders are comfortable with a few short bullets that organize the flow of their remarks and ensure they do not forget a key point or piece of protocol. For example, a small promotion ceremony may require nothing more than a card with the officer's key professional accomplishments, specific family and friends in attendance, and anyone the promotee requests the commander specifically recognize. For more-formal events, a word-for-word script is a must. This includes events for which the commander's remarks are subject to legal, security, or interagency review. If the commander is in a position to make a significant statement of policy, the script of such a speech is often released by the PAO as an additional means of sharing information with a wider audience. In these cases, the script will be marked "as prepared," signifying that it represents the notes prepared before the speech, rather than an exact transcript "as delivered."

Understanding the commander's preference for how they execute a speech is important for an action officer called on to support a speech as it determines what kind of input is more useful and most likely to be incorporated into the commander's remarks.

It is worth knowing the speechwriter. Not only are they plugged into what matters to the commander, but also most develop their own network of staff members who can quickly and authoritatively provide information for speeches. Being on that informal list can create work, but it also offers yet another opportunity to shape, inform, and enable the commander's priorities.

Judge Advocate General

The staff judge advocate general (JAG) is the commander's lawyer. Assigned from the Navy JAG corps, the JAG will offer advice on legal issues involving military operations, organization, and personnel. While the JAG will have the general training in law that comes with a law degree and admission to a state bar, Navy JAGs will also bring specialized insights in areas that matter to the staff:

- Operations. Operational law can encompass rules of engagement, international law, admiralty law, and law of the sea.
- Accountability. When accidents and misconduct cases happen, the JAG is the key advisor to the commander, guiding investigations, helping the commander make proper and informed decisions on disciplinary matters, and ensuring that high-profile events do not become cascading casualties through well-intentioned but improper follow-up actions.
- Ethics. The JAG will also likely be the ethics advisor for the staff, providing training and advice on standards for the commander and staff.

In the present day, very little happens in a staff without the JAG being aware. In the final analysis, the commander bears responsibility and can act against the JAG's best advice, but few commanders will.

Some large staffs will also have a general counsel (GC). The GC is also a lawyer, but a civilian with a different area of legal practice. GCs, who operate under the guidance of the DoN GC, specialize in government contract law, employment and labor law, real estate law, fiscal law, intellectual property law, and arms control issues.

Foreign Policy Advisor

The foreign policy advisor (FPA) is a State Department officer, usually an experienced Foreign Service officer (FSO), who is assigned to the staff. Previously, FPAs were known as political advisors (POLADs). A bit of careless translation, however, and counterparts in authoritarian foreign militaries would regularly mistake them as being similar to their own political officers.

Generally, the FPA will have served in the same region that the staff focuses on, often for multiple tours. Most will accompany the commander on overseas travel, where their expertise in both international and embassy circles can be invaluable.

FPAs will often have or build links to foreign diplomats stationed in the Washington, DC, area or who are local to the staff, and can leverage these ties on behalf of the commander. For example, when a new deputy commander is conducting calls in the Washington, DC, area prior to assuming their position, the FPA could arrange for calls or social events with the ambassador or senior attaché from key partner nations. This direct exchange of insights usually compliments the expertise of the various U.S. interlocutors who are part of the normal briefing circuit. And make no mistake—foreign partners will share their impressions of a newly appointed senior U.S. Navy officer with their capitals, laying the ground-work for more-direct engagements.

The State Department has its own culture and hierarchy, but it is important for military officers to remember that American diplomats, like military officers, also hold presidential commissions—in their case, as officers in the Foreign Service. While many staff directorates will interface directly with the State Department, the FPA will have a special ability to tap into the organization, seeing message traffic from regional diplomatic missions, communicating informally with their peers, and keeping the commander informed of trends that impact operational forces.

Naval Criminal Investigative Service

Naval Criminal Investigative Service (NCIS) represents the U.S. Navy's law enforcement element. NCIS is a unique entity—sworn federal law enforcement agents tasked to prevent the Navy's and Marine Corps' ability to fight and win from being impacted by terrorism, foreign intelligence activities, or criminal activity. As sworn federal agents, NCIS agents have essentially the same arrest authority as special agents of the Federal Bureau of Investigation (FBI) or the Bureau of Alcohol, Tobacco, and Firearms (ATF). The more than one thousand special agents are supported by a similar number of intelligence analysts, cyber specialists, communications experts, and support experts. While there are counterparts to NCIS across all the military services, NCIS is distinctive in being led by a senior civilian who reports directly to the SECNAV rather than to any uniformed officer.

NCIS executes its responsibilities through fifteen field offices located in the United States and overseas. Staff officers will interact with NCIS through a number of different elements.

Major afloat units, such as aircraft carriers, have an embarked agent. The embarked agent is part of the ship's company and remains with the unit throughout its deployment cycle. Embarked agents are jacks-of-all-trades, responding to major crimes, sexual assaults, counterintelligence, and force protection issues. Embarked agents will work with the ship's own master-at-arms force, but have separate authority and responsibilities. An embarked staff will work with the assigned agent throughout workups and deployment, most critically on force protection issues surrounding port visits.

At a fleet staff, staff officers will encounter NCIS agents serving as either the staff counterintelligence officer (SCIO) or counterintelligence coordinating authority (CICA). While superficially similar, the SCIO is essentially an embedded agent within a staff. Their responsibilities extend to the protection of that specific staff. A CICA is at once both a narrower and a broader position. A CICA will focus specifically on counterintelligence issues, but will act as the expert on counterintelligence operations and policy across the staff. In many cases, the CICA will also be the staff action officer on counterintelligence issues, representing the command, and writing and issuing guidance to subordinate organizations.

The last role in which staff officers may encounter NCIS agents is as personal protective detail for key leaders. Personal protection for Navy leaders is not automatic, but is based on an analysis of the threat to the position and individual filling the billet. The protective detail may be a single agent or a team. In any event, including them in all aspects of planning the commander's schedule and movements is essential. This process is usually well-established, but good staff officers will acquaint themselves with it early in their tour.

Security Manager

Every command will have a security manager or security officer. Depending on what activities the command supports or conducts, they may have several. Most staff officers, however, need to concern themselves with only one or two different security offices. The first is the command security manager. The security manager handles both personnel security and physical security. Personnel security is the process of ensuring that people assigned to the command have the administrative authorizations necessary to work with the classified material that their job may require. Physical security includes secure doors, locks, and safes. Physical security of overall installations is a different responsibility, falling within force protection channels.

Special Security Officer

Many staffs also have a special security officer (SSO). SSOs handle security requirements around the use of sensitive compartmented information (SCI). SCI is information about certain intelligence sources and methods and is handled according to a separate control system. SSOs are also responsible for the security, control, and use of any space designated as an SCI facility (SCIF).

The SSO is usually a command position, but will generally operate under the guidance of the N2 or a senior intelligence officer. As a general rule, the security manager and SSO are separate offices, though there should be routine communications between them.

Chaplain

The chaplain's role will vary depending on the size of the staff. In smaller staffs, the chaplain will personally conduct religious ministry and pastoral care for the staff and for subordinate units. In larger staffs, the chaplain will be the manager of religious ministries across an entire fleet or force. These senior chaplains assist and mentor junior chaplains and will support religious ministry teams (RMT) in subordinate commands.

Staff chaplains are often key players in response to crises or tragedies, working with their medical counterparts to surge counselors and religious support to impacted units.

Surgeon or Staff Medical Officer

Like the chaplain, the surgeon's role will vary with the size and seniority of the staff. Staff medical officers engage in planning for contingencies and COPS, ensuring that medical needs are folded into the operation. They track the medical readiness of assigned forces and manage high-interest medical issues such as responses to disease outbreaks. The COVID-19 pandemic dramatically underscored their critical role in keeping the Navy safe and ready for operations.

The Team Doctor

Many fleet surgeons and staff senior medical officers have reached the point in their careers where they are primarily leaders and managers, rather than medical providers. Many, however, still view themselves as the team doctor. Good staff officers know they can be a tremendous resource to take care of their Sailors. Consider the following:

- A lieutenant who faced a devastating cancer diagnosis. A fleet surgeon spent hours talking to specialists with the family, becoming the trusted advocate who helped them make sense of complex choices.
- A Sailor whose pregnant wife was abruptly disenrolled by her private obstetrician due to a change in Navy policy. A fleet surgeon makes phone calls across the bureaucracy, asking simply, "Is this the best you can do for this Sailor?"
- The Pentagon on 11 September (9/11). The three-star Air Force chief of surgery in the courtyard of the building used his skills as a trauma surgeon to triage the wounded.

The senior medical staff became medical professionals to help people. It is completely proper for a staff member facing a significant medical crisis, either personally or to their family, to approach the staff medical officer through their chain of command for support and insight.

Safety Officer

Safety is a key part of Navy processes. Much of what the service does is inherently risky; understanding and managing occupational risk is a responsibility of command. Officers who have served afloat are familiar with the safety officer as an advisor to the commander on safety issues and as the manager of required safety programs. On large staffs, the safety officer performs the same function, supervising safety programs across the commander's assigned forces.

The safety officer on staff will be a key figure in mishap investigations, implementation of safety standards, and the monitoring of mishap, injury, and illness statistics.

Knowledge Management Officer

It is trendy on large staffs to have a knowledge management officer (KMO). The KMO is often attached to the CoS or ED and is charged, in the words of one of the job descriptions, to align command processes, information requirements, and available technology to facilitate staff self-synchroniza-tion, information exchange, and collaboration, as well as to enhance the flow of information across the command and related echelons/services. Practically, such a charge usually dashes against the scope of this task. Staffs are entirely about information, and it is a rare KMO who understands the nuances of the staff processes enough to add foundational value. As a result, the KMO's actual role often comprises little more than organizing the command share drives and creating websites and file-sharing sites.

Comptroller

In simple terms, a comptroller has oversight of accounting and financial reporting for the money assigned to the command. Every Navy command or activity that receives funds that are subject to the Anti-Deficiency Act is required to have a comptroller. The comptroller will establish the inter-nal control system to ensure that all DoD requirements are met, and has a reporting responsibility to the Office of the Secretary of the Navy for Financial Management and Comptroller (OASN/FMC).

The Anti-Deficiency Act

Any discussion of money in a Navy staff will eventually see mention of the Anti-Deficiency Act. The Anti-Deficiency Act is federal law that grows out of a simple premise: the Congress and only the Congress may authorize the expenditure of public funds. Article I of the constitution directs, "No Money shall be drawn from the Treasury, but in Consequence of Appropriations made by Law." This clause is the source of congressional authority over much of the U.S. government, and is called "the power of the purse." The Anti-Deficiency Act guards that power by prohibiting federal officers from spending or obligating the U.S. government for any debt that is not approved by Congress. It also prohibits spending money for a purpose other than as authorized by Congress, and prohibits accepting voluntary services.

What is unique about the Anti-Deficiency Act is that violations carry criminal penalties. While few are prosecuted under the law, Anti-Deficiency Act violations must be reported to the Comptroller General of the United States, the President, and Congress. The report must state if the violation was made as having been executed knowingly or willfully, in which case the letter is also sent to the Department of Justice for criminal investigation. Even if the violation is not deemed criminal, administrative disciplinary action is common and often spells the end of a career.

Given that the requirement to have a comptroller stems from controlling money that is subject to the Anti-Deficiency Act, it is safe to say that avoiding Anti-Deficiency Act violations—and keeping the commander from being mentioned in a report—is the comptroller's primary job.

Beyond keeping the commander out of trouble, the comptroller is also the expert on what money is available to the command and how it can be used.

Sexual Assault and Response Coordinator

Sexual assault and response coordinators (SARCs) exist across all levels of the Navy. In major staffs, an O6 officer is usually assigned the role as a full-time responsibility. At the OPNAV or SECNAV level where the focus is more on establishing policy, a senior civilian may fill the role. Regardless of background, these officers fulfill three roles. First, they administer the Navy's Sexual Assault Prevention and Response (SAPR) program within the headquarters. Second, they assist, oversee, and assess the program across the commander's subordinate forces. Finally, they provide expert advice on the handling of sexual assault cases that involve the commander as a senior reviewing officer. In all of these roles, they will interact directly with the commander, and are always assigned as a direct report to the commander.

Fleet Marine Officer

The Fleet Marine Officer (FMO) is a senior (O5 or O6) Marine permanently assigned as a member of the staff who serves as the critical link between the fleet Marine Force and the fleet. With the recent return of the Marine Corps to its amphibious roots, the importance of these positions has been growing.

Liaison Officers

It is important to understand the difference between a liaison officer and a member of the staff. A liaison officer is a member of the command that sends them. For example, a Navy liaison to an Air Force command works for the Navy commander who sent them, not for the Air Force. A Navy officer assigned to an Air Force staff reports to that Air Force commander. When liaison officers are permanently assigned and integral to the staff, this distinction can be less relevant on a day-to-day basis. It is, however, a critical formal distinction and one that should always be clear.

Naval Special Warfare Liaison Officer

Some staffs have a permanently assigned naval special warfare (NSW) officer who is the staff subject matter expert on special warfare. In other cases, a formal liaison officer from an NSW element is assigned to a staff. NSW officers are notorious for blurring this distinction.

Coast Guard Liaison Officer

Coast Guard liaison officers are generally true liaison officers, working for a Coast Guard district commander who is the counterpart to a Navy numbered fleet commander (NFC).

CHAPTER 6

Getting Started as a Staff Officer

For most officers in large staffs (numbered fleet and above), staff duty centers on owning a portfolio. A portfolio is simply a small slice of the staff's duties. Depending on the scope of the work, the skills of the officer, and the limitations of staffing, an officer will often be responsible for multiple portfolios of different complexity, which can be thought of as primary and collateral duties.

An officer who owns the responsibility to take action on something is called, unimaginatively, an action officer. Joint Staffs (JSs) will often call officers action officers as their title, as in, "He is an action officer in the J5." Navy staffs tend to use the phrase in a more restricted sense; for example, staffs might say, "She is the action officer for the next budget assessment."

The common use of the word "own" to refer to this tasking speaks volumes about the expectations behind this assignment. A staff officer is expected to be thoroughly conversant in the issues surrounding their portfolio, to inform more-senior personnel about the issues, to represent the commander in discussions touching on their area of concern, and to recommend cogent actions to further the commander's intent in their area of work. Performing these duties well requires ownership in the fullest professional sense.

Ensuring a successful staff tour requires work even before arrival at the command. As with any tour, take time to learn about the command and its mission. The basics for most any staff can be found online. What type of staff is it? What command echelon does it represent?

Echelons of Command

It is common to hear staff officers refer to another command by its echelon, as in, "Sixth fleet is an echelon three command."

Echelon simply means how many layers of command lie between a commander and the CNO, with the CNO being considered echelon one. For example, the commander of U.S. Fleet Forces Command (FFC) reports directly to the CNO, thus FFC is an echelon two command. The U.S. Naval Support Facility in Deveselu, Romania, is an echelon four command, whose commanding officer reports to the CNO via the commander, Navy Region Europe / Africa / Central in Naples, Italy (echelon three), and commander, Navy Installations Command (echelon two).

Echelons are a general indicator of the seniority of a command. More important, however, are the documents that define command echelons, the standard Navy distribution lists for the shore chain of command and for the administrative organization of the operating forces of the U.S. Navy (OPNAV instruction [OPNAVINST] 5400.45). These two documents define the chain of command for the entire Navy—a useful starting point for understanding many relationships between staffs.

Another key question is, "What billet will you fill within the staff?" While this seems like a straightforward question, like so many things in Navy staffs, the answer depends. Generally, if you are being ordered to a small staff, to a senior position within a large staff, or have highly specialized skills, your future role will be clear. It is unlikely, for example, that an information professional officer ordered to a DESRON will be anything other than the Staff Communications Officer. However, on large staffs it is not uncommon for an officer to be ordered into an open billet and then assigned according to the needs of the staff.

With this in mind, it is often a mistake to think of your assignment to a specific billet in a large staff as a permanent condition. Indeed, one of the best pieces of advice for an officer looking for new and different work is to create a new portfolio within the staff. The general rule is that every staff has challenges they should be addressing but are not. Simply find one touching on your team's portfolio and set to work. In three months, it will be yours; in six months, no one will remember it was ever any other way.

Along the way, becoming an expert and providing direct advice to senior leaders can and should be a source of pride.

In the case of large staffs in fleet concentration areas or around Washington, DC, the demand for talent usually far exceeds talent that is available. There are often special programs, emerging teams, or senior officers who are scouting talent. Staying connected with seniors and peers in your community can help identify these opportunities.

It is worth asking both the detailer and the officer you are relieving what en route training is required and what might be helpful. Depending on the staff, potential training opportunities include the following.

Tactical Watchstanding Courses

Usually available through Tactical Training Group Atlantic or Pacific, these courses are focused on the duties of afloat staff watchstanders within the CWC construct (see chapter 18):

- Joint Maritime Tactics Course (JMTC): A two-week course intended to provide O4 and above officers the skills to plan and execute strike group combat operations, including joint and combined operations.
- Staff Tactical Watch Officer (STWO) Course: A one week course intended to introduce junior officers bound for fleet, CSGs, expeditionary strike group, and DESRON staffs with watchstanding requirements in a strike group–level operational environment.

Operational Level of War Courses

The Naval War College offers several courses intended for officers who will serve in Maritime Operations Centers (MOCs):

- The Maritime Staff Operators Course (MSOC): Open to officers O1 through O5, MSOC provides five weeks of resident education in the MOC concept.
- Executive Level Operational Level of Warfare Course (ELOC)—ELOC provides O6s an intensive one-week overview of applying the MOC concept as a senior staff member or staff director.

Once you have your orders in hand, make sure you read them carefully. If your billet requires overseas or sea duty screening, attend to this requirement as early as practical.

Getting Cleared

Staff duty is the first opportunity many officers have to see and use some of the Navy and the nation's more highly classified information. Exposure to these insights and capabilities is one of the second-order benefits of a staff experience. Pay particular attention to any language in your orders that outlines a specific security clearance requirement. If your orders state that you will require eligibility for access to SCI, make sure that you are or will be eligible. It is unfortunately not uncommon for officers transferring from commands that are not familiar with these requirements to fail to take the appropriate steps, with awkward results for the service member.

The formula for gaining access to classified information is Eligibility + Need to Know = Access. In execution, there are four steps to this process:

- First, you will be required to complete a detailed form (the Standard Form 86) outlining your résumé, personal contacts, and conduct.
- Second, an investigation is conducted. Records are checked to verify your personal history and financial stability. Your references, family, and coworkers may be contacted to attest to your character and conduct.
- Third, the results of the investigation are passed to the DoD Central Adjudication Facility (DoDCAF), which determines if you meet the requirements (i.e., eligibility) for a specific level of access.
- Finally, if you meet the eligibility requirements and have a need to know for your duties, you can be granted access (i.e., clearance) to that level of information.

While this last step completes granting the security clearance, it does not end the security clearance process. Every member with a security clearance is required to report specific kinds of events (e.g., marriage, foreign contacts, or travel). If required by your billet, you will be subject to continuous monitoring.

Some considerations if ordered to an SCI billet:

- When was your last security investigation and was it sufficient for the billet you are ordered to fill? The rules of background investigations are changing as the DoD updates and automates its approach to reviewing service members for security clearances. If your command has an SSO, check with them on your status. If not, have your command security officer reach out to the SSO at your gaining command or an SSO in your region for advice.

- If you need a new or additional investigation, initiate it as soon as possible. Conducting an investigation is, at best, a multi-month process. In complicated cases, it can take much longer.

- If you have an investigation already initiated or under way, check with your security office to ensure it continues. Investigations cost money, and the requirement for an investigation is often tied to a specific billet. It sometimes happens that a member transfers, leaving the billet for which the investigation was initiated, and the investigation is closed without being completed because the system does not automatically process that the member's future billet also requires this level of investigation.

- If you are currently accessed to SCI information, and are moving to a billet that also requires SCI access, ensure that your gaining command has requested that you transfer in status (TIS): this simplifies the process of accessing information on arrival at the new command, but is not automatic and must be requested by the gaining command.

Bottom line: think of managing your security clearance much like reviewing and preparing your service record before a promotion board. While there are many players involved in the process, no one is as interested in a successful outcome as you are.

In some special cases, your new billet may require a polygraph examination (sometimes called a lie detector test). Generally, personnel routinely assigned to positions that require a polygraph are familiar with the requirement. However, the requirement can now be noted on official Navy orders. If you find such language in your orders, start the process as early as possible, because the lead time to schedule for an examination can be considerable.

Once you arrive, the various security offices will be a key element of your check in. Resist the urge to simply do your own required paperwork—take an extra ten minutes with each office to learn how to stay off the shoals. The security officers can give you the ground truth about security in your new role. Does your office have safes and alarms? Who changes the combinations? What training is required for you and your team each year? How should you report, or even better avoid, security incidents? What are the most common security infractions that the security officers observe?

One area you must understand are any reporting requirements that come with your security clearances. In some cases, you will need to report foreign travel and contact with foreign nationals, including contact on social media. Not knowing these requirements will not mitigate a failure to follow them.

Getting Wired Up

If at all possible, press your sponsor to assist you in having your computer accounts established before you arrive. In some cases, with enterprise-wide systems, that process can be as simple as shifting an existing account from one network node to another. However, while the Navy–Marine Corps Intranet (NMCI) has standardized some accounts in both the unclassified and secret-level domains, it is common for commands to maintain their own systems with unique log-ons, storage, and email addresses. Overseas and afloat staffs will often work on different domains. Many staff positions require access not only to non-classified internet protocol router network (NIPRnet) and secret internet protocol router network (SIPRnet), but also the joint worldwide intelligence communications system (JWICS) and other even more specialized networks. Some systems also require a public key infrastructure (PKI) certificate to access specific websites or data bases that usually require a separate application process from the system itself. In any event, having accounts created and ready before you arrive will usually require completing the required information assurance (IA) training for each information network. The completion certificate from this training will need to be provided to the gaining command IA managers as part of the request to establish the accounts.

Completing the required systems access requests before your arrival can be challenging, but will pay off in your ability to quickly plug in to the information flow during your first days at the staff.

You will also want to learn how to get help with your information technology (IT) systems. For NMCI, the first step is to call the NMCI service desk at 866-THE-NMCI. The NMCI service desk offers support to classified and unclassified systems 24/7, 365 days a year. The new staff officer, arriving from an afloat command where all systems were managed locally, may find the transition to call center support somewhat bewildering. Complaining about the responsiveness and effectiveness of this centralized IT support is a standard staff pastime, but it is the system the Navy has created, so best to learn to use it.

Also, make sure you are clear on the security rules for each IT system. Each system will have an information systems security officer (ISSO) or information systems security manager (ISSM) who can provide training and advice, and who will handle any spillage of classified material between networks.

Paying the Administrative Tax

Arriving at a new command carries with it a host of administrative burdens. Some must be taken care of, and most officers are self-aware enough to ensure their pay continues whether or not there is an effective welcome-aboard process. Depending on the command, however, there are a series of administrative steps that need to be taken to ensure that you are fully functional and ready to serve:

- Being ready to travel. Even in a world of exquisite communications, some conversations only happen face-to-face. That means travel. A good staff officer is prepared to travel, knows how to execute official travel with a minimum of fuss and complication, and how to exploit the opportunities that travel presents.

- Government travel charge card (GTCC). Travelers on official government business are required to pay their expenses using a GTCC. If there is any chance you will travel on official business, you will need one. They take time to secure, so if you do not have one, get one before you have need. The card comes in two varieties: standard ($7,500 credit limit) and restricted ($4,000 credit limit). Getting a standard card requires a fair, but not excellent, credit record. If your credit is less good, or if you decline to have your credit record checked as part of the application process, you will receive a restricted card. Being encouraged to use your personal credit status for official business seems improper, but the reality is that essentially everyone does so.

- Defense travel system (DTS). DTS is the online system for booking official travel. Like the GTCC, if there is any chance you will travel, you should create an account under your new command. If you had an account at your old command, you will also need to take action because the account will be attached to your last command's approval chain and funding codes. Your former command needs to release you, an act that sometimes is more difficult than it should be and one that your new staff cannot complete for you.

- Passports. As a staff officer, you should have both an official and a regular or private passport. Official passports have dark reddish-brown covers and identify the holder as being abroad on official U.S. government business. Regular passports have blue covers and are used by a U.S. citizen on private travel. There is a proper circumstance to use each and you may need either or both depending on circumstances. Both take time to secure. The process can sometimes be expedited to meet an operational requirement, but that process is painful and less reliable. More than once, the decision on which staff officer was sent on a plum overseas travel opportunity has hinged on who already had the correct passport. Buy yourself the option by securing both now.

Taking Charge

So you have arrived on the staff and been given a portfolio. If you are fortunate, your predecessor is still there. At best, you are likely to have a week together, no matter how complex the portfolio. What kinds of things do you need to know?

First, what is their battle rhythm? What meetings, both in- and outside of the staff, require their attendance? Do they write or provide input to any recurring reports or emails?

What references govern this area of responsibility? It is useful to have key references in hard copy for quick reference. Read through them at least once; tab and highlight them as fits your style. Note who issued them and when they were last updated. This will tell you who exercises decision-making authority over these issues, and who might be able to provide expertise. Be warned, however—it is not uncommon for instructions to be woefully out of date, and for the cognizant office to not realize they are not fulfilling their responsibilities. That fact does not necessarily handicap a portfolio, but it does color the operational landscape.

Where is the institutional memory? The textbook answer is that a Navy staff should have a knowledge manager. The reality is that no Navy staff has gotten this process right yet. Most commands no longer keep hard-copy files, yet use digital information management processes that would embarrass a mid-sized company. Fixing that (unless you are the OPNAV N2N6, who is the resource sponsor for these systems) is beyond your mandate. The key insight for the new staff officer is that most transfer of knowledge on arrival will be self-propelled and should be a key element of any staff turnover. To that end, you should determine the following:

- Is there a shared drive? Most staff codes keep a shared drive on each of their computer networks. It is often common to have three: one internal to the directorate or staff element, one that is shared with other directorates to allow collaboration, and one that is common across the entire staff.

- Where is the offline storage? The way the Navy purchases computer systems support means that digital storage is, in many cases, finite. Faced with a shared drive that is full and the need to continue work, it is not uncommon for enterprising staff officers to find other places to keep essential files. In the past, this often took the form of removable media or local drives on individual workstations. Neither are good practice, either from an IT or security standpoint. Removable media introduces a host of security vulnerabilities and is now generally prohibited by security policy. Local drives are not routinely backed up, leaving the staff one electronic failure from a significant data loss. Nonetheless, it is usual practice for departing staff officers to email whatever files they consider essential to their relief, a haphazard and tedious process.

Through whatever mechanism, your predecessor should provide you every memo that was sent up the chain of command concerning your portfolio during their tour, as well as any significant briefings they prepared for senior level information or decision.

After these steps, look at any hard-copy files that the office retains. The reality is that very few staffs still keep centralized files of any kind. What remains is often dated and poorly organized. If you inherit one of those rare cases where there are complete and current files, rejoice. Otherwise, the best course is to close the file drawer and wait. If, after a year, nothing in the file has been essential, consider shredding the lot—or, better, sending the entire cabinet to the command historian.

Finally, absorb as much of your predecessors' contact lists as you can. You should have a list of who else works this portfolio across other parts of the staff, and across other commands and agencies. Ideally, your predecessor will arrange a series of short meetings to introduce you to these key players or leverage a standing meeting to make an introduction.

Since contact and coordination represent an essential element of a staff officer's job, it is important to be easy for others to find and contact:

- Ensure your contact information in NMCI address books is updated.
- Create a full signature block that includes all your contact information on each email system and set it to appear as a default.
- Ensure this updated information is published to the global address list (GAL).
- Create business cards. If your command will not print cards, invest in your own. Good-quality cards can be designed online and professionally printed for the cost of a modest lunch, and are an invaluable tool for making and cementing contacts. Carry them with you and share them broadly, especially when you are new in the position.
- Professional discretion (and operational security, or OPSEC) may suggest you have two sets of business cards—one for U.S. government business with your classified email addresses and secure phone numbers, and one for contacts in business and academia with your commercial phone and NIPRnet address.

Critical Enablers

Much of staff work is receiving, understanding, and conveying information to support the commander. The more you understand about the flow of information in the staff, the more you will be able to create impact.

Most major staffs use an online system for organizing, issuing, and answering the tasks they assign and are assigned. These systems are not intended to take the place of official orders for operational issues, but they are required by policy to be used for administrative actions. All tasking systems have several common elements:

- A standard data format, intended to provide clear tasking
- Rules for who can approve issuing a task outside the command
- Rules for who is the point of contact for tasks at a command
- Rules outlining when a task needs to be answered

Within the Navy, the DoN Tasking, Records and Consolidated Knowledge Enterprise Repository (DoN TRACKER) is intended to be the single Navy-wide system to manage tasks and the paperwork associated with them. The reality, however, is that most staff elements exist at the Venn diagram overlap of several Navy, joint, and specialized tasking systems. Add in that most tasking systems exist in several versions on systems of different classification, and the complexity mounts.

Learning these tasking systems and the processes behind them is first and foremost an exercise in self-defense. In most commands, tasking systems are usually managed by an administrative element that does not understand (and is not expected to understand) the nuances of every complex task. As a result, an incoming task is usually assigned to a staff code. Under business rules set by that command, that staff code usually has a limited time—seventy-two hours is common—to accept, modify, or reclama the assignment of the task.[1] If the code does not respond in that time, they have accepted the task as written, even if it is poorly stated or clearly not in their wheelhouse. Within each staff code, there is usually a small group who, as a collateral duty, check the various tasking systems for new tasks. Given the number of systems and the fact that many staff codes do not receive tasks constantly, it is easy to see how tasks can be missed. In most commands, the office that receives and assigns tasks for the command also produces a status report of tasks completed and overdue. As a result, a not-uncommon source of staff churn is the discovery of a task only once it is pending or overdue.

A good staff officer will learn which tasking systems touch their command, who tasks and is tasked through them, and who in their staff manages them.

Meetings

Staffs have meetings. Meetings within teams, meetings across teams, meetings across commands. Everyone loves to hate meetings. Research, and most staff experience, teaches that most meetings are not an efficient means of conveying information or making decisions. And yet, they remain a key part of most staffs. How should a staff officer make the best use of these gatherings?

First, learn what meetings must be supported. Whether formally articulated or not, most staffs have an established series of recurring meetings that deal with issues of enduring concern. These can be as simply as a DESRON staff huddle after dinner under way, or a nested series of decision-making venues like the OPNAV staff budget review process. Your staff portfolio undoubtedly touches on one or more of these events. For any meeting, you should know a few basic facts:

- Who owns the meeting? This will be the office or officer who set the agenda and often determines who must or may attend.

- Are decisions made in this venue? The answer often depends on who is in attendance.

- What is the classification of the venue? There is nothing more pointless than trying to have half a conversation because the physical space or participants cannot have a fully informed discussion. Find (or create) a venue that supports the seniors present having a full and informed conversation.

- Is there read ahead material? The purpose of read ahead material (sometimes written as RAH) is to allow participants, and especially the senior attendees, to arrive informed about the topic. Read ahead may be nothing more than slides depicting current operations that are available shortly before the daily ops brief. They may be a formal staff package, carefully routed on a strict timeline prior to an event. Properly used, read ahead makes the meeting more effective. Remember, read ahead works on the seniors' timeline, not yours. If read ahead is expected, understand the expectation and the timeline for its delivery. It does no good to deliver material too late for seniors to review prior to the event. If you are attending, budget time to review the read ahead prior to the meeting.

- Consider who should attend from your staff element. For most recurring meetings, who attends is already established. For one-off meetings, the action officer may need to recommend the size, expertise, and seniority of the element's representation. This recommendation will hinge on whether decisions are being made, who is responsible for the issues, or if the command is interested only in watching and taking notes.

- If you are hosting, determine how large the meeting should be. There is a general rule in the business world for determining meeting size known as 8-18-1800: If the goal is to make a decision, there should be no more than eight attendees. If the goal is brainstorming ideas, the number can go up to eighteen. If the goal is a one-way conveying of information, eighteen hundred people in a meeting can work. Smaller usually makes sense. However, in a military setting, there is one additional dynamic—who is really in the meeting. Arguably, if the meeting includes seniors and observers where the split between the seniors, who are the only attendees allowed by custom or formal direction to speak, and the observers is clear, the functional size of the meeting is the number of seniors.

Managing Meeting Uncertainty

A Navy four-star, legendary for his effectiveness in staff positions, used to mentor young officers to never walk into a meeting without already knowing the outcome. Years later, his advice was repeated to a senior civilian who had worked as the admiral's deputy several times over decades. The former deputy rejoined, "Of course—when the admiral didn't know what was going to happen in a meeting, he sent me!"

Sending a trusted deputy to a difficult meeting is a varsity staff technique for dealing with uncertainty. The deputy should be knowledgeable and able to represent the command with vigor. If the decision is not favorable, or if the command position has ruffled too many feathers, the commander often has the option of reopening the issue by calling the other seniors involved directly, even if the issue was officially decided at the meeting in question. Such a move is not hanging the deputy out to dry; acting as a foil in public discussions is part of the role of a trusted deputy.

General Meeting Skills

Know What Venues Are Available

On a flagship or in a small staff, finding a venue may be straightforward. In a large staff, or in the Pentagon, there may be dozens of competing meetings on any day. Find (or create) a list of conference rooms that can be scheduled, who schedules them, and what classification level they can support.

Know Who Needs to Be There

Juggling schedules to get the right folks in the room is a challenge. Determine up front who must be in attendance. In many cases, it will be the commander or another senior official, in which case others will usually modify their schedules to fit the senior's availability.

Know When the Meeting Must End—and Who Will Keep Time

If you are hosting the commander, know when the meeting ends and what the next event on their schedule is. If the next event cannot be moved, the front office staff will often call it a hard stop. A hard stop means that, even if your meeting starts late because the commander is delayed, it will still need to end on time. In many cases, the EA will watch the clock and intervene to remind the team and the commander of the time. However, the best staff officers have the situational awareness to do so themselves and will not presume that they can run over their allotted time. Even if the commander is still engaged and interested, use the line, "Sir/ma'am, we want to be respectful of your time. We can get back with you later if you need," as a polite opportunity to reset—or to receive an explicit invitation to continue.

Know How to Set Up and Run the Audiovisual Equipment

In most cases, the audiovisual (AV) systems are set up by whoever is using the venue. Learn how to do so for the venues you will use, then arrive early and ensure the equipment is configured. Little is more frustrating than delaying a senior leader while your computer profile loads onto a conference desktop for the first time.

Consider the Use of Video Teleconferences

Video teleconferences (VTCs) allow the benefits of a face-to-face meeting to be shared between decision-makers across the globe. They also add a layer of friction to the already challenging dynamic of meetings. Running a VTC is much like running a meeting, but has its own challenges.

Remember Time Zones

Nothing creates animosity across the fleet like scheduling a meeting with globally deployed forces solely at your convenience. While it is sometimes unavoidable, even four-star commanders try to find times that are within or near working hours for the other staffs involved if at all possible.

Remember Classification

The U.S. Navy uses multiple VTC systems at multiple classification levels. Ensure you have scheduled the right one for your purpose.

The Microphone Is Always On, and the Camera Is Always on You

Or at least smart officers act like they are.

Make an Impact

You are the Navy's expert on your account. That may seem a daunting statement, but your job as the action officer is to make it real. Becoming a respected expert is likely more attainable than you may expect. Odds are that no one else in the service is focused on the same problem that you are, certainly no one from the same command echelon and with the same instructions and imperatives. Even your predecessor, who may have been the expert six months ago, has likely moved on to other challenges and is rapidly growing out of date. You have the contacts, sit in the meetings, watch the positions develop. Fold in some basic hard work—the initiative to do the reading, reach out to peers and specialists, and ask the second-, third-, and fourth-level questions—and your commander will quickly be referring to you as "my expert" on the issue.

Arleigh Burke on Getting the Facts Straight

4 January 1957

MEMORANDUM FOR OP-03B

Subj: Categorical Statements

1. You started your presentation on the need for a change in the Planning Cycle for Shipbuilding with a categorical statement which, if I remember correctly, was about as follows:

   "This cart must start in 1957 to get a shipbuilding program in 1960. I realize this is a long time, but I would like to call to your attention that the period of gestation of elephants is two years, and big things cannot be accomplished quickly."

2. The Encyclopedia Britannica states:

   "The gestation period for elephants is not accurately known, but it is between 18 and 20 months."

3. Compton's Encyclopedia states:

   "The gestation period for elephants is about 22 months."

4. Avoid categorical statements unless you can prove them. There is always somebody who checks them!

ARLEIGH BURKE[2]

Selling Your Portfolio

Part of owning your portfolio is being prepared to sell it. Most naval officers recoil from the word "sell," and rightly so. Every staff has the officers who have fallen in love with their program, and who push an idea beyond what is productive or in the larger interest of the Navy. But a competent staff officer, possessed of insight and thoughts on how to best address their issue, needs to be prepared for fleeting moments when clear communication could have a profound impact.

You should have an elevator speech. It is a simple image: You and the admiral get into an elevator. The admiral eyes you and asks, "What do you do?" What would you say about you and your portfolio in the thirty seconds you have traveling between floors? Thirty seconds of talking is eighty to ninety words for most people, or eight to ten sentences. Going through this drill forces you to identify the essential issues, boil these complex issues down to the key points, then to distill from these points what a senior should consider and what action a senior can and should take to make a difference.

Disingenuous? Hardly. Good seniors want to hear from their staffs— and they prize clear, impactful communications. The most impactful "spontaneous" communications are rarely completely spontaneous. Going through this drill will leave you prepared for most situations where a senior suddenly offers an opportunity for discussion.

Closely related to the elevator pitch is the question, "What should I be thinking about?" Some commanders will ask their trusted staff this question directly. Even if they do not, answering the question is a useful tool. A staff officer should know what their commander is thinking about, at least as relates to their portfolio. Invariably, there are significant issues that have not yet been raised to the commander's level or that are prioritized behind the urgent issues of the day. Once identified, the staff can consider how to place these issues in the commander's field of view. For the individual staff officer, it is another level of preparation for senior-level interactions. A clear, cogent explanation of such an issue conveys that the officer knows the commander and their priorities, and is thinking ahead on their behalf.

Checklist for Preparing and Reporting Aboard

- On receipt of orders, read your full orders, noting requirements for
    - training, and
    - security clearance.
- Research your new command, learning its
    - history,
    - mission,
    - place in the food chain, and
    - current commander.
- Reach out to your new command and
    - ask for a sponsor, and
    - determine who you will relieve, if known.
- Prior to arrival,
    - submit paperwork to establish computer accounts.

- After reporting,
  - move GTCC account to new command;
  - register in the DTS and shift your profile from your previous command;
  - determine if a passport is required;
  - find shared drives, files, and other sources of institutional memory;
  - get business cards; and
  - learn applicable tasking systems.

CHAPTER 7

Communicating as a Staff Officer

S taffs are about enabling commanders to make decisions. They carry out that mission by providing information and advice. How to find information, evaluate it, and synthesize it into cogent thought is a theme throughout this guide.

To have an impact, however, you need to be able to share your information. Like the last tactical actions that close a kill chain against an adversary, communicating information is the key step enabling the staff to deliver impact. Like a precision guided weapon, effective communication will deliver the right information to the right place at the right time. Fail this step, and all the previous work was for nothing.

In this chapter, we will consider some of the key means staffs use to communicate. Some readers will wonder why this chapter exists. Most officers are literate, anyone can sit through a meeting, and PowerPoint is used in many grammar schools. Nonetheless, there are at least two reasons to step back and consider these tools.

First, staffs today make heavy use of tools that did not exist even twenty-five years ago. The impact on staff dynamics and culture has been significant and is worth considering, and perhaps deliberately managing. Most staff officers use a tool because it is what they used last time, and because it is close at hand. A bit of thought can help you, as a staff officer and naval leader, pick the right tool for your communications, realizing the second-order effects of that choice.

Second, in the same way a ship is known by its boats, a staff is known by its communications. New staff officers across the service are continually finding ways to repeat basic communications mistakes. At best, these errors result in less professional communications. At worst, miscommunications cost time, waste effort, and increase risk to our forces. A bit of time invested can keep you from the most common pitfalls.

Spreading the Word

In a graphic age, naval staffs remain the preserve of the written word. How these words are formed and conveyed has changed, but the basis of communications remains the written word.

The advent of email has radically changed the dynamic of Navy staffs. On one hand, communication with other staff elements, subordinates, and colleagues has never been easier. Communication that once required a formal letter through the U.S. Postal Service or a record message through a naval communications system can now happen in the course of a few minutes. As dealers in information, email should be a boon for staffs.

Just to be clear: the Navy considers email to be a specialized form of Navy correspondence. The *Navy Correspondence Manual* states that email may be used "for informal communications in place of telephone calls or to transmit formal correspondence." If email is used for formal correspondence, it is supposed to conform to all the *Correspondence Manual* requirements to include "SSIC [Standard Subject Identification Code], serial number, date, and signature authority." By this standard, email is essentially never used for formal correspondence, at least in the legal sense. As for the millions of informal emails that the Navy generates each hour, the *Navy Correspondence Manual* notes, "There are no specific guidelines for informal correspondence; however, keep it brief, use good taste, and observe traditional customs and courtesies."[1] Good advice, but hardly complete. A large body of customs have grown up around emails. Like all military customs, they may not be enforced as regulation, but their violation can have real consequences.

The basic rules are simple:

- Chose the right computer system. If the topic is operationally sensitive or classified, move the conversation to the appropriate secure information processing system. Do not talk around sensitive or classified information.

- List your addressees in order of seniority, following the pattern you would in a naval letter or message. This practice is not only courteous, but also allows recipients to quickly see the most senior addressees on a long address list.

- Close professionally. While not directive, the strong norm is that juniors sign an email to seniors with "Very respectfully," while seniors sign "Respectfully" to juniors. There are other practices; save them for when you are more experienced.

- Create a signature block that includes your full name, position, command, and phone number, at a minimum. Where appropriate, include your email address on other classified systems. Then, use this block on every email. Online directories do not always update reliably, are often not reachable from across systems domains, and your regular contacts will sometimes transfer or have their email systems crash. You want to be easy to find when others have a question about your work.

- Digitally sign every email. Every official email system has a means to include a DoD PKI digital signature that increases confidence that an email is actually from the sender it claims to be from. A digital signature is required for any email with an attachment; it is good practice in every event.

- Encrypt when appropriate. Digital encryption helps protect personally identifiable information (PII) and sensitive information. It is, however, not a substitute for using secure communications systems for classified information.

- Use your "out of office" function and identify alternative points of contact for time-critical issues. In fact, if you will be absent for more than three business days, DoN regulations require that you enable an automated email response. You would not, in an operational setting, hold up essential communications, so do not do it in the staff.

So much for the basics. Where staff officers often get in trouble is when they forget a couple truths about emails:

- An email sent is an email out of control. As a wise senior counseled, "Once you hit send, you don't own it . . . but you will live with it forever." Staff lore is full of examples of "private" emails that were forwarded to audiences beyond where the author intended.

- "Reply all" is the staff equivalent of a public Twitter post. It is not uncommon for an informational email to have dozens or hundreds of addressees. Unless you know each and every one, treat any response as a public announcement. Otherwise, you may find that the lieutenant you do not know buried in the carbon copy (CC) line is the deputy EA to your boss's classmate.

- Tone and emotion translate badly into emails. You may intend to express a touch of irritation, impatience, or disappointment. When your email is read out of context, you may convey much more than you intended. If you feel the need to correct, upbraid, or wire brush someone, do it in person. It is both more effective and less likely to come back at you.

- Emails are forever. Every email sent on a U.S. government system is essentially archived immediately and permanently. It may be inaccessible to the user or the command and appear to be permanently deleted, but, if required for an investigation, it almost always still exists.

  Rules for success:

- Know the three lines. Emails are addressed To, CC, or blind carbon copy (BCC):

  - Sending a note To someone is the equivalent of making an action addressee on a naval message. You are conveying that the information is of particular concern or that they need to take action on its contents.

  - CC, or carbon copy, is a reference to the days of typewriters when a typist could make a limited number of additional copies of a letter by inserting carbon paper between the sheets. These were shared with people who needed to know about the correspondence but did not necessarily need to act on it.

  - Many three- and four-star officers will not read or acknowledge emails on which they are CCed unless the sender is senior to them, and many commanders have a rule that their staff should never CC them on emails. The thought is that if it is not for their direct action, it is not worth investing their limited time.

  - BCCing someone on an email provides them a direct copy of the note while preventing others from seeing who else is receiving it. BCCing can be used for mundane reasons, such as sending an invitation to a large group without revealing who exactly was invited to an event. It can also be a subtle way of allowing peers and seniors to see a correspondence. For example, an O4 action officer sending a note to another O6 on the staff with a reputation for being prickly might BCC their O6 boss. CCing their O6 boss might elevate the discussion sooner than is appropriate, and might also convey that the O4 is not empowered to have the discussion. The BCC hedges against the other O6 going directly to their boss and catching them unawares—without the baggage of obviously bringing them into the discussion. However, be aware that some senior officers believe that showing who an email is addressed to is a matter of integrity, and react very badly to finding someone was BCCed on an email to them.

- Know who responds. In most staffs, when the commander sends an email To someone, that is who they expect to respond directly to them. A good commander will CC the chain of command between, and the response will certainly CC the chain, but it is the commander's discretion to direct a question to whomever they believe can provide a quick and cogent answer. For example, the commander wants to know details of an upcoming operation. They might send the question directly to the operations officer, CCing the deputy commander and MOC director, but not expect the operations officer's response to be chopped through (reviewed and approved by) each.

- Acknowledge. Any time a senior sends you an email with you on the To line that requires any delay to answer, acknowledge it immediately, even if the answer must follow later.

- Brevity wins:
  - State why you are writing. A number of staffs require emails to begin with the lines "FOR DECISION" or "FOR INFORMATION ONLY," allowing the senior recipients to quickly triage communications from their staffs.
  - Put the bottom-line up front (BLUF). Many staffs require the first line after the salutation to explicitly say BLUF, followed by one or two lines summarizing the info and any decision to be made.

– Discipline yourself. A number of seniors will cite the seventeen-line rule, and require their staffs to frame any issue in an email of seventeen lines or less. Seventeen lines is a good rule of thumb, in part because it is the size of the preview pane in most email handling programs and allows the recipient to read the email without opening it.

Why Seventeen Lines?

Staff lore is that the seventeen-line limit comes from the Joint Requirements Oversight Council (JROC), a senior body chaired by the Vice Chair of the Joint Chiefs of Staff that approves major DoD acquisitions projects. The justification for major defense programs—for example, purchasing ships and aircraft over decades at the cost of billions of dollars—is restricted to seventeen lines. The thought process from seniors is that, if buying the *Zumwalt*-class guided missile destroyer (DDG) can be explained and justified in seventeen lines, so can most staff actions.

- Use tear lines. Sometimes you will need to offer more detail to your audience. Use the rules above, holding to your seventeen lines, then note as appropriate, "More detail on this issue is found below." Then, below your signature, include the additional text that amplifies your brief summary.

- Explain attachments. Unless you are simply passing a product between action officers, do not send attachments without an explanation. If the point of your communication is buried in an attachment, most of your readers are going to miss it unless you make it clear up front. Cite every attachment in the same way you would cite enclosures in a naval letter or a reference in a naval message. For example, "As detailed in the attachment, the command intends to _____."

- Remember the *Washington Post* test: Simply ask yourself if you would be happy seeing your words in the *Washington Post*. If sent on an unclassified network, emails can easily leak into the hands of the press or public. Even if not shared directly, unclassified communications are generally subject to release under the Freedom of Information Act (FOIA). If you are dealing with a sensitive or controversial topic, always remain completely professional in written communication. The rule is that if you would not want it to be cited—with your name—on the front page of a major newspaper, do not write it.

Voldemort and the Fleet

Years ago, the *Washington Post* rule was mostly for senior officers and officers serving in Washington, DC. No more. The list of naval issues of interest to the press and public has only grown, and the existence of searchable digital records (of which your emails are part) has made the internal discussions of Navy staffs open to the public (and our adversaries) at a scale never before seen.

In one case, a major news event created required action across many commands. It was quickly communicated that no email dealing with the response should name the entity that inspired it. Staff officers quickly dubbed the entity involved "Voldemort" after the villain in the Harry Potter books whose name was too terrible to be uttered. The directive was well-intentioned, but could have itself become an embarrassment or, worse, been seen as an improper effort to conceal discoverable information in anticipation of a FOIA request or investigation.

Transparency serves democracy, and our conduct, public and private, should always be beyond reproach.

Be careful of personal email accounts. Today, every naval officer has one or more personal email accounts. Compared to U.S. government email systems, they offer a list of advantages. Commercial web-based email services are easier to access than the clunky web interfaces to official NIPRnet accounts. They are easy to access from smart phones. Often, they allow the movement of file types that are restricted on government systems due to security risks. They are a transportable between commands in ways that NMCI has never achieved. And yet, using a personal email system for official business is an extraordinarily bad idea.

The security of nongovernment email systems can never be ensured. Thus, using personal email creates a presumption that you have made the information vulnerable to hackers and criminals. Furthermore, using your personal email for official business potentially opens your entire personal email account to public scrutiny.

Staff officers have official email addresses to do official business. While in most cases it is possible to access web-based personal emails from government computers, you should not develop the habit of using these programs for anything other than personal business. Your official business is the Navy's business. The Navy needs access to it if necessary and you owe the Navy using the tools and safeguards it has built into official information systems when doing official business.

If this rule seems pedantic, consider the consequences. In 2018 the leading candidate for the position of CNO withdrew his nomination after it was disclosed that he had conducted official business with an officer who had been removed from the CNO's staff under an allegation of misconduct. Over the course of months, the candidate had corresponded with the officer via personal email, soliciting his advice on official business. The fact that this correspondence was conducted via personal email did not change its official nature.

When handling email, follow these rules:

- First, ask if email is the right tool. In many cases, you are better off to pick up the phone or walk down the hall. There is no substitute for direct communications, especially if you are dealing with an emotional issue. While we live in a digital culture, we fight alongside shipmates; talking is what turns email contacts into shipmates.

- Build a reputation for discretion. You usually get to burn your shipmates only once before you are cut off. If it explicitly says "Do not forward," do not forward it. If you are BCCed, do not reply to the email. If it seems sensitive, keep it in confidence. Understand there are layers to sharing: within your team, up the chain within your command, outside the command. Going to a broader circle with an issue before it is internally coordinated can complicate an issue enormously, and is usually not appreciated by the seniors. If in doubt, ask.

- Handle flag correspondence delicately. As a staff officer, you may be privy to correspondence between senior officers. Unless expectations are clearly understood (e.g., routine reports sent by email), treat these as privileged communications: they are for your information but not for sharing.

- Delegating email access. It is not uncommon for seniors to delegate access to their email to their front office staff. When sending an email to a flag officer, you should assume that their EA, at a minimum, will see the correspondence. In most cases, they trust their EA's discretion (see chapter 4), and you can as well, but when dealing with issues of exceptional sensitivity, such delegated access may be a consideration.

Regular Reports

Regular emails, often heavily formatted, have taken the place of record message reports for many commands. For example, most naval component commanders send an email update to their CCDR and the CNO by email each week. Many shore commands update their chain of command with an email each week or month.

Taken as a whole, the proliferation of these email reports is probably responsible for more staff work than any other single development. For the fleet commander to send an email to the CNO, the fleet staff requires inputs from each direct-report subordinate unit; these units collect reports in turn and so on down the chain of command. At each step, the higher headquarters edits the response. If the fleet commander is sending a note to CNO each Friday, the fleet staff will want inputs Wednesday so they can be edited on Thursday and delivered to the fleet commander on Friday morning. That means subordinate inputs are written on Tuesday or earlier, which means they need to be updated for what has transpired in the intervening seventy-two hours.

Following is what a good staff officer needs to understand about these reports:

- The reports rely on standardized formats. Each command has a format for their reports, usually driven by their higher headquarters' format, the goal being for the senior headquarters to be able to cut and paste from subordinate reports. Collect examples of these formats and make your inputs conform to them.

- The reports are widely shared. While the report is for the higher headquarters commander, their key staff is also usually CCed. These seniors may routinely resend the report to their key subordinates, and so on and so on. This phenomenon is great for broad situational awareness, but these notes should not be mistaken for the seniors' private discussions.

- Version control of the reports. Given that each report is usually a composite of inputs, good staffs create a clear process with strict version control on the draft product. A good staff officer knows this process, while an exceptional staff officer knows who can reach into the process when last-minute updates dictate.

- Using these reports to get ahead of a major command by taking credit for an action. It is not uncommon for multiple commands to support a major event or action. Often this support is a significant event for these specialized commands. They report their work to their chains of command, who wrap up their reports and push news of their good work up to their seniors. Great—until the report from the supporting element gets ahead of the report from the supported operational command who ran the overall operation. Very little vexes a fleet commander like a supporting chain of command telling the CNO about their success outside of the context of the wider operation.

The Art of the Ghost Email

Staff officers are commonly tasked to produce ghost emails (GEMs) for their seniors. The term comes from the publishing term "ghost writing," when someone writes a book published under the name of a more prominent individual. Where in an earlier era the staff would have written a memo to be endorsed and forwarded by the senior, today the staff will deliver their GEMs for the senior to edit and send over their own signature. The process is an accepted part of a staff officer's role.

Effectively ghosting an email requires that an action officer emulate the format and style of the senior who will send the email. It is accepted practice to go to a senior's EA or flag writer and ask for examples of their email style. Examples include mechanics such as how they address their bosses and how they sign emails to different audiences, as well as the senior's distinctive voice, making ghosting emails not unlike speechwriting.

For example, assume you run a program that requires support from subordinate commands. You brief your commander, and part of your request is that the commander might send an email to these commands to raise their awareness of the requirement. You then provide the commander with a GEM that sounds nothing like their normal tone, but they are busy and perhaps only somewhat invested in the issue, so they send it without edits. Any savvy subordinate will recognize it for what it is: a ghosted email that the commander did not think enough of to edit into their own voice. You raised the profile of your program, but you also communicated that it is clearly not commander's business.

The goal of a proficient staff officer should be to produce an email that is in the senior's voice and that requires no editing, allowing the senior to simply press "send" to complete the staff action.

Live Hand Grenades

Part of writing a GEM is creating the address lists for the email. The nature of most email programs means that the drafter could have an email, per-haps routine, perhaps controversial, addressed to people much senior to themselves that is one mouse click away from launching. So, a word to the wise: Start the GEM by selecting the senior as the "from" addressee, a little-used function in most email programs. Usually, since you will not have permission to send from the senior's account, this action will create a safety against the email sending before it is final. Compose the email, then address the "to" fields last and, once it is addressed, treat it like a live grenade until it is safely forwarded.

There are better ways for admirals to learn your name.

Directive Authority and Emails

Email communication long ago moved from administrative to operational tool. One of the challenges of email is that almost anyone can send a note to anyone else. While tasking can come from multiple places, clarity of C2 requires that orders directing operational action come from a recognized authority, be transmitted to a standardized group of recipients, and be recorded in a standardized way. In some cases, authority is evident (it is from the commander, for example), but even then, direction for operational actions will usually be retransmitted from a single point. In most MOCs, the battle watch captain on duty has the responsibility to transmit orders to subordinate commands. This role is discussed further in chapter 13.

Covering Your Six

In an earlier age, staff officers used memoranda to provide contemporaneous documentation of conversations to cover themselves against future questions of who-knew-what-when. Today, a signed email offers future proof of the time of and participants in a conversation in a similar way. These CYA emails can be a useful tool for a staff officer. However, a CYA email will generally be recognized for what it is and may be taken as a sign of a lack of trust. This impression may be accurate and useful, but should be used carefully and with due regard for likely reactions.

Naval Messages

If email is being used for operational orders, regular reports, and higher headquarters direction, what remains of naval messages?

The question is somewhat muddy. When established in the early twentieth century, naval messages were used for communications that needed to be delivered electronically. Their strict formatting rules were created to allow rapid transmission in an era when naval messages were sent manually by Morse code over a high-frequency fleet broadcast. Strict formatting continued to allow early forms of automated data processing systems to manage them in bulk. Today, naval messages are often edited on the same desktop computers that handle our emails, and are processed by systems that will not fail to deliver the message because of one incorrectly inserted character in the body of the text. Truly, the technical distinction between a naval message and an email is limited and often only understood by information professionals. Nonetheless, naval messages remain uniquely authoritative, in part because of their formality. The fact that naval messages are often called "record messages" speaks to our view of their permanence: they are how we record what matters.

For Navy staffs, naval messages remain in use for the following:

- Operations that require high-confidence delivery within a set time

- Reports to joint systems or elements that only interface through joint message handling systems
- Official communications between commands where the releasing authority must be explicit to ensure the veracity and authority of the message
- Establishing official orders force-wide in an archived and footnotable way (e.g., record message addressed to All Navy [ALNAVs] or operational tasks [OPTASKs])
- Standardized, formatted inputs into legacy data-handling systems
- Conveyance of permanent change of station orders for personnel
- Messages marked "Personal For" between commanders
- Bravo Zulu messages[2]

In an era of emails, "Personal For" messages remain in use as a way to pass guidance, insight, and concerns with the formality of a naval message to a restricted audience.

Picking the Right Tool

A savvy commander can use the nuances of naval communications to get the word out in effective ways. One fleet commander wanted to jumpstart discussion of major warfighting issues. Their views were somewhat controversial, and the commander wanted broad discussion and impact without having them mired in coordination. Their tactic—issue a series of "Personal For" messages marked as "Personal for Commanding Officers" rather than to one or two recipients, while sending the message information to higher headquarters. Hundreds of subordinate commanding officers, suddenly in receipt of a "Personal For" from a four-star, promptly generated the buzz that was desired. The higher headquarters listed as information addressees could not argue that a message from the fleet commander to their own subordinates should have been coordinated, but given the animated readership in the fleet, the higher headquarters read them and made them part of their warfighting thinking.

Memorandums and Point Papers

Sometime in the 1980s, the U.S. Navy decided it was going paperless. Technologically, it was possible. A quick check of the current budget for paper and printer supplies, however, testifies that culturally it is not happening anytime soon.

While much of this expenditure is people printing emails and PowerPoint briefings (more on these later), the tradition of the memorandum and point paper remain alive, and with good reason.

Email lends itself to brevity and speed. Complex issues deserve a nuanced and thoughtful treatment, and an explanation of how we arrived at the present, an exploration of competing options, and a consideration of alternative views. That fact, not simply tradition, is why many staffs insist certain issues be addressed via longer written products.

Writing, whether a tight one-page point paper or a fifty-page study, has two critical effects. First, writing forces the author to think systematically. Even when produced on a tight timeline, memos and point papers inherently take longer than writing an email, offering a window for new thought. Organizing text requires a thorough approach. Where the terseness of briefing slides or emails can cover for omissions or unsupported analytic leaps, it is much harder to obfuscate in prose.

Second, memos and point papers are usually routed as hard copies. Where emails can be shot-gunned to dozens of addressees, memos and point papers tend to be routed sequentially. This allows each level of the chain of command to consider the comments of those along the way. And where an email generally carries an expectation of immediate action, a memo or point paper has no such expectations.

While most naval officers have experience writing as part of their college studies, many arrive at a staff tour some years from their last confrontation with a blank sheet of paper. Do not despair. Writing is like any other learned skill. While some folks have more of a knack for it than others, the discipline naval officers bring to their profession provides a good basis for becoming a competent writer. A few quick basics:

- Learn the formats. The *Navy Correspondence Manual* outlines the accepted formats for written communications. Knowing which format fits the task at hand is no different from an aircraft mechanic knowing which wrench to reach for. Some lazy staff officers simply write text and hand it to the nearest yeoman, if one is available, to have it formatted. While a yeoman is a great asset to ensuring your correspondence is correctly formatted, they cannot make a letter read like a memorandum or vice versa.

- Use the tools. Today's computer software includes a range of spelling and grammar checkers. Like any instrument, they are limited and imperfect, but useful and, like most instruments, an amazing number of operators choose not to use them.

- Find critics. Your shipmates are also writers. Enlist them to polish your prose. You will learn who is exacting and methodical—the perfect ally for the detailed study—and who can do a rapid "is-this-good-enough" chop on an overdue paper. Do the same for others.

- Read about writing. There are numerous excellent short texts on how to approach professional writing; some titles are found in the Further Reading list at the end of this book. Find a text, read it, and think about writing as a discipline no different from learning to conn alongside.

Standard Subject Identification Code

Every naval letter receives a Standard Subject Identification Code (SSIC) on the top right of the first page. The SSIC identifies the topic of the letter. For example, any letter with a code between 3000 and 3999 concerns operations and readiness, while a letter with a code between 4000 and 4999 concerns logistics. The SECNAV Department of the Navy Standard Subject Identification Code (SSIC) Manual section M-5210.2 provides the entire detailed list.

The basic structure of SSICs has been essentially unchanged over the past hundred years. A researcher who was looking for U.S. Navy unit awards during World War II at the National Archives was told that OPNAV records were hard to use because they were filed according to a unique naval system. Recognizing the SSIC system, the researcher simply requested the 1650-series files—the SSIC for awards—and quickly found the desired information.

SSICs strike some as being archaic in a digital era. In fact, in managing the volume of information generated by the U.S. Navy over decades, they are the original metadata tag, connecting information between both originators and years to form a coherent Navy story.

Coordination

Formal coordination is the process of offering other staff elements the opportunity to review and comment on a document that touches on an area of their expertise. At the unit level, every naval officer is familiar with getting chops on a document such as an outgoing message. The coordination process simply codifies this requirement. It is usually formalized at the numbered fleet level and assumes increasing importance that the larger and more senior the staff is. This process indicates who must coordinate on a product, the level of authority they exert over the document being reviewed (for example, are they required only to review, or is their concurrence required?), how long they have to review, and who within the organization must sign on behalf of the staff element. Usually, a staff element reviewing a document can concur, concur with comments, or non-concur. They return the document with a list of inputs and corrections in a staff comment matrix. This comment matrix lists the comment, its significance to the office requesting the change, and why it ought to be accepted.

Within the Pentagon, formal coordination is a hard requirement for most products. It is also a powerful tool for slowing staff actions. Depending on the staff culture, staff sections can ignore coordination deadlines, offer hundreds of minor edits (each of which must be reviewed), or demand that any change, however minor, be subjected to another cycle of formal coordination. At its most cynical, this obstructionism is intended to push resolution of an issue beyond the tour of a military officer who is advocating for change, or into a different budget cycle, or is intended to simply raise the cost of challenging an entrenched interest.

Non-concurring in the flag-level review when the staff element concurred at earlier stages is generally considered poor form unless the product changed significantly between reviews. While it sometimes happens for legitimate reasons, it is normally a sign that the staff element did an incomplete job in the earlier stages. Other staff elements will quickly determine when "concur without comment" is shorthand for "concurred without reading."

Getting a routine product through formal coordination will require significant patience. Moving a significant or controversial product requires a next-level understanding, including understanding:

- Who is the traffic cop? Most staffs have an office—the flag secretary in a smaller staff or the director of the Navy staff at OPNAV—who moves formal staff packages and enforces the rules. They are the ones who can keep a staff code from burying a document, or, if the staff element is recalcitrant, authorize the document to proceed without their formal concurrence.

- Who is required to concur and who is simply reviewing? The reviewers will have opinions, and, while they should be considered, opinions are not usually directive. The list of organizations that must concur is usually much smaller than the list of interested organizations.

- Why is the staff element non-concurring? In many large staffs, a staff element may only non-concur with a document under the authority of a different staff element for very specific reasons, such as if it outlines a process that is contrary to law. Otherwise, the staff element may object, but it cannot prevent the further consideration of the document. A surprising number of staff officers do not know these rules; the best use them to their advantage.

- Check the reviewers who are always required. In most staffs, there are several offices that are always required to review documents; examples are the JAG or GC, the comptroller, or the congressional liaison. Since they see every paper going to the commander, they have a deliberate process for review—and are usually backlogged.

Memorandum of Understanding and Memorandum of Agreement

Memorandums of understanding (MOUs) and memorandums of agreement (MOAs) represent a specialized form of written staff communication. The phrases are often used interchangeably, but they are not the same. An MOU is a statement of a general understanding between two or more parties. It neither includes a commitment of resources nor binds a party to any specific action. An MOA is an agreement between two or more parties, and includes specific terms agreed to and a commitment by at least one party to act. It includes either a commitment of resources or binds a party to a specific action.

Most staffs are party to multiple MOUs and MOAs. The administrative or legal officer should hold copies of all of them and be able to provide a list. Knowing what MOUs and MOAs touch on your portfolio is an advanced staff officer skill. Consider two examples:

- A joint command, looking for cost savings, wanted to unilaterally discontinue supporting a fleet activity. Only after weeks of discussion did the fleet staff recall that an MOA had been signed between the two commands years prior. The existence of the MOA allowed the fleet to negotiate a transfer of resources that softened the cost of assuming the responsibility.

- A failure in mission support from a shore command contributed to a costly fleet mishap. The accident investigation discovered that the shore command's support was provided under the terms of an MOA that had expired years before. Support had continued, driven by habit and good intent. Nonetheless, the investigation viewed that the fact that the fleet staff did not know the terms of the support MOA, much less that it had expired, as a strong indicator that the staff had been negligent in its oversight role.

MOAs and MOUs are effective tools for clarifying and recording agreements between commands, services, and, sometimes, between international partners. If you need to negotiate an MOA or MOU, start with a discussion with the JAG. The JAG will know who has authority to sign for the command and be able spot legal pitfalls. For example, an MOA that obligates money or assumes liability is subject to Anti-Deficiency Act requirements that must be clearly incorporated.

PowerPoint

PowerPoint is a presentation software produced and sold by the Microsoft Corporation; it is a registered trademark of Microsoft Corporation. Since its first release in 1987, use of PowerPoint software has become a ubiquitous feature in government and business. Some version of it is part of the standard software suite on almost every desktop or laptop computer used in the U.S. Navy. There is a widely cited figure that some 30 million new PowerPoint presentations are created each day; it often seems as if Navy staffs account for 25 million of that figure. More than one staff has made patches in the style of carrier landing emblems proclaiming the wearer has completed "1,000 Hours of PowerPoint."

PowerPoint presentations really fill two independent roles that need to be considered separately. The first is when the PowerPoint presentation is intended to facilitate an oral presentation of information (e.g., a briefing). That is, of course, what it was designed to do. The second is when the presentation is the product, and is intended to be transmitted and to stand alone.

With that, we need to consider a few things about the software that staff officers love to hate. The reality is that PowerPoint has a number of inherent limitations that drive the way we use it. The key is to understand these limitations, use its strengths, and not allow the medium to drive the staff process.

Since you are going to need to use PowerPoint in some form, there are some basics that are worth having firmly in hand:

- Find the format. There is no Navy-wide format for PowerPoint presentations, but commands often have one. Find it and start with that as the basis for your work. Changing formats later is like changing out the engine in an automobile: it's possible, but is difficult to accomplish and usually not completely successful.

- Avoid formats with colored backgrounds. A blue background may look good in some cases, but printing any solid-colored slide costs the taxpayers in ink and printer supplies, takes longer to print, and often makes the slides busy and visually distracting.

- Always mark classification. It is important to mark the classification of the overall presentation on the first slide and then the classification of each individual slide. This rule holds even for unclassified slides. Slides take on a life of their own; they may be copied, retained, moved between different computer systems, or folded into future presentation. Do not make the next staff officer guess the classification.

- Include a point of contact. Your slides may unexpectedly travel around the world. When they arrive, you want any questions they raise to find their way back to you.

- Watch the gutters. PowerPoint includes notes pages that allow sources and briefing notes to be included. It is also possible to park graphics and text off slide. These are not seen when slides are displayed or printed, but are part of the electronic file. Use them as you need in building a presentation, but be sure to check them prior to sharing the file, lest you share more than was intended.

- Avoid white text. If you were wise enough to avoid a colored slide background, white text should not be needed. White text has an unfortunate habit of being moved around while a presentation is being built. If it is parked off the colored background, it will disappear into the white of the screen. Usually this is just inconvenient, unless the text is an early draft or represents a classification issue.

Thinking about Data Visualization

Data visualization is a fancy phrase that refers to the use of graphs and pictures to represent information. Every naval professional who learned navigation and piloting is intimately familiar with the idea, even if they do not realize it. Maps and charts are a specialized, highly developed form of data visualization. One of the first things a novice officer learns is that each form of visualization—what we call chart projections—has its own advantages and disadvantages. Cartographic and hydrographic information, painstakingly gathered through years of surveys, can be rendered useless if not represented in the right projection and scale.

Naval staffs face similar challenges. They exist to gather and create data. If those data are not presented in a usual format, at best they will be ineffective.

Did PowerPoint Destroy the Space Shuttle?

During liftoff on 16 January 2003, the space shuttle *Columbia* was struck by a small piece of foam insulation that detached from the liquid fuel tank under the stress of launch. The impact damaged the shuttle orbiter's thermal protective cladding. Sixteen days later, the orbiter disintegrated on reentry, destroyed by the thermal stress on the compromised area. All seven astronauts, including three Navy officers—pilot CDR William McCool and mission specialists CAPT David Brown and CAPT Laurel Salton Clark—perished.

Engineers from NASA and Boeing assessed that the shuttle might have been damaged in the 16 January launch. Expressing their concerns to their chain of command, these experts relied on PowerPoint to express their ideas. Reviewing these internal debates about possible damage, the *Columbia* Accident Investigation Board wrote that "when engineering analyses and risk assessments are condensed to fit on a standard form or overhead slide, information is inevitably lost." In one particularly critical presentation, it was "easy to understand how a senior manager might read this PowerPoint slide and not realize that it addresses a life-threatening situation."[3]

Edward Tufte, a noted scholar of data visualization and PowerPoint critic, dissected this key briefing, observing that the densely worded slides lacked precision, obscured the assumptions behind the engineering analysis and the limitations of testing, and, most critically, did not convey the potential impact of a failure.[4]

The limitations of PowerPoint were aggravated by pressure to conserve senior leaders' time—a pressure every Navy staff officer experiences. "The initial damage assessment briefing . . . was cut down considerably in order to make it 'fit' the schedule. Even so, it took 40 minutes. It was cut down further to a three-minute discussion topic" at a more senior meeting.[5]

Whether PowerPoint was a cause or symptom of a dysfunctional bureaucratic culture, the loss of *Columbia* is an excellent cautionary tale that conveying information badly within a staff can have tragic consequences.

One of the first questions a navigator asks is, What chart is right for the task at hand? A staff officer working to convey ideas needs to start the same way. In a number of cases, the answer will be given to you. For example, in many theaters, briefs seeking approval for operations are always supported by slides created using the same format. If the format is suitable, this standardization can allow the audience to sort information quickly. The quad slide represents a particular evolution of this process, essentially creating four slides shrunk onto one.

So, the commander liked your briefing and wants the boss to see it. The problem? Your masterpiece exceeds the size limit for email attachments. Now what? We will skip the question of whether PowerPoint was the right tool for the task. It is done and now you own the problem. Really, there are only a couple tactics that can help at this moment:

- Delete all the backup slides. Unless they are critical—and in that case, they are not backups.

- Compress the file. The instinct when placing graphics and images into a presentation is to select the highest resolution available. That step avoids grainy images, but often increases the size of the presentation file significantly. Once your presentation is complete, use the compression function in PowerPoint to reduce the size of all the graphics to the level needed for display or printing.

- Shift to a different file type. PowerPoint allows you to save a presentation as an Adobe Acrobat file. Acrobat files are usually much smaller than PowerPoint presentations. Acrobat is also a normal software load on Navy computers, so your colleagues should be able to read it, but they will not be able to manipulate it. If that meets intent (and sometimes it is useful to make manipulating your slides harder), try it.

- Use a sharing site. Both SIPRnet and JWICS have file sharing services as a part of their basic architecture, which allow massive files to be uploaded and shared. Such tools are less consistently available on NIPRnet. Using commercial file sharing services for official use is improper and insecure. There are some official file-sharing services available to any DoD element through other services. Check with your N6 on the current state of the art.

- Fragment it. Worst case, send the brief in multiple chunks. Just be sure to number each email and indicate the total number of slides being sent.

Why do we keep using PowerPoint?

- PowerPoint will help ensure that a briefing meets minimums. Let's face it: PowerPoint makes it less likely that a briefing will crash and burn. If the slides meet minimums, talking to the material in them will usually keep you in the fight.

- It lets you kill two (or more) birds with one stone. On many staffs, a set of presentation slides can serve as read ahead material to prepare seniors for a briefing, visuals for the briefing, and a record of the discussion and decision that can be shared afterwards.

- The boss expects it. Why they expect it is a good question for commanders to ask themselves.

Briefing PowerPoint Slides

Ostensibly, most PowerPoint presentations are intended to support a briefing. In many cases, the way we use PowerPoint suboptimizes the time the staff is investing in the presentation. A widely quoted statistic asserts

Briefing is an essential staff officer skill. Here, a Seventh Fleet staff officer shows how it is done, 1960s style. *Naval History and Heritage Command*

that the average PowerPoint slide contains forty words. That is at once too many and too few:

- Too many: Slide text creates an invitation for the audience to listen and read at the same time. Few people multitask effectively in this way; they will either listen or read. In either case, they will miss information.

- Too few: Forty words (or even a slide full of words) is often not enough to explain a complex issue. Nuance falls between the bullet points, perhaps even without the audience noticing. And the usual formula of text and a picture complicates this dynamic even more. The human eye naturally goes to the picture, even a poorly drawn or irrelevant picture that is only there to fill out a slide.

Next-Level Briefing

There is a better way. It involves separating the briefing from the PowerPoint and being mindful of how our brains work.

Recent research has footnoted what many briefers know instinctively. First, human beings think in narrative. We are natural storytellers. Our first complex lessons come to us as children in the form of stories. A story forms a frame for information, allowing complex ideas to fit into context. Stories can also touch the emotions, creating a call to action beyond what even compelling data can create.

Second, as human beings we are wired to remember what we see. Vision is the first of our five senses that we use to find patterns in the world. It routinely consumes more than half of our mental resources. In fact, after most staff briefings, the average audiences can describe the layout of the conference room more thoroughly than the details of the briefing. Why? Because the simple tasks of walking in, assessing who was there, and finding a seat forces them to look at it.

The best briefers leverage both of these insights. They do the hard work of analysis, find what they need to convey—and then turn it into a story. Like any good story, it has a beginning, middle, and end. It may or may not follow a strict chronology, but if it flashes back (to, for example, why a project was started), it needs to move relentlessly forward.

A good story in the hands of a competent storyteller needs no visuals. The storyteller can create them in the mind of the audience. Nonetheless, visuals can help as frames and memory aids.

There are multiple ways to exploit the power of visuals. One effective technique is to use a few carefully crafted graphs showing quantitative data. Usually, the briefer will verbally unpack the data, articulating its origins, relevance, and implications. Once that is done, the briefer then moves to a blank screen, refocusing the audience on the speaker. The novelty of a briefing without a large number of slides usually creates attention in and of itself. A contrasting technique is to use a large number of images with little or no text. The briefer moves quickly through the narrative, with a cascade of images tying directly to the story and creating an association with the key points.

Some of the best examples of this approach are TEDtalks. TED Conferences (TED is short for technology, entertainment, design) offer a forum for experts to talk about complex topics to interested non-expert audiences. These are usually fifteen to twenty minutes long, about the length of an executive briefing, and are often excellent examples of how technical issues can be crafted into compelling narratives. Most TED presenters use either a few carefully crafted displays of data or a collection of compelling images.

Varsity Briefings: The Downside
Varsity briefings have pitfalls:

- Creating the narrative first and falling in love with the story. Narrative can be too convincing—to both the commander and the analyst. Once human beings create a narrative that explains a problem, the tendency is to find information that supports the story. Information that contradicts the story is marginalized and discounted. This confirmation bias is natural and pernicious. The intelligence community refers to narratives as a type of mental model (sometimes also called frames or mind sets). The advantage to articulating the narrative, however, is that it offers an opportunity to challenge the narrative deliberately. Structured analytic techniques such as an analysis of competing hypotheses, devil's advocacy, and quality of information checks offer means to ensure ideas are being tested appropriately. These techniques have been taught in the operations analysis and intelligence communities for decades, but can be applied across many situations.

- It is labor intensive. Superficially, this style of briefing looks easier than the usual staff approach since it involves fewer slides or slides without words. The reality, however, parallels French philosopher Blaise Pascal's comment in a letter to a friend that he would have needed more time to write a shorter letter; combining brevity and clarity requires thought, and thought requires time. Crafting three compelling graphics that tell a complete story is vastly more difficult than filling twenty boilerplate slides.

- It is not portable. Since the briefing, and not the slides, is the product, it is more difficult to package up and share with other audiences.

- It places an extraordinary burden on the briefer. The briefer cannot read the slides, but rather must know the story and tell it with confidence. This is a feat most staff officers can learn—consider that almost every parent learns to tell stories to their children—but it does require practice.

- It will cause concern. In a world where staffs are conditioned to briefings looking a certain way, telling an EA that you are coming with sixty slides for a thirty-minute brief—and that you intend to talk for only twenty minutes—will cause concern. Ensure you have the top cover to get in the door the first time and then ensure you deliver, and you will never have a problem with that office again.

The Elevator Pitch

Chapter 6 introduced the idea of having an elevator pitch about your portfolio. Good staff officers develop a short pitch for any complex project or briefing that they are leading. Why have a thirty-second pitch on a thirty-minute brief? First, because it will force you to distill your own thinking into short, compelling phrases that capture the bottom line. Second, you will typically need to pre-brief other seniors before your main presentation. Often, they will not want to hear your entire talk, but just the essential elements. In these cases, you can give them your elevator pitch and invite discussion. Finally, outside events may disrupt your big event. Schedules run over, operations intrude, and your thirty-minute window may shrink to eight minutes. A clear elevator pitch to a busy senior may gain the result you were looking for now. Even if it does not, it will allow the senior to establish the priority of your next briefing opportunity rather than your briefing being punted indefinitely into the future.

The Handwritten Note

The last form of staff communications is perhaps the most archaic, and potentially the most impactful: the handwritten note. In an age when every form of writing has become digital, a note, written by the sender, stands out for the time and deliberate effort involved in sending it. A number of senior leaders make the habit of sending a short note—often only a couple lines—to congratulate their staff on births, marriages, or professional accomplishments, or to send sympathies on personal losses. Others take it a step farther and use handwritten notes to convey short Bravo Zulus and encouragement.

You do not need to be a flag officer to pick up this habit. Appropriate note cards are available inexpensively from the stock system, print shop, or at the Navy Exchange. Then grab a pen. If you learned formal Palmer penmanship, great. If not, no need to worry; just strive for something legible. And say thank you to your shipmates and colleagues.

In the long run, it could be the most powerful communication tool of all.

Professional Writing

A staff tour can be the ideal moment to begin writing on professional topics. Most staff officers have experience on current challenges facing our Navy and have time to think about the best ways to address those challenges. They have also usually been writing regularly, honing a skill that may have been used less during operational tours.

Writing on professional topics shares hard-won insight with the wider Navy, helps establish a professional reputation, and contributes to the development of the naval profession. With the growth of the Internet, there are more venues than ever for thoughtful writing to find an audience. The editors at the U.S. Naval Institute *Proceedings* are approachable and are used to working with new authors of all pay grades; they are great resources for anyone considering contributing to a professional journal.

Need a way to begin? When asked about how he starts his writing process, CAPT Peter Swartz, one of the foremost naval strategists of his generation, says, "I get mad. . . . After I calm down, I reflect on whether I have a better answer."[6] What in your professional experience makes you mad? Where do you have a better idea? Share it—and make the profession better!

CHAPTER 8

The Business of Running a Staff

Personnel, Resources, and Congress

A Navy staff is a Navy command, which needs to be run like any other command. While the fundamentals are the same ashore or afloat, there are a few peculiarities to staffs that are worth understanding.

The Commanding Officer of Troops

A large staff will have dozens or hundreds of enlisted Sailors assigned. Sailors need a host of administrative and command functions performed on their behalf; special request chits, transfers, evaluations, promotion recommendations, and, in some cases, discipline. Raising these issues to the level of the commander is not an effective use of the commander's time. Many staff elements may have only a few Sailors, meaning their care is likely to be a collateral duty. Despite the best of intentions, this arrangement may mean lost opportunities for the Sailor. The solution is to appoint a staff officer, usually the flag secretary, as the commanding officer of troops or staff commanding officer. This officer will act as the commanding officer for all routine matters for all assigned enlisted Sailors, to include conducting non-judicial punishment.

Correctly handled, the commanding officer of troops construct ensures consistency of administration across the Sailors assigned to a staff. Key to its success, however, is communication between the Staff commanding officer and the leadership of the individual staff elements where the Sailors work each day. Little is more awkward than a post-major command staff officer differing with the comparatively junior staff commanding officer about one of their Sailors, especially in cases that concern discipline.

Determining Staffing

It is more difficult to provide personnel for staffs than for operational units. With operational units, there are clear bounds—for example, what equipment is to be operated and serviced, how many people can embark a ship? Once established, the staffing for an operational unit will evolve over time, but rarely will the basic organization change. Operational units often have a life cycle. A class of ship or a type of aircraft is placed in service, used, and then retired. The next class or airframe may bring different personnel requirements, which are considered in the course of their adoption.

Staffs are different. A staff is elastic, subject to shifts based on mission and intent, and has no set life cycle. As mentioned earlier, the tendency is for staffs to grow over time. To assess and resource staff requirements, the Navy has two processes for shore and afloat staffs, respectively, that should be familiar to staff officers.

Shore Staffing

The Shore Manpower Requirements Determination (SMRD) is the formal process for evaluating the labor force needs of shore-based organizations, to include staffs. Most staff officers will experience at least one during their staff tour. SMRDs, like the labor force system it informs, are complex. The staff N1 team will take lead on the process, but it is important to understand the basics to ensure it is well-informed.

The SMRD is a critical step in assigning additional resources to a staff. It is, however, not usually a solution for the near term. Rather, the processes informed by the SMRD will result in resources in coming years. Doing an SMRD well is a classic way to pay it forward; it will benefit the next cycle of leaders assigned to the staff.

The SMRD starts from the work assigned to the staff. The basic statement of a shore command's work is its Missions, Functions, and Tasks Statement. Per OPNAVINST 5400.44, missions, functions, and tasks are separate items:

- Missions are what the activities [commands] are to accomplish.
- Functions are detailed requirements derived from the principal elements of command's mission.

- Tasks are requirements levied on an activity that are not directly derived from the activity's mission but that are required by a policy directive or written tasking.

The Missions, Functions, and Tasks Statement is approved by the command's immediate superior in command (ISIC), based on the mission statement approved by SECNAV on its establishment and forms the basis for its initial resourcing.

The staff's workload will change over time for many reasons. These include the assignment of new missions by higher headquarters, the need to correct identified fleet deficiencies, changes in technology, or the deployment of new equipment. Changes to existing operations plans (OPLANs), MOUs or MOAs, status-of-forces agreement (SOFA) and interservice support agreements (ISSAs) could also change staff requirements and personnel needs. Thus, the Missions, Functions, and Tasks Statement is required to be updated every three years. If that update process is handled well, the SMRD process will be much easier, because only changes to the staff workload since the last update will need to be documented.

Early in the SMRD process, the N1 provides a listing of requested changes to staffing along with supporting documentation. This paperwork drill matters—all taskings used in determining labor force requirements must be supported in writing by a requirement for the task from a higher authority.

The key point where most staff officers interact with the SMRD process is during the command visit. During this phase of the SMRD, a large team of labor force experts will visit the command to gain an on-the-ground sense of the command's needs. The team will

- evaluate the effectiveness of the staff organization,

- validate the command's statement of their work loads,

- look for potential efficiencies, and

- analyze the risk involved to reducing or eliminating existing lower-priority tasking.

One factor that complicates this process are the many bureaucratic techniques used by staffs to add to their labor force outside the formal system. Many staffs use contract personnel to support staff functions. Contractors, as noted elsewhere, are easier to hire and can be funded from a variety of budget sources as a quick solution to a staff need. In other cases, military personnel are assigned on revolving temporary duties (TDYs), essentially creating the effect of a permanent military billet by stealing personnel from other, usually subordinate, commands. Any enduring work should properly be reflected in the next SMRD and evaluated for inclusion in formal personnel resourcing.

Afloat Staff Staffing

As the name implies, SMRDs are only conducted for shore commands. The basic needs of an afloat staff, as for all afloat Navy commands, flow from the command's Required Operational Capability/Projected Operational Environment (ROC/POE) documents, which are published as OPNAV 3501-series instructions. Those documents are the afloat counterpart to the Missions, Functions, and Tasks Statement. They outline what the command will be required to do and under what circumstances it will be required to do it. These requirements are then reflected into an Activity Manpower Document (AMDs). That document should then be used as the basis for the command's share of available personnel.

Dealing with Congress

Most military officers have encountered members of Congress inquiring about specific issues raised by service members who write to their congressional representatives. Staff duty, however, often brings new and more substantive ways to interact with the legislative branch.

As part of its oversight role, Congress will often ask about specific naval programs and issues. Sometimes these questions are posed directly to the Navy Office of Legislative Affairs (OLA). Other times the requirement for a congressionally directed report is written into law. In any event, these questions are normally tasked by OLA to the Navy staff with expertise in the area. Answers are sent back to OLA, where they are reviewed, formatted, and passed to Congress through a formal system that tracks these responses.

Sometimes a staff will be called on to support the testimony of a senior leader before Congress. Leaders may be called on to testify before their confirmation to a new position, as part of an annual budget cycle, or in response to a significant issue. Testimony may also be accompanied by questions for the record. These are questions from Congress that need to be answered in writing. In support of testimony, OLA normally identifies issues of interest and requests supporting papers from the relevant Navy commands. These papers often have strict limits on length, format, and classification, which ensure that the DoN presents consistent and professional responses. They are also often produced on a tight timeline.

Finally, members of Congress and their staffs often travel to visit DoN commands as part of their oversight role. Such visits require significant support and senior-level engagement. A good staff, however, views these visits as opportunities. Every good commander knows there is value in "putting eyes on" a challenge and talking to Sailors on the deck plates. Congressional travel is the legislative equivalent. The impressions formed during visits can be critical to the future of Navy programs and budgets.

In any congressional visit, the delegation will be accompanied by a military escort officer. This officer, who is normally a congressional affairs officer drawn from the service with the most equities in the visit, should be the first point of contract for background and insight on the delegations' interests.

Congressional staffs and staffers come in many roles. Some are essentially interns; other wield influence that will make or break major service initiatives. The nuances of personal versus professional staff—who has what authorities and influence, who is experienced and who is new to the system—matter. These boundaries can be important; which committees oversee certain activities may have been the topic of long and contentious negotiation between their leadership, and violating these lines may raise enmity well beyond the topic at hand. Learn the lay of the land before engaging with Congress or hosting a congressional visit.

Congressional visits also present unique security issues. It is often necessary and appropriate to talk to members of Congress and their staffers about classified material. However, the rules for sharing classified information between the executive and legislative branches are unique and most security officers are unfamiliar with them. In some cases, what can be shared varies with the visitor's role and committee assignments. The bottom line: in hosting a visit by Congress, ask about security clearances early, and include the OLA escort officer in the discussion.

While dealing with Congress can be complicated, a staff officer will do well by following four basic rules:

1. Seek professional advice.

The OLA exists to help the DoN and Congress communicate. The officers detailed to OLA are normally assigned a portfolio and know the Hill in general and the players who care about that particular area. Other major Navy and joint commands have small offices that manage congressional engagements. Find these experts and leverage their insights.

2. Be positive.

Attitude matters. Congress is the nation's board of directors. Congress's role is essential to the constitutional system that the U.S. Navy serves. It will be apparent if a congressional interaction is viewed as an intrusion rather than an opportunity to inform decision-makers. Such an attitude undermines the good work of other Navy leaders.

3. Be responsive.

When Congress asks, answer. Sometimes congressional questions are tough. They are designed to be. Answering slowly never makes the news better, and creates the impression that the command is not being forthcoming.

4. Be honest.

It will be apparent if a staff officer is being less than fully candid. Congress is a place where members and staffers may remain for decades, and a reputation for dissimilation will follow you—and your commander.

CHAPTER 9

Civilian Personnel

Most officers will have encountered Navy civilian personnel by the time they reach their first staff tour. They may have been Naval Academy instructors, port engineers, or the clerk at a local personnel support detachment. For most, however, a staff will be their first extended experience with civilians in a professional setting.

The U.S. Navy hired Charles W. Goldsborough, its first civilian employee, as chief clerk in 1798. Goldsborough served until 1843, becoming "influential because he was an intelligent repository of tradition and experience."[1] Today, the Navy employs almost 275,000 civilian personnel whose work is essential to every function in the service. In our distributed fleet model, the days of clean divisions between uniformed operators and civilian support have blurred. At the senior levels, Navy civilians inform, shape, and sometimes make critical decisions with service-wide impact. The highly effective staff officer understands the basics of their structure so that their communications, leadership, and management exploit the distinctive strengths of the civilian work force and avoid common pitfalls.

Federal civilian employees follow a set of personnel rules that are different from their uniformed counterparts. For the uninformed, these differences can be a source of frustration. Such officers often rue that they "can't move, hire, or fire" a specific civilian. Often, they can (more on that later), but it is worth recalling why this system exists. In nineteenth-century America, civilian jobs in the federal government—including in the Navy—were political prizes. With each change of presidential administration, a new set of political cronies replaced those already in the jobs. Competence was often a secondary concern, and no citizen could trust that a decision

Taking a pause from administering a growing navy, senior civilians of the Navy Bureau of Supplies and Accounts pose circa 1893. *Naval History and Heritage Command*

was made apart from political influence. The creation of the Civil Service in 1883 was intended to professionalize the work of government and notably predates the promotion of commissioned naval officers by merit.

It is also worth remembering that civil servants take an oath to the Constitution that is almost word for word the oath taken by military personnel. The service element of civil service is real for the vast majority of Navy civilians, and the best officers remember and enlist that fact in their leadership. While allowed different latitude than uniformed personnel, federal civilians also accept limitations on their personal lives, including on their political activities and sometimes on employment after leaving government service.

Civilian employees come in two major categories: general schedule (GS), and excepted service (GG). For most purposes, the two are interchangeable, the main difference being how each is hired. GG positions allow more-flexible hiring processes, but are restricted to certain organizations. Within the Navy, the NCIS and naval intelligence are the main users of excepted service positions.

Often, civilian employees will be referred to by grade. These grades (GS-1 through GS-15, or GG-1 through GG-15) correspond to the complexity and level of responsibility represented by the position the civilian occupies. For purposes of protocol, OPNAVINST 1710.7A (Social Usage and Protocol) directs how these grades correspond to military officer grades.

Civilian Pay Grade	Military Grade Equivalent
GS-7	Ensign (O1)
GS-7, 8, 9	Lieutenant j.g. (O2)
GS-11	Lieutenant (O3)
GS-12	Lieutenant Commander (O4)
GS-13 OR -14	Commander (O5)
GS-14 OR -15	Captain (O6)
SES, SL, ST	Flag or General Officer

The key difference between the civil service and the military, however, is that, despite these equivalency charts, there is no civilian equivalent of "general military authority," which is the phrase JAGs use to describe the authority of any military officer or non-commissioned to exercise authority over junior personnel, regardless of their respective chains of command. General military authority is an ancient concept, created to allow military officers to take charge in the chaos of combat. The civil service, created for a different purpose, can exercise authority only with a defined chain of command.

What does that mean for a staff officer? First, a civilian GS-15 is not a Navy captain. However, if the system is working as intended, the captain and the civilian GS-15 should be leading similar levels of the organization, exercising comparable levels of authority within their chains of command, and facing similar levels of professional challenge. Second, protocol equivalencies usually describe a level of experience and often authority within the chain of command that merits an appropriate respect. The GS-15 comptroller, for example, cannot take charge of a working party the way a chief or lieutenant can; they can shift a couple million dollars from one budget account to another (or not) in response to your boss's requirements. A smart staff officer will respect their position accordingly.

Exactly what challenges and authority a civil servant has are found in their position description (PD). Every civil service position must have a position description. This document does exactly what the name implies— it describes the scope and responsibilities of a specific civilian position. Getting the position description correct is essential to getting what the command needs from its civilian workforce. The critical job elements in the position description will determine what pay grade is appropriate for the job, what skills should be assessed in the hiring process, and what performance objectives indicate an individual's success in the position. Each position will be placed within a series, which can be thought of much like an officer designator. For example, intelligence analysts of all kinds fall under the 0132 series, while law clerks are designated 0904. The position description should be updated every time the position is filled or when the duties of the position change significantly.

Like uniformed personnel, civilians are regularly evaluated on their performance. There is a tendency on larger staffs to create a system where most of the evaluation of civilians is done by other civilians. This arrangement minimizes the administrative burden for the uniformed staff, but care needs to be taken that it does not inadvertently create two separate chains of command.

Another distinctive feature of the civilian personnel system is the requirement for accounting for work time. Civilian employees are required to work a specific number of hours, usually forty per week for full-time personnel. There is considerable flexibility to shape these hours, allowing, for example, a civilian to work more than eight hours each day and take a day off every other week. Telework from home or remote locations is also possible, and, after the experience of the COVID-19 pandemic, it is increasingly seen as a useful option that builds command resiliency. The intent behind these flexible work policies is to allow the Navy to keep talented individuals by allowing civilian employees to craft a work arrangement that meets both mission and personal needs. How these policies are implemented for a specific employee is determined by their command, and every supervisor of civilians should be familiar with these policies.

However civilian working hours are set, they must be formally accounted for. This accounting is usually done through an electronic time card system. It is common for an officer to be appointed as a timekeeper. The timekeeper certifies time cards for civilians under their leadership. It is a basic duty, but one where staff officers sometimes encounter problems. Most commonly, civilian employees will claim forty hours a week, ignoring that they are working more hours in support of the command mission. In fact, when audited against entry logs or computer log-on times, it is common to find Navy civilians are working well beyond their official forty hours. If not accounted for by the command, this represents a breach of trust on two levels. First, if the work is in fact mission essential, the command owes appropriate compensation to its employees. Civilian overtime work must normally be approved in advance, and civil servants in the grade GS-1 through GS-15 receive overtime pay. A command that refuses to approve overtime or compensatory time but expects extra work to accomplish its mission is violating multiple regulations that exist expressly to prevent supervisors from acting capriciously, starting with the certifying official's promise that the time card is "true, correct, and accurate." Second, if a command requests to establish new civilian positions to handle an expansion of the workload, the first question normally asked is if there has been a need to use existing employees beyond their normal workload. If that work is not documented, justifying the requirement for more employees is much more difficult.

Less common are civilians who are working less than their assigned hours. This is referred to as time card fraud, and is a form of theft from the government. Documented time card fraud is one of the quickest ways for a civilian employee to lose their position, but most cases should be detected and resolved by the certifying officer long before it rises to this level.

Bottom line, time cards are a certified report, no different from an aircraft maintenance book or a ship's sounding log. They should be handled with the same attention to detail and integrity.

The fundamentals of leading civilians are no different from leading Sailors. Communicate mission requirements and establish clear expectations. Provide positive, constructive feedback. Recognize excellence and address deficiencies with training and accountability. The tools available for each of these tasks are different with civilians, but they are clearly articulated in official instructions and are intended to create the same effects. An unfortunate number of officers do not learn even the basics of these tools, and approach civilians as difficult, exotic, and best left alone. One senior civilian who is often asked by senior officers to help with civilian personnel challenges notes that his first question—"Have you talked to your civilian about the issue you have with them?"—is often answered in the negative.

Like uniformed personnel, civilian personnel need to be trained and developed. Civilians are eligible for a range of training opportunities. In some cases, these are the same schools attended by uniformed members, in other cases they are distinctively civilian opportunities. These opportunities can come with travel and tuition costs, and the command should budget for them each year. Where uniformed personnel often go to school between commands, civilians do not rotate on a fixed schedule, meaning that they will only have such opportunities if their command offers them time and support. Professionals value training and education. Offering such opportunities will not only make the command more effective, but also can help retain valuable civilians who might make more money outside the government. Civilian personnel should have an individual development plan (IDP) that outlines their plans for continuing professional development and the command's willingness to support. Most commands, however, do not invest the time or resources required to meet this requirement.

Recognizing excellence in civilian personnel is every bit as important as in the uniformed ranks. Notable specific actions can be recognized with time off and financial awards. Consistent superior performance can be recognized with formal civilian awards such as the Navy Meritorious Civilian Service Award. There is also a formal process for awarding annual bonuses to civilian personnel. A set percentage of the total payroll for the command is set aside and awarded to personnel in that pay pool each year. This process is established in law and regulation, and is intended to create incentive for superior performance. In most commands, well over half of the civilian workers receive an annual bonus, with the amount varying over an accepted range, usually not exceeding 5 percent of an employee's annual salary. A military supervisor may take some time to get used to the idea of money as an incentive, but it is a key part of the civil service culture. Financial awards can also be a bit like officer fitness report (FITREP) rankings; while confidential, often much of the command knows who received what. Similar competitive dynamics can emerge.

Civilian personnel, like military personnel, sometimes demonstrate poor performance or misconduct. Dealing with performance issues is a key element of leadership. Unfortunately, it is common for military officers to fail to address these issues, either from a perception that significant action against a civilian is impossible or from an unwillingness to do the work involved. The irony is that these same uniformed leaders would be completely comfortable addressing a thorny performance issue with a senior enlisted or junior officer that involves that same level of administrative burden.

Why is this the case? Firing or disciplining a civilian employee is, by design, a deliberate and formal process. When a military leader identifies a performance challenge with a civilian employee, they commonly use familiar informal tools to address the situation. Only when these fail, and the situation deteriorates, do they consult with the experts in their human resources office (HRO) or N1. That office asks for specific documentation of the performance issues, which usually does not exist. The officer then realizes that, formally, the process to hold the civilian accountable for their performance is only beginning. Faced with an extended, multistep process, the military leader often decides to pass the challenge to their relief, who begins the cycle again.

Documentation is the key to being able to formally address a civilian performance challenge. How to produce correct and effective documentation will vary widely based on the employee's status. In most cases, an employee's poor performance must impact a critical job element—another reason that position descriptions need to be accurate. The fundamentals of this process will be familiar to any Navy leader who has written a counseling chit.

Many civil service positions require a probationary period of up to two years, during which removing an employee is significantly easier. This tool should be used as intended to ensure poor performers do not become a permanent element of the civil service.

Most major staffs have civilians in senior leadership positions. These senior civilians come in several varieties. Most are members of the Senior Executive Service (SES), a cadre of professional civil servants established to provide leadership at the highest levels of the federal bureaucracy. Civilians classified as SESs are generally selected after decades of successful service and must be approved by the Office of Personnel Management (OPM) as meeting key leadership criteria before they can be appointed. The level of responsibility they are entrusted with carries with it their recognition as flag-level personnel for protocol purposes.

Within the U.S. Navy, many fleet and major commands have an SES as ED and CoS. SESs commonly head major acquisition programs, defining and purchasing the Navy's next ships, weapons, and aircraft. Within the Navy staff, it is common for major staff elements to have a military head and a civilian deputy. These deputies often have many decades of experience in that staff area, often within the same organization. While the head of the organization will provide leadership, guidance, and direction, most will lean heavily on the experience and insight of their deputy. While not exactly the same, in the best cases the relationship parallels effective commanding officer/executive officer, or commander/command master chief teams.

For the new staff officer, it is important to understand the scope of authority that can rest with senior civilians, especially outside of military operational commands.

How *Not* to Get What You Want

A carrier strike group (CSG) commander decided he needed a change to the support provided by a national intelligence agency. Such a change would have involved altering both policy and resources with theater-wide impact and ought to have been passed through the fleet to the OPNAV staff and then to the agency involved, allowing deliberate and informed coordination. Faced with an impatient commander, however, the CSG staff socialized (which is to say, sent, ostensibly as a courtesy notification that a formal request was forthcoming) the request via email directly to the agency. Receiving a response from an unfamiliar civilian, a senior

CSG staff officer replied that his commander expected a response from a senior uniformed counterpart. The agency involved has a general officer assigned to their leadership team, but in a limited role, primarily as a liaison to support specific operational functions. The agency director and all the decision-makers who control policy and resources are senior civilian officials, one of whom had sent the email to the CSG staff officer.

Having given what was seen as a patronizing response, the CSG staff self-identified as having no understanding of how decision-making worked in this realm, much less the implications of their request—and the snubbed senior civilian leaders directed their subordinate two-star to respond that the CSG commander's request would not be entertained.

The post-9/11 era has seen a growth of contractors in government service. Once upon a time, contract personnel on staffs were unusual, and were normally limited to specific support function. After 9/11, the DoD received a massive influx of overseas contingency operations (OCO) money from Congress. OCO is sometimes called cost-of-war money, and is intended to defray the unexpected costs of military operations. At the same time, the DoD was called on to support new missions, requiring different skill sets and shifts in personnel. Enter the contractors, who emerged as a convenient device to solve two problems.

First, overseas contingency operations money is non-recurring. While the DoD has received money classified as overseas contingency operations for the past twenty years, it is legally reauthorized each year and cannot be spent on permanent personnel, either uniformed or civilian. However, those funds can buy services, to include labor. Second, contractors avoid the tedious route of authorizing new billets or navigating the civilian hiring process. They can be added and, in principle, removed from the work force rapidly.

Today, most major staffs, including afloat staffs, have contractors embedded in their ranks. In some places in the DoD, more than half of a major staff is contracted. Common examples include

- systems administrators provided as part of a larger IT services contract;
- subject matter experts working on a per hour or per project basis to address specific issues;

- operational planners and targeteers hired through a contract to allow a rapid surge in support of a new operational requirement; and

- administrative support staff whose billets were cut in a headquarters staff reduction effort decades ago, but were deemed valuable enough that the staff funded a contract out of operational funds.

Contractors, however, come with their own rules and considerations. Technically, the staff does not have a relationship with the individual contractor. Rather, it has a legal relationship with the firm that is under contract to provide a service. That contract defines the relationship; it is subject to the same general rules that cover a multi-billion-dollar program.

It is common for contracted personnel to stay with a command for years, even decades. In many cases, the firm holding the contract will change, but the new firm will hire workers from the last firm, keeping familiar and trusted people in the command providing the same services. Good leaders foster inclusion, treating all their employees— uniformed, civilian, and contracted—as valued professionals. Over time, contracted employees become part of the team. That should always be the case, but it is important to recall that, with contracted employees, you cannot directly reward them. Their pay, leave, and work schedule are all set by their contract—a contract with the U.S. government, not an individual staff officer (or even a commander). You generally cannot offer them awards, often to include team awards. Formal feedback on their performance goes to their firm, which is then in a position to reward their success or address their shortcomings. They cannot receive challenge coins purchased with government funds. Some leaders, under the influence of very cautious JAGs, will not even give contracted personnel challenge coins purchased with their own personal funds, interpreting such a token of thanks as an improper preference for a specific government contractor. Bottom line—get advice from your JAG, consider how much risk you are willing to take, and find a way to lead your entire team; it may take some creativity.

The second issue is to understand what a contracted employee can and cannot do. Contracted employees in some cases exercise significant authority. However, they cannot conduct functions that are inherently governmental. An inherently governmental function is defined in law as "a function so intimately related to the public interest as to require performance by Federal Government employees."[2] What is inherently governmental is a policy decision, and it can be unclear. For example, commanding forces and conducting combat operations are inherently governmental. Providing security can be either contracted or inherently governmental, depending on how much discretion the position entails. Contractors are specifically limited in their ability to obligate and spend government funds, whether a major acquisition or the command's official credit card. They are also prohibited from setting policy or representing the command. Over time, competent contracted employees build trust and attract more responsibility. In some cases, they may be former military or civilian employees, and so are competent and comfortable with authority. With the best of intentions, it is easy to slowly move beyond the language of the contract and beyond what is appropriate for contracted employees. If you supervise contracted employees, it is good practice to review what their statement of work describes and their actual roles in your staff.

Key Points for Success with Staff Civilians

1. Find a native guide. Talk to your N1, civilian personnel director, or a senior civilian about expectations and the tools available to manage and shape your civilian workforce.

2. Partner with a civilian counterpart. Your civilian peers will often have more and different professional experiences in their field than you. Those who have come into civilian service after a career in uniform may be uniquely positioned to help explain the relationship between both institutional cultures. Take advantage of their insights. Ideally, form a relationship that lasts beyond your tour.

3. Attend to the basics. Listen, communicate, and, if in a leadership position, lead—both your military and civilian personnel.

CHAPTER 10

Working with International Partners

T he U.S. Navy fights alongside its allies and partners. Through allies and partners, we shape the development of maritime security around the world, and leverage the strength of like-minded navies to accomplish goals that no one nation, however powerful, could achieve alone. Having worked with foreign navies at sea, most U.S. Navy officers understand this reality. Staff officers often have a new and different opportunity to influence international partners, even if the word "international" appears nowhere in their job title. International engagements present the staff with their own expectations, opportunities, and pitfalls.

International Engagements

The term "international engagements" covers a multitude of events, from working-level operational coordination to elaborate diplomatic events. Each has its own patterns and requirements.

Watch-to-Watch Communications

If the objective of international engagements is for like-minded navies to work together for common goals, routine communications between 24/7 watches are perhaps the highest form of engagement. The fundamentals are straightforward, but not simple: the staffs of two operational commanders with a common area of interest coordinate, usually via a secure communications mechanism. In these cases, form truly follows function. A number of nations want the cachet of communications with U.S. counterparts, but the invariable rule is that these arrangements work only if there is a real operational requirement for routine interaction. Otherwise, a secure communications circuit, installed at significant cost in time and money, will sit unused except for periodic communications checks.

Communications circuits can be voice or data, point-to-point or networked. In any case, any communications circuit between navies should come with a clear standard operating procedure (SOP) that outlines the following:

- What organizations(s) are on the other end of the circuit.
- Who in the U.S. Navy staff is authorized to use it.
- What information may be shared.
- Whether the circuit is monitored reliably.
- Any language issues that can be anticipated. Some partners can do business in English 24/7. Some claim to be able to do so, but, in reality, language challenges can be expected, especially outside duty hours. With others, we transmit documents and emails in English, they in their language, and business waits for an available translator.
- What is to be done with information received from the partner navy.
- Who maintains the circuit and repairs it in the event of an outage.

Within the staff, senior officers in the N2, N3, N5, and N6 should be familiar with what means are available to communicate with partners. A crisis involving risk to forces or life is not the moment to ask how critical information can be passed.

Key Leader Engagements

The term "key leader engagement" (KLE) proves the U.S. military tendency to create an acronym for everything. A key leader engagement is the most fundamental form of international engagement—one senior decision-maker talking to another. It is part and parcel of what Navy leaders do every day. They can be informal office calls, a discussion on the sidelines of a larger event, or a full-blown ceremony with all the naval, protocol, and diplomatic formalities. In any event, they will require preparation and support from the staff. In a major command, key leader engagements are often scheduled as part of an overall engagement plan, usually created by the staff N5. The goal of the schedule is to ensure that key partners hear from their friends in the U.S. Navy on a regular basis, and not just when we need something.

Staff Talks

For most staff officers, the most common kind of international engagement is a meeting with a counterpart staff element. These are often scheduled on a recurring basis, nominally once or twice a year. For some afloat staffs, staff talks are more opportunistic, occurring when the staff visits the foreign partner in conjunction with a port call. In any event, staff talks are generally headed by the commander or deputy commander, and cover a range of operational issues of common concern.

Specialized Staff Talks

Deeper relationships with partners require more-detailed interaction than can be supported by a single senior-level event. At numbered fleets and naval components, it is common for key staff elements to maintain relationships with foreign counterparts. For example, the N4 may keep a regular dialogue with logistics staffs in major partner nations. These counterparts sometimes conduct sidebar discussions on the periphery of larger staff talks, and sometimes they conduct dedicated events involving extended meetings.

Subject Matter Expert Exchanges

Subject matter expert exchanges (SMEEs) represent engagements on more specific topics below the level of staff talks. For example, the fleet N2 staff may assemble a team of experts on maritime domain awareness (MDA) to travel to a foreign partner, visit their maritime surveillance center, and exchange insights on best practices for monitoring illicit activity in coastal areas. Subject matter expert exchanges are often held away from headquarters and closer to the deck plates than staff talks, allowing a candid view of each other's work. Because they are also generally held at a working level, these engagements are an excellent opportunity for more-junior officers to have the experience of leading a team representing the U.S. Navy to a foreign partner. Also, because the focus is on execution rather than policy, it is often useful to leverage a number of U.S. Navy commands beyond the cognizant staff to provide the required detailed expertise.

Multilateral Engagements

The U.S. Navy is part of a web of international partnerships, ranging from longstanding treaty alliances to informal meetings of regional navies.

CAPT Lex Walker, commodore of Destroyer Squadron 7, pauses for a selfie during a community engagement in Vietnam. *U.S. Navy*

Representing the U.S. Navy to each of these events falls to a lead staff, who assembles and prepares the team.

Receptions and Social Events

U.S. Navy units host a number of social events with international partners. These events help build informal ties, create venues for deeper interactions, and allow a wider range of staff members to interact than events that are more formal. Most common are events hosted on board a visiting warship, which may include both senior members of the staff as well as junior members of the wardroom, chiefs' mess, and Sailors.

Given the wider attendance, it is good to familiarize more-junior members of the staff with the norms of such events:

- Invitations will specify if they are for anyone other than the member. Do not presume by bringing a spouse or guest unless it is clearly expected.
- Ensure you are in the correct uniform.
- Storage for covers is often provided, either on the pier or just after coming on board. If convenient storage is not available, invitations often request that covers not be worn.

- After boarding a foreign vessel, there is generally a short receiving line consisting of the foreign ambassador or local consul, embarked flag officer, and commanding officer of the hosting vessel. Greet them, offer a brief thanks for their hospitality, and move on. Service members precede their spouse or guest through this line.

- After all guests have arrived, there are usually welcoming remarks by the hosts, and often a welcome from the senior U.S. representative. Remarks may be followed by a short program of entertainment offered by the ship's company, such as music, dance, or martial arts demonstrations.

- Remember, the purpose of these events is to meet foreign counterparts. Do not simply talk to the same people you see every day. If it is an event sponsored by a U.S. host, make it part of your duties to ensure the foreign guests you encounter find someone with whom they can share a story or refreshment.

- Do not overstay. Most receptions run two hours, and there is usually a clear sign when the formal event is ending. Thank your hosts and move on.

International Fleet Reviews

International fleet reviews (IFRs) are a traditional way for navies and nations to mark major events. These reviews have been held to mark anniversaries of navies being founded, coronations, and major international arms expositions. They are usually one-off events, and require a designated U.S. staff to attend planning meetings, assess and recommend the level of U.S. Navy participation, and lead execution of the event. Many international fleet reviews also include a conference or meeting of senior commanders or chiefs of navies, creating a further venue for international contact.

Americans have a reputation for being arrogant, insular, and culturally insensitive. We also have a reputation for openness, enthusiasm, and professionalism. Every foreign interaction is an opportunity to build—or erode—a positive image of our Navy and nation.

In general, a simple rule is to always act like serious professionals dealing with other respected professionals. This approach requires an attitude of humility and openness. Every navy, including our own, has limitations in personnel, resources, or policy. Each also offers unique strengths and experiences. A navy with few platforms may use them in flexible and innovative ways. No matter how good our insight on a region, we will never have the nuanced understanding that comes from living there. A willingness to listen will invariably be rewarded.

Preparing for International Engagements

Professional mariners would never conduct operations at sea without adequate preparation. Staff work is no different, but international engagements place a premium on careful preparation.

It is common for our foreign partners to have more experience in international engagements than our staffs. In general, other navies keep officers on active duty longer, allowing them to spend more time in specific jobs. In a smaller navy, most officers will have had the experience of meeting foreign counterparts regularly throughout their careers. Finally, it is not uncommon for other navies to develop a cadre specializing in what are known as "American issues." These officers often become regular interlocutors. As a result, U.S. Navy officers new to a region or issue often find themselves engaging foreign partners who are deeply versed in the specific issues at hand. Very often the partners across the table will have been in every meeting since an issue was first raised years before. They will know the United States' previous positions, the U.S. players, and what they want out of the discussion. If the U.S. staff is unprepared, they will fail to recognize opportunities to advance our common interests, or, alternatively, will fail to protect U.S. equities. Either outcome squanders the investment of time and prestige our Navy has made in the discussion.

Fortunately, the highly effective staff officer can draw on a host of professionals to prepare for international engagements.

Desk Officers

Most major staffs have desk officers assigned to manage the relationship with a region or set of foreign partners. Often housed in the N5, these billets are increasingly filled by foreign area officers (FAOs) with significant experience in the region. Regardless of designator, a competent desk officer will be able to identify the major players in the relationship (both the commands and the personalities) on both sides, articulate the command's interests in the relationship, and explain where and how the command has engaged the partner in the past. They should also hold records of the command's previous meetings with the foreign partner. In many venues, it is common for both sides to craft a memo recording the major topics of discussion and the action items each side intends to pursue in support of each other. There should also be private notes reflecting the tone of the discussions. Familiarity with these notes is an essential start to preparing for an engagement.

Scene Setters

Desk officers will also often have access to scene-setter messages in advance of a major meeting. On major staffs, the desk officers will craft scene setters in support of the commander's engagements. For the most senior engagements, the U.S. Embassy or defense attaché office will send its own scene-setter message, offering their view of the situation in the country and the likely issues that will be raised in the engagement. Given the seniority of their intended audience, these documents are generally carefully crafted and very well-informed and can be a valuable resource to the staff. For example, the scene-setter message sent from a defense attaché office to the Joint Staff ahead of the Chair's most recent visit to their host country will also offer a visiting CSG staff high-level background before a port call and counterpart visit.

Defense Attaché Offices

More than one hundred defense attaché offices (DAOs) represent the U.S. DoD in foreign capitals around the world. Many of these have naval officers assigned as attachés. Military attachés represent the DoD to their host nation, advise the ambassador, and partner with the representatives of other U.S. agencies in the embassy to carry out U.S. policy.

Attachés are an essential source of insight before, during, and after an international engagement. As naval professionals who live on the ground and have regular contact with the host military, they can provide a level of current information and nuance that no other source can offer. Since they support every U.S. military engagement with their host nation, they can place a staff's engagement in the context of the larger DoD effort, and consider how an interaction by another service or command may impact the staff's event.

Attachés are also in a position to leverage the entire U.S. Embassy country team. The country team consists of representatives of all the major U.S. government agencies with offices in that embassy. Generally, the first day of any significant in-country international engagement will involve a stop at the U.S. Embassy. When an event is being supported by U.S. officers from different commands, this stop represents a critical chance for the U.S. participants to exchange information and synchronize before engaging the foreign partner. It also allows the visiting team to be aware of the big picture in that country and get a last update on the lay of the land. At a minimum, a visiting team should meet with the defense attaché office. If the visit is senior enough, a meeting with the full country team and ambassador or deputy chief of mission is also appropriate.

Within the staff, it is useful for a single office to take lead on engaging the defense attaché office. On larger staffs, this task usually falls to the country desk officer. Defense attaché offices are relatively small organizations, and even the largest generally have only one or two officers from each service. In the era of rapid and direct communications, it is easy to overwhelm a defense attaché office with multiple inquiries. It is also worth remembering that, while the staff's engagement is important, it is highly likely that the same attaché who is supporting it is also supporting a more senior visit, an international conference, or a port visit in the days prior.

During international engagements, it is always appropriate to keep the attaché in the room. The attaché represents the Navy the other 364 days of the year, and will likely be tasked to support any follow-up actions with the partner navy. Ensuring they are in the discussion, informed, and credible is simply good staff work.

Liaison Offices

The U.S. DoD supports liaison offices in a number of major international organizations. Some of these, like the U.S. Mission to NATO, have the status of diplomatic missions headed by an ambassador. Others consist of a single officer assigned to the staff of the international organization. Regardless of size, these offices provide a service similar to a defense attaché office for U.S. government elements engaging with their international organization.

When engaging these representatives, it is important to understand the distinction between a liaison to an organization and an element of that organization. For example, the U.S. Mission to NATO represents the United States to the alliance. Separately, U.S. officers are embedded in the NATO staff. The latter are not there primarily to represent the United States, but to do the work of the alliance as part of a multinational team. While they can be a tremendous source of insight, their role—as agreed by the highest levels of the U.S. government—is different.

Foreign Policy Advisor

Discussed separately in chapter 5, the FPA, if assigned, can be a key link to the wider U.S. foreign policy community, as well as a source of deep personal experience in international engagements.

Protocol

The command protocol officer, discussed separately in chapter 4, can provide valuable insight on the practicalities of arranging an engagement, especially if it is being hosted by the U.S. Navy.

Working with Interpreters

Finally, a foreign engagement often involves working in a language other than English. Scope the engagement and determine early what type and level of language support the event will require. Get the terminology right. Interpreters work with oral communication, while translators work with written documents. It is less common to need a translator, but they may be necessary to render slides and papers into another language during staff talks or formal negotiations. Interpreters are often necessary. There are different levels of interpreters, and considerations in using each.

Heritage Speakers

Heritage speakers are U.S. Navy personnel who speak a foreign language due to their family background or the place where they were raised. Heritage speakers are often pressed into service to interpret for low-level or informal interactions. Heritage speakers are rightfully proud of both their family roots and their service, and interpreting can be a personally rewarding way to honor both those ties. Before pressing a heritage speaker into service, however, a few challenges need to be considered:

- Not all heritage speakers have taken the Defense Language Proficiency Test (DLPT) in their language, meaning that it can be difficult to gauge their actual level of skill. Even a competent speaker may be challenged with conveying nuances of politics or technical systems. Furthermore, understanding two languages and interpreting between them are different skills. Not every speaker of a foreign language can turn complex or unfamiliar ideas into lucid English rapidly, for an extended period, in front of a senior audience.

- Do not put a native or heritage speaker in a difficult personal position. Some may have come to the United States seeking political stability or economic opportunity, perhaps under difficult circumstances. They may have family still overseas. Communicating with a senior officer from that nation may be uncomfortable for them, and potentially the foreign guest. In the worst case, with less friendly foreign counterparts they may have ties that create counterintelligence concerns if exposed to foreign officials.

Interpreting More than Words

A brilliant female U.S. Navy junior officer was also a heritage language speaker, raised in a traditional culture where deference to male elders was expected. Warfare-qualified, competent, and confident, in any normal professional context she was forceful and effective. Knowing her language skills, the staff decided to use her as an interpreter for a visiting flag officer from the nation where her parents were born. In that formal setting, her interactions immediately and unconsciously shifted to the cultural norms in which she was raised. She became quiet and deferential to the senior foreign officers present, to the point that she was challenged to deliver the direct and forceful message that her commander needed to convey.

An awareness of the cultural and human dynamics of language interpretation would have cued the staff to ensure that she was more effectively prepared for the task.

Professional Interpreters

A few staffs that are located overseas and that have a primary liaison mission have professional interpreters. For some of our most senior engagements (for example, CNO counterpart visits), the staff may hire an interpreter through the Department of State.

If you are fortunate enough to have access to a professional interpreter, realize the significant asset that they can be for your engagement. In some cases (though not all), these professionals will have a security clearance and will be familiar with the full range of what the U.S. Navy is trying to accomplish with a partner. They may have the experience of having been in the room for dozens or hundreds of meetings with senior counterparts. In general, a professional interpreter will not share impressions or insights during an event unless you ask specifically. Bringing them into the team, however, can be an excellent force-multiplier:

- Invest time up front. Make time to sit with the interpreter and go over the planned schedule of events and topics. Ask if they have met any of the foreign counterparts before. While a professional interpreter will not divulge the substance of discussions with other commands, they will often share impressions of personalities and suggest approaches.

- A professional interpreter will look for topics where they are not familiar with the specialized vocabulary and will invest time in preparing. If you intend to have a specialized technical discussion, make sure you highlight that fact.

- Realize that, if you are working with a paid or contracted interpreter, this preparation time will add to the cost of their support. It is worth the investment.

Foreign Disclosure

Few staff processes are as poorly understood as the disclosure of non-public information to foreign partners. All international engagements involve some sharing of information beyond what is available to the public. The process to do this correctly is simply a matter of professional survival. To be blunt,

- disclosure of U.S. classified information to foreign personnel without authority and with intent to do harm is *espionage,*

- disclosure of U.S. classified information to foreign personnel without proper authority is a *security violation,* and

- disclosure of U.S. classified information to foreign personnel with proper authority is an *effective partnership*

Yet despite this fact, a number of commands (and, in cases, commanders) are willing to cut corners on the foreign disclosure process. Mishandling, or, as is sometimes seen, ignoring the foreign disclosure process will result in unauthorized disclosures of sensitive or classified information. These are security violations, and must be formally investigated as such with all the ensuing consequences and potential career implications.

This reality does not mean that a staff officer should be afraid of foreign disclosure or foreign engagements. Naval officers routinely handle exacting processes with significant consequences. Rather, they need to understand that this is one of them.

Any command that conducts significant foreign engagement needs a foreign disclosure officer (FDO). The FDO may be a full-time employee or on a collateral duty. In any event, serving as an FDO requires formal training and designation. An unfortunate number of commands designate an officer as FDO without investing in their training, which is a recipe for failure. Commonly, commands designate their FDO from the intelligence team under the theory that all FDO issues involve classification and the intelligence team understands classified information.

A common failure scenario goes like this: A well-meaning staff officer builds a briefing for scheduled operational talks with a foreign partner, then drops it on the FDO shortly before the event with a request to "FDO it." The FDO is an intelligence officer, who is confronted with a briefing on an operational topic on which they are not an expert. Since the slides have no notes or references, the FDO does not know where the information in the brief originated. Was it derived from a publication? A database? Collected by sensors? In each case, the rules for foreign disclosure are different. Unable to determine the origin of the information, the FDO cannot even begin the process for authorizing release to a foreign partner. In other cases, the FDO can determine the origin, but authority to disclose the information is held at a higher echelon—in some cases outside of the Navy or the DoD. The process for reviewing such a request can be long, and is not generally sympathetic to commands that submit requests shortly before a routine need. The result: the brief is not available for the staff talks, to the embarrassment of the staff and the loss of an opportunity.

How to avoid this chain of events?

First, start with release in mind. When building a product that may need to be released to a foreign partner, footnote it as if you are writing a term paper. This sourcing allows the FDO to find the original classification authority (OCA) for the information. That authority ultimately determines the releasability of the information. Ensure classification markings are correct and detailed. If one line of a slide is not releasable, mark it clearly to prevent the entire slide from being considered not releasable.

Next, ensure your FDO also has subject matter experts to assist. For foreign disclosure purposes, classified information is considered in eight categories:

Category 1: Organization, Training, and Employment of Military Forces

Category 2: Military Materiel and Munitions

Category 3: Applied Research and Development Information and Materiel

Category 4: Production Information

Category 5: Combined Military Operations, Planning, and Readiness

Category 6: U.S. Order of Battle

Category 7: North American Defense

Category 8: Military Intelligence

These categories cover all the activities of the DoD. No single staff officer can be an expert on all of them. The best foreign disclosure programs designate foreign disclosure representatives (FDRs) for each category that impact their command. Thus, in our scenario, the FDO in the intelligence team, who is an expert in category 8 information, would be able to call on a trained foreign disclosure representative in the operational team familiar with category 5 information to help in the disclosure process.

Third, start early. If you follow steps 1 and 2, and the information requested is within the authority of your FDO to disclose, the process can be extraordinarily rapid, taking even just minutes in operational cases. If authority is held elsewhere, understand the process can take days or even weeks.

Finally, understand that the foreign disclosure process exists to perform the difficult process of balancing legitimate competing interests. What information the U.S. Navy is permitted to share is determined through a complex interagency process. It is common to hear seniors attack the process as slow, bureaucratic, and inconsistent with the U.S. reliance on allies and partners. It is rare for these same seniors to do their part to enable the process.

Hand-in-hand with foreign disclosure rules, every foreign engagement requires basic attention to OPSEC. No navy shares everything it does with even their closest partners. Bring nothing into an international engagement that you are not willing to share. Assume you will mislay your notebook, that anything you write will be seen, and that every counterpart understands English, even if they never speak or evidence that fact.

International Representatives on the Staff

Many U.S. Navy staffs and commands have foreign officers attached to their structure. Being permanently assigned to a U.S. Navy command is often a highly sought-after position among our foreign partners, and the officers they send are, more often than not, the best and brightest of their wardrooms. If used correctly, these embedded officers can be a significant enabler of international operations and engagements. In the best cases, they are also officers with diverse professional and operational experience that they can share if asked. Need to understand diesel-electric submarine operations, operations in the Arctic or on a jungle river, the challenges of leading draftees, or handling alcohol responsibly on board ships that are under way? There are foreign officers with these experiences and more serving in U.S. Navy staffs today who will gladly share their expertise.

These officers come in two varieties, each carrying important distinctions and limitations.

Foreign Liaison Officers

Foreign liaison officers (foreign LNOs) are representatives of a foreign navy to the command in which they work. As such, they are expected to maintain communications with their own navy, to pass information that may assist in working issues of common interest, and sit in meetings as the representative of their navy. Always and everywhere, they work for their navy.

Professional Exchange Program Officers

Professional exchange program officers (PEPs) are part of the U.S. Navy unit in which they are placed. They are given specific responsibilities within the command and function as an integrated part of the team. As such, they can represent the U.S. Navy command (rather than their own navy) in meetings and discussions. PEP arrangements exist only with our closest partners, and are regulated by law and formal agreements.

Every foreign officer assigned to a U.S. Navy staff must have a U.S. officer who is designated as their contact officer. This officer is responsible for the administrative care of the foreign officer. Most critically, they are also responsible for managing their access to U.S. classified information.

Gift Giving

Americans almost never give gifts to each other in an official capacity, and ethics rules make doing so fraught with peril. These ethics limits are appropriate; gifts can signify preference and favor and shape behavior. For exactly these reasons, it is common to exchange gifts with foreign partners. Because these gifts are intended to be part of representing the United States to foreign partners, they are often called "representational gifts." On a large staff, the PAO and foreign area officers should be well-versed in the process. Nonetheless, any staff officer who might be responsible for a foreign visit needs to know how this process works.

First, it is important to understand that the gift exchange is often important to the U.S. seniors involved. At the least, they do not want to be seen as unprepared or ungenerous. A competent staff officer will always work with foreign counterparts to determine if there is going to be a gift exchange, will brief the U.S. senior on the gift they will be giving, and will have the gifts staged and ready. The experienced staff officer will know which foreign guest is likely to surprise their U.S. friends with an unexpected gift. Many U.S. attachés supporting counterpart visits travel with small, unmarked gifts ready for just such an eventuality.

The U.S. Navy has some limited funds for gifts for foreign visitors. The specific rules for these funds are beyond the scope of this book, but there are some basic guidelines. Gifts, and the money for them, are accountable and ruthlessly audited. Consider that, in some cases, the Navy is using

The right gift for the right occasion: CDR Hank Adams, commanding officer of USS *Stethem*, receives a gift of flowers and the full attention of his Korean hosts during a port visit. *U.S. Navy*

taxpayer money to buy fine crystal, challenge coins, and alcohol, and the level of scrutiny is completely understandable.

Not every command receives these funds. A DDG hosting foreign visitors may not receive money for representation gifts. If the commanding officer wants to reciprocate the plaque given by a visiting foreign flag officer, they will often pay for the gift out of pocket. U.S. attachés sometimes receive money for representational gifts, but it is often limited and subject to specific restrictions. A staff should understand these limits and never assume that some other command will fund or provide representational gifts unless specifically agreed beforehand. It should also ask carefully. A subordinate command that dips into its own funds to support the admiral's desire to give a gift may be crossing an ethical line that places the commander at risk, especially if a tone-deaf staff officer has conveyed that such support is expected or assumed.

The type of gift exchanged depends on the relationship and the length and significance of the visit. A brief office call between fleet commanders, for example, may be followed by the presentation of a challenge coin, ballcap, or plaque. A formal office call between heads of navies (the CNO and their foreign counterpart), especially one that is part of a larger counterpart visit program, may include a larger gift. These gifts are often chosen for cultural significance, such as a piece of porcelain, a small statue, or a ship model. Ideally the gift can be the topic of a short explanation, offering a chance to share a piece of history with a foreign friend. Many CNOs have given their counterparts reproductions of the Truxton Bowl, a historic porcelain piece produced in the nineteenth century for the frigate *Truxton* that is currently on display at the U.S. Navy Museum at the Washington Navy Yard.

While official gifts follow normal patterns, occasionally seniors offer something extraordinary, either from a desire to impress or from real affection. For example, during one CNO counterpart visit, a commander of the foreign navy's first aircraft carrier was part of the official delegation. Knowing their pride in that first carrier and that the carrier commanding officer read English, the CNO staff acquired a history of U.S. Navy aircraft carriers written by ADM James Holloway, a legendary naval aviator. They then visited the retired admiral to have him inscribe the book personally to the foreign visitor.

On the other hand, careless gifts sometimes miscarry. For example, wherever possible give gifts that are made in the United States. Giving a partner a gift that is clearly marked as having been made in another country is never a good look. One staff presented a European ally with a gift that was tastefully wrapped in the colors of the local opposition party, to the embarrassment of the senior receiving it. Alcohol can be an appreciated gift under the right circumstances, but requires an awareness of both the culture and the individual recipient.

Once the gifts are given, the PAO or protocol officer, if assigned, will take custody of the gift. The gift is then logged and often photographed. If necessary, it will be inspected by an appropriate security office. Usually, the small ship model does not include a hidden microphone, but if it is going to sit on the commander's desk, the Navy needs to be certain. The value

of the gift is then estimated. The estimation process may be straightforward for commercially available gifts, or more difficult ("Is that really an
antique?"). As a general rule, a senior may accept any gift from a foreign
counterpart, with the obvious exception of gifts that are immediately dan-
gerous or illegal. Whether the recipient can retain the gift is another matter.
U.S. officers may generally only retain foreign gifts under a certain value
($415 at the time of writing. This amount is revised every three years.). The
JAG will also review the gift, looking at the source ("May this source give a
gift legally?"), the value, and other considerations,

The gifts are then returned to the senior for disposition. A very senior
officer (the CNO or a fleet commander) may host many foreign visitors
each month, and receive dozens of gifts. In these cases, the senior often
receives a binder each month with a page for each gift. The page includes
the context for the gift, a photo, an estimated value, and a blank space for
the senior to direct what they want to do with it. If the value of the gift is
under the legal limit, the senior may keep it. If it is over the limit, the senior
may pay the U.S. government the difference in value, essentially buying the
gift from the taxpayers.

Many of the most senior officers do not keep all the gifts they receive;
there are simply too many. In these cases, the gift may be retained by the
command or disposed of officially. Large staff protocol offices have a gift
locker retaining gifts from important foreign partners. These gifts will be
stored until that foreign senior, or another senior from that nation, visits
again, when they will be retrieved and displayed in the commander's office
or conference room.

The important thing to remember is that gifts are a tool for communication and relationships. For some partners, they are important and appreciated signals. The best partners are the ones where the common mission
becomes the driving force. As one foreign partner remarked, "I knew we
were real friends when we stopped giving each other plaques."

CHAPTER 11

Managing Your Career within a Staff

Officers land in staff jobs for a host of reasons. Whatever path leads them there, for the most part they arrive having been successful so far in their careers, and wanting to continue their service after their time in the staff. It is worth a great deal to make the most of a staff tour professionally, and thus to earn the opportunity for continued service and increased responsibility.

Staff tours offer excellent opportunities for learning and developing as a naval officer. Generally, staffs deal with broader issues than those found at the unit level. Even the smallest staffs comprise a professionally diverse group of experts. On a large staff, just about every career specialty is represented. When their decades of previous assignments are considered, there is usually someone on staff with personal expertise with every activity conducted by the U.S. Navy, however obscure or esoteric.

Senior officers know this fact from firsthand experience and they expect high-performing subordinates to take advantage of the experience of others. Indeed, this expansion of professional contacts and perspectives is one of the reasons a staff tour is often seen as a prerequisite for senior positions and command assignments.

Some positions inherently offer a broad view of the staff. For example, the director of a major N-code or an EA will sit through enough staff-wide meetings to understand the scope of the staff's activities. Personnel not in one of these positions, however, need to proactively seek out these opportunities. There are a host of approaches, but a simple request to sit with someone and hear about what they do for the Navy rarely fails. Senior leaders on the staff can build this culture by encouraging staff officers to back-bench meetings, hosting brown bag talks by other staff elements, and forcing officers to think and work broadly.

The best staff officers not only learn from other experts, but also develop the habit of active collaboration with personnel from completely different backgrounds. When mature, this breadth of insight goes beyond just bringing multiple staff codes into a meeting: it represents an understanding of the full scope of the Navy's resources and skills.

On a large staff, many officers will hold two or even three jobs in a nominal three-year tour. Since most staffs have jobs of different complexity, there is often an informal progression through these positions. Learning the staff should also involve identifying these local norms and considering what challenges an officer might want next. Few staffs have enough consistency in their staffing to allow a formal multiyear plan for this progression, but the officer who knows what they want and asks for it has better odds of getting it. Often, the first prerequisite for a tough, rewarding job is to ask for it.

One of the most difficult things for new staff officers to comprehend is that there is always opportunity available on a staff; this is even more true on a large staff. It is astonishing the number of officers who arrive at a staff tour believing that the horizon of their experience will be defined by the title and scope of action that they inherit. In some cases, an officer lands in a challenging and well-defined position. COPS, for example, follows well-defined patterns and instructions, presents constant demands, and is well understood and valued by seniors. In other cases, a job may be both challenging and poorly defined. The officer who is given responsibility for a new program with a high level of command interest may have ample challenge and opportunity. But what of the officer in the less-challenging billet? Experienced officers know that every staff has more worthy work within its missions, functions, and tasks than it can perform with the personnel at hand. A winning approach for officers looking for broader responsibility is to identify a problem within their skill set that the staff is not currently addressing. Develop an idea, green light it with the immediate chain of command, and move to meet the need. Usually, within a month the staff has welcomed the improvement. In six months, no one will remember any other arrangement and the portfolio will be permanent.

Fitness Reports

Most staff officers have significant experience with the professional evaluation of officers, usually from both sides of the process. Nonetheless, FITREPs on a staff have some special considerations.

Probably the first and most critical question for any individual officer is who signs their FITREP. Ideally, an officer should understand this process before accepting orders to a staff. FITREPs on afloat operational staffs are almost universally signed by the commander. Numbered fleets, whether afloat or ashore, similarly tend to have the three-star commander personally sign FITREPs. Career-wise, this arrangement can be a significant benefit of taking staff orders. Paper from a senior unrestricted line officer, whether an O6 commodore or the vice admiral commanding a fleet, carries weight in selection boards.

On larger staffs, the evaluation of officers may be delegated below the commander. The arrangement varies, but generally the commander will evaluate direct reports (the EA, special assistants), with other officers being evaluated by the deputy commander or CoS. Within OPNAV, officers are usually evaluated by the Deputy Chief of Naval Operations (DCNO) responsible for their N-code. While the arrangements vary, they are required to be formally articulated through a delegation of reporting senior letter or instruction. Once delegated, these arrangements can be changed, but only with formal notice that resembles any other change of reporting senior arrangement. Some staffs view this formality as an unnecessary burden, but it is a simple requirement of fairness to the officers being evaluated. The instructions governing delegation of reporting seniors within staffs are complex and have changed, becoming much stricter in recent years. It is worth consulting the most recent edition of BUPERSINST (Bureau of Naval Personnel Instruction) 1610.10 to ensure compliance with current guidance.

In most staffs, subordinate leaders recommend up their chain of command the relative merit of the officers under their span of authority. Some part of the leadership will then come together in one or more ranking boards to produce a rank-ordered list of the officers in and across competitive categories. For example, at one major staff most FITREPs are signed by the directors of the various N-codes. Nonetheless, the N-code directors come together with the CoS to produce a rank-ordered list of officers that assesses the relative merit of officers across the entire staff. The list is then submitted to the deputy commander for approval. Such a process allows officers who are not in the same competitive category to be compared. This list supports soft breakouts—language in the FITREP that explicitly cites the officer's merit relative to officers across competitive categories—which are especially critical for those officers who are alone in a competitive category. For example, even on a large staff an O4 JAG is almost certainly a competitive category of one. If this officer is in fact exceptional, their ranking relative to the sixty other O4s on the staff is an important factor in their future promotion potential.

A ranking board is an interesting test of staff dynamics. Generally, the flag secretary or administrative officer will provide the members a list of all the officers being evaluated, often with their seniority, promotion status, and previous ranking and trait averages outlined. Sometimes an EA or CoS will act as Chair. Each of the members will engage as an advocate for their personnel. Such advocacy is expected and, if absent, is an immediate down-check on the officer in question. A top-tier competitive ranking, however, is usually the result of advocacy by other board members endorsing an officer from outside their purview. Much depends on the officer's reputation outside of their staff code, the acknowledged difficulty and impact of their work, and the ability and willingness of their chain of command to advocate forcefully for their performance.

Since the process is informal, it can in no way bind a reporting senior. If the commander signs the reports, the comparative lists are recommendations to inform their judgment. Similarly, it cannot actually require a delegated reporting senior to write "#6 of 27 officers" in an officer's report.

On large staffs, there are special cases that will shape the flow of FITREPs. Every staff and reporting senior will handle them differently based on their values and experience:

- One-of-one officers. As mentioned, there are a number of critical staff members who are usually the only officer within their grade and designator. Because they will never receive a hard breakout—a direct comparison to other officers in Block 45 and 46 of their report—soft breakouts and the reporting senior average are key to providing a report that recognizes excellent work.

- Greatly differing experience within pay grades. A large staff will have officers at different points in their career who are within the same competitive category. For example, at a numbered fleet there may be ten O5s, some of whom are new and aspiring to command, others who are post-command and looking to O6 and major command opportunities. The latter will generally be given more responsibility based on their professional experience and thus will fare better in the ranking process. If the command is not careful, they will inadvertently cause an entire cadre of junior O5s to be noncompetitive because they are permanently ranked below their seniors. The mitigation for this situation is for the reporting senior to be explicit in their comments. The explicit statement "#4 behind three stellar post-command officers—ready for command now" can often mitigate the hard math of such a competitive group.

- Non–due course officers. An officer is said to be due course when they have successfully completed the expected requirements for their next career milestone and have not failed to select at a statutory or administrative board. Large staffs often have a number of officers who are non–due course. In some cases, these officers have come to the staff in the hope that strong paper from a senior officer can place them back on track. In other cases, they are continuing to serve pending statutory retirement.

One word to the wise on non–due course officers. In general, competition in Navy selection boards is fierce, growing more challenging as staff becomes more senior. Essentially, every officer will fail to select at some point. Furthermore, with the removal of the above-zone designation in officer selection boards, more and more quality officers are making their next grade after failing to select, sometimes more than once. Some of the finest staff officers in the Navy are "off track" but are still highly experienced and personally committed to making the Navy better. Being non–due course may impact an officer's professional future; it does not limit their contributions to the command they are at. It is sometimes the case that officers at their terminal pay grade are more fearless in advocating for what they believe to be the right things, which is a trait savvy senior officers will value. Being smart, motivated, and at terminal pay grade can be a powerful combination.

Mentoring

Every officer on staff should develop several mentors, and, indeed, the diversity and seniority of staffs offer unique opportunities for mentoring relationships. Mentors can provide not only insight and advice, but also advocacy, actively linking promising officers to new opportunities. The best senior officers actually introduce their juniors to mentors. However, even in the best of circumstances, an officer will need to be proactive in seeking mentorship:

- Identify who has insight you need. Looking toward command? Find the officers who have recently completed successful command tours, and the senior officers who trained them. Trying to understand how resources work? Look around for a logistician.

- Ask. Few professionals will turn down a request to share their wisdom and experience. Even if they do not have the time for a recurring relationship, most will share an hour and a cup of coffee.

- Find a broker. If the reach across grades or communities is too daunting, find an intermediary who can make the introduction.

- Diversify. Seek out mentors (and mentor others) from completely different professional, cultural, and organizational backgrounds.

- Pay it back. While seeking mentors for yourself, make sure you also take time to look for the younger professionals who could benefit from your mentorship.

CHAPTER 12

Intelligence

I want you to be the Admiral Nagumo of my staff . . . to see the war, their operations, their aims, from the Japanese viewpoint.

FADM Nimitz to his N2[1]

Navies exist to fight. Fighting inherently involves an adversary. For operational staffs, the adversary is potentially real and present just over the next horizon. For staffs working acquisitions, that adversary is often theoretical; an opponent who might be faced decades in the future, armed with weapons not yet designed. Nonetheless, the adversary is always a defining element of our profession.

As central as that fact is, the adversary is never represented in our discussions unless they are consciously and deliberately brought into the staff process. That duty—what ADM Nimitz called "being the enemy"—is the core function of the staff intelligence team at every level of command.

The culture of naval intelligence is distinctive within the U.S. intelligence community, and grows from the way in which naval intelligence is embedded within Navy operational staffs. In most other services, intelligence support is typically provided by separate commands, often answering to a separate chain of command. The U.S. Navy has made the N2 staff element the locus of operational intelligence support, with key capabilities organic to the fleet.

The Pacific War and the Culture of Naval Intelligence

When the PACFLT was established in 1940, LCDR Edward "Eddie" Layton became the first fleet intelligence officer. A Japanese linguist and student of naval intelligence, Layton struggled to detect and understand imperial Japanese navy movements in the growing tensions of 1941. It was clear that conflict was coming—but exactly when and how was not. Years after the attack on Pearl Harbor, Layton learned that key leaders in Washington had insights from breaking Japanese diplomatic communications that pointed to an imminent attack in the Pacific— insights not shared with the Pacific Fleet commander.

After the attack on Pearl Harbor, the code breakers who worked in Pearl Harbor, led by Layton's good friend, LCDR Joe Rochefort, defied instructions from their chain of command and focused their efforts on breaking Japanese operational codes of immediate tactical use to the fleet. Their efforts enabled the victory at Midway.

Rather than celebrate the initiative and brilliant success of the Pacific code breakers, the OPNAV bureaucracy reacted with anger. Two OPNAV staff officers, Joseph and John Redman, who occupied key positions in the operations and communications elements in the Navy staff, were more interested in asserting control over information to build their own bureaucratic standing than in serving the fleet. Unable to admit that the code breakers in Hawaii had defied their instructions in order to provide Nimitz decisive insight before Midway, John Redman instead fired LCDR Rochefort.

Rochefort, the most brilliant Navy code breaker of his generation, eventually commanded a floating dry dock.

What generations of naval intelligence officers have taken from this experience has shaped naval intelligence ever since: essential intelligence support must report directly to the fleet commander, and essential insight, regardless of its sensitivity, must be used to inform naval operations.

Being an Intelligence Customer

Intelligence support is a complex subject, laden with specialized knowledge, acronyms, and closely held secrets.

Nonetheless, the best Navy commanders have developed an understanding of using intelligence as a tool. As with any tool, they understand its strengths and limitations. Because each aviation squadron has its own squadron intelligence officer, aviators often develop this understanding early in their careers. For other unrestricted line officers, a major staff tour may be the first time they have ever met an intelligence officer or enlisted Intelligence Specialist. Knowledge is power, and the United States invests billions of dollars each year to ensure it knows more than any other nation about things it cares about. Learning how to leverage that investment is a useful benefit of a staff tour.

When slicing intelligence into understandable chunks, it is usually divided by collection discipline—how the information is acquired—or by the audience who uses it. Both are useful distinctions, but for Navy staffs the audience is the first and most important consideration.

Intelligence Support to Operations

After all, the line drawn between intelligence and operations is quite tenuous and is there for convenience only.

Arleigh Burke, August 1945

When supporting operations at the tactical to operational level of war, the intelligence team must first answer five questions about the adversary:

1. Where are they?
2. What are they doing?
3. What can they do?
4. What do they typically do?
5. What will they do in this case?

These five questions cross the entire scope of operational intelligence support. The first two questions—Where are they? and What are they doing?—are descriptive, conveying what is happening now (or as near to the present as possible). "What can they do?" entails the complete technical assessment of the adversary—the range of their weapons, the speed of their ships, the effectiveness of their electronics—but also the proficiency that enables their use of technical capabilities to their fullest extent. To understand "What do they typically do?," naval intelligence must understand what constitutes normal operational behavior. Does the adversary do an underway replenishment before conducting high-speed operations? Or is an oiler in proximity to adversary combatants unusual? Finally, knowing the answer to "What will they do in this case," or "What is normal and what is possible?" helps the intelligence team be predictive, informing the commander about what they are likely to encounter in their own future operations (FOPS).

In recent years, the information warfare community has come to use the term "battlespace awareness" to represent these functions. The danger, of course, is that battlespace awareness focuses on only the first two of the five key questions for tactical-level maritime intelligence. Naval intelligence professionals traditionally use OPINTEL (operational intelligence) to describe comprehensive intelligence support in the maritime environment. Though the term is shorthand for operational intelligence, in Navy circles it does not mean intelligence at the operational level of war. Rather, World War II staffs coined the term to distinguish intelligence to support naval operations from strategic intelligence. While naval intelligence will use the correct joint and information warfare community lexicon when required, the term persists in the fleet both for intellectual clarity and as a bit of naval heritage.

The task is straightforward, but not simple. Whether the adversary is an opposing fleet or a network of terrorists, they do not want to be found or understood, and will use tools and tactics to avoid detection.

A Sailor captures a view of a nearby contact. Collection is the first step of the intelligence cycle. *U.S. Navy*

Answering these questions requires that the intelligence team complete a series of steps that guide its actions. In its simplest form, it is represented as a cycle.

It is critical that this cycle starts with the commander's requirements—what the commander needs to know in order to protect friendly forces and operate against the adversary. The intelligence team must understand what matters to the commander. One senior naval intelligence officer described this imperative as "deep penetration of the customer," and taught a generation that it was as critical as "deep penetration of the adversary" for naval intelligence professionals.[2]

The commander's intelligence needs are codified in doctrine as priority intelligence requirements (PIRs). PIRs should be tied to decision points. The unfortunate reality is that, for most staffs, PIRs are often an afterthought to CCIRs (see chapter 13). Admittedly, in the dynamic operational environment, keeping PIRs current is a challenge. However, the process of developing PIRs can force essential conversations between the commander, the senior staff, and the intelligence team. The intelligence team owes the commander feedback on the PIRs, including an honest assessment of the extent to which they can be met, what resources are required to do so, and where they cannot be satisfied with confidence.

For their part, good commanders understand that intelligence is not free. Any command, whether a DESRON or a fleet, possesses finite tools to learn about the environment and adversary. While off-board capabilities may be available and significant, they are ultimately limited by the capacity of the staff and its supporting data systems to make sense of the information available. The commander who turns the PIRs into a laundry list on which everything is a priority has missed the point; setting priorities includes accepting risk from limited insight on lower priorities.

Intelligence Operations

Intelligence operations are the specific actions taken to gather information about the environment and adversary to aid the force. They can take the form of explicitly tasking a ship's sensors, using tactical unmanned aircraft, ship's signals exploitation space (SSES), embarked human intelligence (HUMINT) collectors, or a host of other assets organic to the fleet. It also involves the coordination of requests to intelligence collection assets operated by other units, the joint force, or national intelligence agencies. This process of collection management examines the commander's intelligence requirements, assesses what information already exists, and pairs those requirements with collection operations that can fill the gaps as required.

An essential distinction in intelligence collection is between organic and inorganic collection assets. Simply, organic assets are an inherent part of the command, and answer to the commander for their tasking. Think of these as a ship's lookout: they will look where they are told, for what they are told. Inorganic assets are assets that are operated by another command. In this case, all a commander can do is ask. Even if an inorganic asset is put in support of a commander, it can always be taken for higher priority tasking.

Intelligence teams come in many shapes and sizes. Individual units may have an embarked Intelligence Specialist or collateral duty intelligence officer, usually tasked with the most basic functions. A DESRON or aviation squadron is the smallest staff element with direct intelligence support, usually in the form of a single junior officer providing direct support to the commander. At the amphibious ready group (ARG) or CSG level, each staff will have a more senior intelligence officer (lieutenant commander or commander, respectively) and a small team of other professionals. These teams will form the backbone of a full afloat intelligence center. In the case of the CSG, the intelligence elements of each embarked squadron will come together to populate a carrier intelligence center (CVIC), while in the case of the ARG, the embarked Marine element will create a joint intelligence center (JIC). In each case, the resulting organization is a cross-organizational team, with all the strengths and leadership challenges inherent in such a construct.

Intelligence support to planning is inherently different from intelligence support to operations. At the basic level, planning relies on much the same information as operations—adversary disposition and capabilities, for example. Where planning is unique is that planning often relies on assessments of what an adversary will do in a future circumstance that has not yet come to pass. For example, if the adversary's territory is invaded, will they resist fiercely or collapse believing that defeat is inevitable? Can adversary forces adapt creatively to unexpected events? If damaged, do they seek to break contact and repair forces for a long-term fight, or press on, believing aggressive action offers the best chance for success? These questions are distinctive because rarely can answers be simply observed by an intelligence collection system or cleanly extrapolated from existing information. Rather, they require thoughtful assessment and a willingness on the part of the intelligence team to go beyond what they can footnote. This willingness is often outside the experience of intelligence analysts. Senior planners and commanders will need to set the ground rules so that their intelligence teams learn to provide this kind of support. As one fleet commander observed to his intelligence staff, "Even if you don't 'know,' I have to plan. I would rather have your assessment than me making [stuff] up!"

Tradecraft and Intelligence Support

In the years following both 9/11 and the Second Gulf War, the perception of significant intelligence failures caused the implementation of tradecraft standards across the intelligence community. These requirements to explicitly cite sources has arguably made intelligence assessments more conservative, and has complicated the kind of imaginative work required to support planning and strategic decision-making. Naval intelligence teams that are an organic part of operational units have more latitude in this regard, both formally and culturally, which is a distinction essential to supporting an operational commander.

One of the key ways in which intelligence teams provide this support is through red teaming. While the term "red team" carries a host of meanings, in the context of naval planning a red team provides interactive feedback to planners, usually during the war gaming phase of the planning process, by emulating the adversary's operations and decision-making. NWP 5–01 *Navy Planning* directs that the N2 provide red teaming support to planning.

One of the challenges in red teaming, especially on a small staff, is that much of the intelligence team may have been closely tied to the process that developed the plan. If an operational planning team (OPT) was formed, intelligence team representatives should have been embedded at the outset. These are often the analysts best equipped to support the planning, and the temptation is to have these same intelligence analysts act as the red team during war gaming. Instead, these team members should remain with the planners, providing intelligence support, while other intelligence analysts provide outside feedback to the process. Where time allows, use of outside experts from the Office of Naval Intelligence or theater joint intelligence operations center (JIOC), or an outside team such as the Pacific Naval Aggressor Team (PNAT), a red team operated by the PACFLT staff, can be useful.

Intelligence at the Operational Level of War

Major fleet commands are distinctive in working at the operational level of war. The operational level of war is distinctive largely in its time horizons. The placement of major fleet assets, their logistics support, and their integration with the joint force require a view that looks days and even weeks into the future. In the face of a dynamic adversary, confidence in specific predictions deteriorates rapidly over time. The best commanders know that intelligence can rarely offer certainty at the operational level of war. What a skilled intelligence team can do is offer an intellectual cone of courses, defining the adversary's options, the likelihood of each occurring, and assisting the commander in orienting friendly forces in time, space, and purpose to respond to and exploit each possibility.

In many theaters the scope of potential threats at the operational level of war has driven a federated approach to intelligence support. This approach is most developed in the Pacific Fleet Intelligence Federation (PFIF), where three fleet staffs (Pacific, Third, and Seventh Fleets) coordinate intelligence functions across the entire area of responsibility. Each fleet provides indications and warning to the forces under its own OPCON, but also focuses on a specific geographic area, providing situational awareness to the other nodes in the federation. Supported by common processes and data standards, this approach maximizes the limited intelligence capacity organic to the fleet.

Intelligence Support to Acquisitions

Many Navy staffs—OPNAV, TYCOMs, and systems commands—are occupied with the work of conceiving, designing, and building the Navy of the future. This task offers unique intelligence challenges. Designing an aircraft carrier or submarine is the work of decades. Once built, these platforms are expected to remain in service thirty or even fifty years. Building them to meet threats more than half a century away requires an extraordinary type of intelligence support; it would be like asking someone a year before the Wright brothers' first flight in 1903 to conceive the first flight of a nuclear-capable B-52 in 1952. In fact, the unique nature of naval platforms means that the intelligence teams that support the acquisition of those platforms work on the longest time frames of any part of the U.S. intelligence community.

Because of the time frames and the amount of money and congressional interest in acquisitions, intelligence support to acquisitions is a formal process. DoD acquisition regulations require intelligence input at specific gates, input that is supposed to set the terms for the development of the system.

One of the key tasks of the intelligence community is informing acquisitions programs of threats that could critically impact the survivability or effectiveness of the system under development. To support this challenge, a formal process exists to identify the key developments that could force a change to the acquisition program, ranging from a minor change in the design to a complete cancellation. These developments are called critical intelligence parameters (CIPs). If a CIP is met, the criteria is said to be breached. In many cases, a CIP breach requires a notification to appropriate committees in Congress.

As the speed of technology development increases, there is a growing focus on acquisitions agility. A key question for acquisition-focused staffs in this environment is how to respond to dynamic intelligence insights within a highly formalized support process.

Using the Naval Intelligence Team

Intelligence, like every staff function, is a function of the commander, and the commander sets the tone for how effective it can be. Military intelligence professionals often joke that there are two kinds of operations: operational successes and intelligence failures. While humorous, the commander who uses the intelligence team as light entertainment or as a chew toy for operational frustrations will assume more risk than is necessary, risk that is driven by failing to position the intelligence team to support their needs.

Commanders will often tell their intelligence officers, "I don't want to see you without the N3 with you." It is sound guidance: intelligence exists to be used, and most often the operations officer is the one who must make use of it. Great commanders also say the reverse. If intelligence needs to inform, enable, and drive operations, an operations officer without the N2 is half a team.

Similarly, the best customers of intelligence understand that it is a process and relationship rather than a product. A fully developed operations or planning product that includes a placeholder reading, "Insert N2 input" is evidence that intelligence is not being well integrated or exploited within a staff.

As part of building this relationship, a good intelligence officer will often answer a question with another question, ensuring that the intelligence team knows not only what is being asked, but also why and how that information will be used, allowing them to fully support the effort.

Asking the Right Questions

Few navies achieve the level of information dominance over their adversary that the Royal Navy created during World War I. Monitoring Imperial German Navy communications, the Royal Navy was often able to detect the German fleet preparing for sea and to have Royal Navy units under way in response before the German fleet had departed port.

Despite that penetrating insight, intelligence was considered a marginal staff function and was not fully integrated into operations; this construct failed the Royal Navy at a key moment of the war.

On 31 May 1916, it was apparent that large elements of the German navy were preparing for sea. ADM John Jellicoe's forces were already under way in response. The key question was whether the German fleet had departed port yet.

At that juncture, CAPT Thomas Jackson, the senior admiralty operations officer, entered the intelligence center and asked where call sign DK was located. The officer on duty responded that call sign DK remained in port. CAPT Jackson then communicated to ADM Jellicoe that the German fleet was still in port.

It was not.

When the German fleet got under way, German navy shifted the call sign DK, normally used by a senior afloat commander, to a shore radio station in an effort to deceive anyone listening. The British naval intelligence team knew that the German fleet was under way, using a different radio call sign.

But that was not what CAPT Jackson had asked.

Jackson had built a long and prickly relationship with the intelligence team, who had learned that the irascible captain was best handled by giving him exactly what he wanted. They would never ask (or be told) why particular information was important, and thus why they were never positioned to give him—and through him, the fleet—what was really needed.

On the morning of 1 June 1916, the Royal Navy met the German fleet at sea. As a result of the faulty intelligence passed just three hours prior, they were not anticipating the encounter. The ensuing Battle of Jutland was a costly draw for the Royal Navy, and was an unsatisfying result that better handling of intelligence might have changed.

Intelligence Networks

The complexity of the threats faced by the U.S. Navy means that no single command, however focused or well equipped, can understand all the aspects of every potential adversary. Thus, the intelligence element of any staff should be thought of as part of several networks, formal and informal, that they leverage to serve their command.

Operational Networks

Any Navy operational command will be tied into an operational intelligence support structure. For example, a carrier intelligence center supporting a CSG may provide information to and receive information from a numbered fleet intelligence team, a theater undersea warfare commander, and a joint intelligence operations center in the same hour. In fleets with multiple MOCs, each MOC will usually be assigned a specific geographic area within which it provides intelligence support to the entire fleet. In the Pacific Fleet area of responsibility (AOR), this arrangement is codified as the Pacific Fleet Intelligence Federation, and extends to each fleet unit that has a significant intelligence element.

Strategic and Technical Networks

Beyond operational channels, it is common for intelligence elements to coordinate with subject matter experts from the Defense Intelligence Enterprise and wider intelligence community. The Office of Naval Intelligence, for example, acts as the service intelligence center for the entire U.S. Navy, supporting technical analysis and in-depth insight on naval systems and platforms. The best experts on trade with a country under United Nations sanctions may reside in one of the many three-letter agencies headquartered in or near Washington, DC. A good N2 has extensive contacts, often developed during previous tours with these agencies, to leverage in support of their commander.

Finally, intelligence is fully effective only when it is integrated into a staff environment that allows deep professional candor. Naval operations are about warfare. Success in combat is the final metric, and it is determined by the adversary's ability to fight. That ability is an objective yardstick, and the commander must allow it, and not the desired outcome, to be the standard for the command.

CHAPTER 13

Operations

Operations are the heart of the Navy; taking ships to sea and deploying forces to defend the nation. In any staff with an operational mission, the N3 will normally consider themselves to be first among equals in the staff pecking order.

Since every line officer begins their career conducting operations, there emerges an expectation that controlling operations at the staff level should be straightforward and intuitive. In reality, while prior operational experience is useful and important, guiding operations from a staff requires a new and different outlook.

How a staff deals with operations hinges on two factors: time and command. Operational time divides into three bins: current operations (COPS), future operations (FUOPS), and future plans (FUPLANS).

COPS are what is happening now and in the immediate future. Perhaps the best way to think of it is that COPS are those operations that will continue without any further orders from higher headquarters. For example, a transit of a politically sensitive waterway, once in motion, will continue according to plan unless orders or conditions change.

Future operations are operations that may be necessary in response to a change in current circumstances—the "What if?" For example, during the transit mentioned above, orders are received to join with a friendly foreign navy in the area and conduct visible operations. For anything beyond a simple exchange of signals, the higher headquarters will need to set out at least basic information and guidance.

FUPLANS handles operations beyond the scope of what is currently in execution. For example, the units conducting the transit will conduct a second series of presence operations in a different area in the coming weeks, likely making a port call beforehand and requiring dedicated underway logistics support. That task will likely fall to FUPLANS.

It will be obvious that the line between each of the three processes is, of necessity, elastic. Naval doctrine is wise enough not to define a hard-and-fast timeline for what falls within each process. Generally, COPS needs to stay focused on monitoring and directing COPS, and should pass planning and replanning efforts to future operations (FOPS) or the maritime planning group (MPG) whenever possible. If properly constructed, FOPS and FUPLANS have planning expertise and the time to reach across the staff for specialized expertise. The natural tendency of hard-charging COPS officers, however, is to retain control of as much of operations as possible.

Guiding and directing these three processes is one of the key roles of the operations officer or director for operations (N3). Depending on the staff construct, the N3 may also be designated as the director of the Maritime Operations Center (MOC-D or DMOC) or as Director, Maritime Operations (DMO). As a fine point, a MOC-D directs the MOC within a command; a DMO directs operations across a command's span of authority and is a more senior position. Large fleet staffs will have both a MOC-D and a DMO. Regardless of titles, naval doctrine specifies that the N3 remains responsible for "the direction and control of operations, beginning with the mid- and near-term horizon planning through the completion of specific operations."[1]

Operations Watches and Current Operations

Naval operations continue around the clock. As a result, control over COPS is normally exercised through a watch run by the N3 team. Afloat, this may be the flag plot. At the fleet level, COPS will be run through the Fleet Command Center (FCC), which maintains operational situational awareness for the commander. The FCC will be a critical part of the MOC construct, which is described more fully in chapter 19. However, the FCC is a place and a watch team, whereas the MOC is a structure and a concept. Some officers will use the two phrases interchangeably, but that is incorrect.

The N3 will typically have a cadre of mid- and senior-grade petty officers, mostly operations specialists, sufficient to stand the FCC watch.

Management of these Sailors can be a challenge since there are often just enough on the staff to fill the watch bill. They are, however, usually on shore duty and are drawn from ratings that spend most of their careers at sea. Spending most or all of their shore tour on a 24/7 watch can come at the cost of the educational and personal opportunities that normally are part of such assignments.

Senior watch standers are normally drawn from across the staff. Every unrestricted line officer assigned to the staff will normally qualify as battle watch captain (BWC). Staff codes with their own 24/7 watch standing requirements (for example, the intelligence team), usually qualify on that watch. Once qualified, duty several times a month is common. This construct has the advantage of spreading the watch burden outside of the N3 team and of ensuring most staff codes have a stake in this critical staff function. It does, however, often create a strong variability in experience, competence, and engagement among the senior watch standers that must be managed.

However they are assigned, the battle watch captain acts as the commander's direct representative for all COPS. They and their team will do the following:

- Manage the common operational picture
- Monitor execution of maritime operations
- Act as the central node for handling, tracking, and recording information
- Maintain a record of significant events and pending actions to a level of detail capable of reconstruction
- Track CCIRs
- Coordinate and assess ongoing operations

To execute these functions, the FCC team must be knowledgeable of and closely tied to other watches within the command and the watch teams at higher and subordinate commands. The battle watch captain also acts as the sole authority for issuing operational orders (OPORDs) such as fragmentary orders (FRAGOs), execute orders (EXORDs), and daily intentions messages (DIMs) to subordinate commanders. This function ensures that the operations team is cognizant of all orders being issued by the command, and ensures they are recorded and tracked.

Foundational to these processes is a clear understanding of command relationships. Each battle watch captain needs to understand how their command relates to each entity with which it interacts. In brief, there are five basic command relationships:

1. Combatant command (COCOM). In joint command structures, CCDRs exercise COCOM as a type of command authority over assigned forces. COCOM provides sweeping authority to, among other things, organize and use commands and forces and to assign tasks. The CCDR cannot delegate COCOM, and so a Navy command will never have COCOM over another unit. All U.S. Navy commands except those that are service retained fall under the COCOM of a CCDR. As a point of clarification, DoD uses three acronyms for the same words when used for different ideas:

   a. CCDR = the combatant commander (person)

   b. CCMD = the combatant command (organization)

   c. COCOM = combatant command (authority)

2. Operational control (OPCON). Inherent in COCOM, OPCON may be delegated; it allows a commander the authority to organize and use commands and forces, assign tasks, designate objectives, and give authoritative direction over all aspects of military operations necessary. However, OPCON is limited to accomplishment of an assigned mission. That mission may last for months, but is not indefinite in the way COCOM is.

3. Tactical control (TACON). TACON is an authority over assigned or attached force and is limited to the detailed direction and control of movements and maneuvers within the operational area necessary to accomplish assigned missions assigned by a commander exercising OPCON or TACON of the force.

4. Supported or supporting. A unit may be in support to another specific unit (direct support), two or more units may support each other

(mutual support), or a unit may provide a category of support across an area (general support). In any event, a supported or supporting relationship is a formal command relationship that can be created only by a common superior in the chain of command.

5. Administrative control (ADCON). ADCON is authority over administration and support. It is most commonly associated with the services (e.g., Navy, Marine Corps, etc.) that address organization resources and equipment, personnel management, logistics, individual and unit training, readiness, mobilization, demobilization, and discipline.

It is important to remember that many close foreign partners often use similar phrases, but with different nuances that must be understood when working with coalition forces.

Staff Operations: Basics Matter

No other FCC task is so foundational as is keeping track of the units under the staff's OPCON. The procedures by which control of a unit is maintained and passed between commands—how units CHOP (change of operational control [OPCON])—can seem unnecessarily rigid, even pedantic to the new staff officer. Far from mere formalism, however, these procedures have been learned and relearned in tragedy.

In the closing days of World War II, the heavy cruiser USS *Indianapolis* was returning to the western Pacific after repairs had been made to damage from kamikaze attacks sustained during the U.S. invasion of Okinawa. *Indianapolis* carried the nuclear material for the first atomic bomb to Tinian, and was then routed to Guam. After a brief port call there, *Indianapolis* was to report to Task Force 95 at Leyte for ten days of training with the expectation that it would then be sent north to join the forces gathering for the expected invasion of Japan.

Just after midnight on 30 July 1945, almost exactly midway between Guam and Leyte, *Indianapolis* was torpedoed by the Japanese submarine *I-58*, and sank within twelve minutes. While damage to the ship prevented any SOS message from being sent, *Indianapolis* was scheduled to arrive at Leyte the morning of 31 July, less than thirty-six hours after the sinking.

By 1945, the U.S. Navy had a well-developed search and rescue system, and survivors afloat in such a quiet sector of the Pacific could expect to be rescued quickly.

Unfortunately, however, *Indianapolis* fell into the seam between three Navy staffs. The Marianas Sea Frontier Headquarters in Guam, who had assigned *Indianapolis* the route to Leyte, assumed it was proceeding along the assigned track. Once time-distance calculations indicated it should be out of their waters, they ceased tracking. The Leyte Gulf Naval Operations Base Port director knew *Indianapolis* was scheduled to arrive, but recently, in an effort to reduce the burden of routine message traffic, their higher headquarters had ended the practice of sending arrival messages for warships. Junior personnel noted that the ship never appeared, but reasoned that if no arrival message was required, no message indicating a non-arrival was required either. Task Force 95 knew *Indianapolis* was scheduled to report to them, but had failed to read an earlier message tasking them with providing the planned ten days of training. As a result, they did not know why *Indianapolis* had been routed to them and assumed that such a capable heavy cruiser had likely been diverted to the invasion fleet gathering near Okinawa.

With no one taking responsibility for monitoring *Indianapolis*, it was not until an aircraft on routine ASW patrol spotted survivors that anyone actively inquired after its whereabouts. Even then, it took hours to understand where the survivors were from and the scope of the rescue effort required. By that time, the surviving crew had been in the water for four days, their numbers slowly whittled away by exposure, thirst, and sharks. Of the 1,195 Sailors on *Indianapolis*, approximately 890 went into the water alive after the sinking. Only 316 survived their ordeal at sea. More than twenty years later, their commanding officer, haunted by guilt even in retirement, committed suicide.

The loss of *Indianapolis* has been a source of controversy since her sinking. Several excellent books explore the multiple aspects of responsibility; the commanding officer's accountability, whether intelligence about Japanese submarines in the area was handled correctly, and if the cruiser should have been zigzagging or been provided an escort.

One element, however, is beyond debate. If any one of the three operations teams involved had tracked *Indianapolis* with competent attention, hundreds of survivors would have been found alive days earlier.

As the FCC monitors ongoing operations, the COPS team works in close coordination. COPS spaces are often physically in or adjacent to the FCC. COPS will conduct short-term operation planning as required, moving into action when the task exceeds the capacity of the FCC team on watch. COPS will also function as the back office for the FCC, conducting tasks such as updating CCIRs, preparing the daily operations briefs, and drafting and releasing intentions messages. COPS also acts as the continuity on operations that extend over several watch cycles.

Future Operations

FOPS focuses on branch and contingency plans to ongoing COPS. As discussed, the line between COPS and FOPS is blurry. Generally, FOPS

Bad staff work has consequences: Ambulances staged pierside in Guam await survivors from USS *Indianapolis*, 8 August 1945. *NARA*

planning requires significant coordination across the staff and outside the lifelines. In some ways, FOPS functions as a dedicated, standing OPT able to handle both the detailed integration of ongoing operations and planning branches created by a rolling series of operational challenges.

Air Operations and Fires Planning

Because they fall under rigid joint processes, air operations and fires often fall within their own specialized operational processes. Where air operations or fires are a staff focus, the N3 will often have a dedicated team that can engage with each issue.

As outlined in chapter 19, the U.S. Air Force components under each CCMD act as joint force air component commander (JFACC) for all air operations in the designated theater. The N3 team will manage a process to engage U.S. Navy air operations with the joint air tasking cycle. The air tasking cycle is a seventy-two-hour process that produces an air tasking order (ATO) covering twenty-four hours of air operations across the entire area of operations.

CHAPTER 14

Maintenance, Logistics, and Readiness

Maintenance, logistics, and readiness are three distinct functions, but share common elements. The extent to which these three functions animate a staff will vary according to the staff mission. For example, a deployed DESRON will concern itself with all three, but usually in the limited sense of being a broker and customer of support services for units conducting operations. A major fleet staff may be intimately engaged in all three across a significant part of the Navy, to include planning for the next several years.

Maintenance

Maintaining the nation's investment in its ships, submarines, and aircraft is a significant responsibility. While maintenance, like all other activities, is the ultimate responsibility of the commanding officer, a multitude of staffs manage and direct maintenance activities.

The policy of the Navy is to maintain its ships

- in the highest practical level of material readiness to meet operational availability requirements while minimizing the total cost over the design life of the ship;
- in a safe material condition;
- to ensure shipboard habitability;
- to meet required environmental standards; and
- to meet the ship's expected service life.

Ship maintenance across the Navy is run by Naval Sea Systems Command (NAVSEA). Similarly, aircraft maintenance is the purview of Naval Air Systems Command (NAVAIR) The TYCOMs are responsible for the maintenance of ships that are assigned to them. Ships are typically assigned to TYCOMs during long maintenance periods and in the early phases of their work-up cycle. Both of these staffs are discussed in chapter 22.

Despite the existence of these specialized staffs, the fleet commanders and their staffs have a key role in managing and directing the maintenance of their forces. To understand that role, it is important to first understand that maintenance availabilities—periods when a ship is dedicated to repairs or modernization—fall into two categories: CNO and non-CNO availabilities.

Fleet commanders and their staffs assign and schedule non-CNO availabilities. CNO availabilities are scheduled by OPNAV N83, and while fleet commanders can influence these schedules, they are charged with making ships available for them to the maximum extent possible.

One of the key elements that the fleet staff will manage is the scope of the work to be performed during a maintenance period. Work can be based on time—think of changing a home furnace filter every six months—or on material condition. What work is needed based on material condition is usually identified before the availability by the ship's company or by inspection teams.

Orchestrating this effort is the fleet maintenance officer, usually designated N43 at major staffs. The fleet maintenance officer at FFC and Pacific Fleets is usually a flag officer. In the Pacific, for example, the N43 overseas maintenance execution across some 60 percent of the Navy. Policies and processes for execution of fleet maintenance are determined by the fleet maintenance board of directors. The group is made up of the senior fleet maintenance officers from FFC, Pacific Fleet, NAVSEA, and OPNAV N83.

Logistics

At numbered fleets and naval component commands, the fleet logistics staff represents the key link between the tactical logistics requirements and strategic logistics capabilities. NWP 3–32 *Maritime Operations at the Operational Level of War* pointedly notes that logistics is actually conducted at the tactical and strategic levels. At the operational level, the logistics staff synchronizes these resources in time, place, and purpose to support the commander's overall operational design.

Logistics takes different forms over time, but navies survive on their stores. Here, a capital ship of the New Steel Navy takes on coal. *Naval History and Heritage Command*

It is often said that amateurs study tactics, but professionals study logistics. The ability of the U.S. Navy to act as a forward-deployed force, operating across the sweep of the world's oceans, is built on a series of logistics innovations and the daily work of the professionals who keep the supplies moving to the fleet. In our recollection of our history, we often forget the impact of logistics. Consider that, in the dark days of early 1942, the PACFLT did not commit all the battleships it had available to the desperate fighting near Guadalcanal. The fuel requirements of the older oil-fired ships were simply too high for the fleet's limited number of oilers to support.

It is clear that logistics is fundamental to supporting operations, and must be incorporated into the earliest stages of the planning cycle. Developing a plan and then passing it to the logistics team to assess wastes valuable time. Such a disconnect can also increase risk to the force, since the natural habit of planners is to try to adapt the developed but suboptimal plan, sometimes by ignoring the logistics challenges.

In addition to embedding logistics experts into other OPTs and planning efforts, the N4 organization maintains several mechanisms to monitor and direct logistics efforts. To support this task, the N4 organization will maintain several staff elements. The overarching logistics element is the Logistics Readiness Center (LRC). When required by operations, the LRC will be a 24/7 watch within the MOC. The LRC maintains visibility into the logistics requirements of the force, ultimately enabling the commander to make decisions about the use of finite resources. The LRC then coordinates, commands, and controls logistics support elements in accord with the commander's operational scheme of maneuver. The senior logistics officer will generally chair a logistics coordination board at least once each day as a forum for discussing and aligning logistics issues across subordinate commands.

While this mission may sound straightforward, it is not simple. An LRC must support the following:

- Supply
- General services
- Distribution
- Maintenance and battle damage repair
- Contracting
- Ordnance
- Petroleum, oils, and lubricants
- Transportation
- Civil contingency engineering and facilities
- Mortuary affairs
- Coordination and integration of host-nation support

As needed, the LRC will establish sections that address each of these requirements. In many cases, key strategic supply structures supporting operations are part of the joint force. For example, much essential petroleum, oil, and lubricants (POL) movement is coordinated by the Defense Logistics Agency (DLA), while key strategic lift fall under the command of U.S. Transportation Command (USTRANSCOM), a global CCDR. This reality requires the logistics staff to move routinely between service and joint structures more than most other staff elements.

As the Navy faces the renewed challenge of high-end warfare, fleet logistics has been called on to adapt. Much of the current supply system is communications intensive, and is required by its nature to interface with commercial IT systems. Cognizant that these links will be unreliable in conflict, fleet logistics planners should develop preplanned logistics processes that can be executed with minimal communications. These measures are in many ways a return to how logistics were managed in earlier times, when the ability to make and coordinate detailed supply requests was not assumed.

USS *Benfold* takes stores from USNS *Charles Drew* in the Philippine Sea, 2021. *U.S. Navy*

Readiness

Logistics, maintenance and training combine to produce readiness. Readiness—the preparedness of naval forces to conduct their assigned missions—is the critical metric of how much of the nation's naval power can be brought to bear in operations at a moment in time. As such, senior level officers will focus on readiness metrics, and the professional ability of much of the service is dedicated to creating as much readiness in the force as possible.

Readiness reporting across the Navy and DoD is formalized in the Status of Resources and Training System (SORTS) and the Defense Readiness Reporting System (DRRS). Together, these automated systems measure the readiness of individual units to perform their assigned missions. SORTS was introduced in 1986, and was the subject of congressional criticism and review in the late 1990s. DRRS was intended to replace SORTS in its entirety; however, today SORTS remains as a reporting system for individual units. These unit data are then aggregated into DRRS.

The heart of the unit level assessment is the C rating. Every unit is assigned mission areas. While the exact mission areas vary depending on the unit type as identified in the unit ROC/POE instruction, at a minimum a unit will be assessed on personnel, supply, training, and equipment. Based on a formula that measures material and non-material factors, each area receives a C rating. These mission areas are then aggregated into a C rating for the entire unit. C ratings are expressed on a four-point scale, with one the best and four the least ready. For overall scores,

- C1 means the unit can fully carry out its wartime mission;
- C2 means the unit can carry out most of its wartime mission;
- C3 means the unit can carry out portions of its wartime mission; and
- C4 means the unit needs additional resources to perform its wartime mission.

Within DRRS, the readiness of individual units rolls up into an assessment of readiness within a group, squadron, unit type, or mission area. For example, a TYCOM might regularly measure the readiness of both individual units and specific types of aircraft across the entire globe.

DRRS status is managed by the Under Secretary of Defense for Personnel and Readiness, and is briefed to the highest levels of the DoD. It is used to assess long-term readiness trends across forces. It is also provided to Congress to help its members understand both the DoD's needs and its stewardship of the taxpayers' resources.

One of the most direct impacts on a unit's C rating is its material condition. Degradation of major systems is required to be reported via a casualty report, or CASREP. Like C ratings, CASREPs are graded by severity from one to four, with one being a minor fault and four being an impact to the unit's overall mission. CASREPs are the subject of much guidance, direction, and folklore. On one hand, CASREPs are intended to help the system help units with their material issues. Each TYCOM has resources in the form of money, expert advice, and spare parts, which is earmarked to repair causalties. Generally, these resources can only be unlocked if and when a CASREP is issued. It is not uncommon to find a support team ready to help troubleshoot and repair a casualty on a deployed unit to be waiting on their phone for the date-time-group of the CASREP so they can depart for the airport. On the other hand, there is a perception that superior units have minimal CASREPs. Certainly, if a casualty is the result of carelessness or error, sending a message to the world explaining the failure is not pleasant. It is, however, part of the job. Senior officers generally understand casualties happen, often having had the experience themselves. When a higher headquarters discovers a casualty that ought to have been reported, however, the benefit of the doubt is lost. The immediate, and unfortunately often correct assumption, is that the unit was trying to avoid self-reporting an error. Similarly, low balling CASREPs will also hurt a unit's reputation. Sending a report for a minor fault, only to have to update the CASREP to reflect a major casualty, can be the result of honest troubleshooting—the extent of a crack, for example, may not be apparent until other equipment is removed—but it will attract attention.

Honor, Courage, and Readiness

With so much attention to readiness, a brief word about the integrity of the system is in order. Superior commanders drive readiness and material excellence. Not every unit has the resources to be C1 even under the most extraordinary leadership. Across the Navy, there is real pressure to present the best possible account to the joint leadership and to Congress. The only protection against that pressure is the integrity of the leaders in the system. ADM James O. Richardson, commander, U.S. Fleet, in 1941, wrote, "It takes great intestinal fortitude for a military officer to report to his senior that some of the units of his force are not ready for war. Too frequently such a report results in his detachment and the ordering to his billet of some officer whose abilities are thought to be of a higher order or, in case where the truth is offensive to the seniors affected, the ordering of someone whose conscience is more elastic, or standard of readiness markedly lower."[1]

Richardson was removed from fleet command nine months before the attack on Pearl Harbor, in part for vigorously informing his chain of command that permanently placing the fleet at Pearl Harbor caused it to be less ready for combat.

In 2017 PACFLT lost seventeen Sailors in two tragic collisions at sea. Subsequent investigations revealed that neither unit involved was fully ready for the missions they were conducting. Some of these deficiencies had been formally reported, others had not. Certainly, the aggregate impact of these deficiencies was not effectively articulated up the chain of command or perhaps was not acted on once received. While many factors entered into these accidents, readiness reporting and the willingness to act on a report was a central factor.

CHAPTER 15

Plans

Plans and planning are what make staffs unique. Staffs may direct action, but the actual execution is the work of others. Planning—synthesizing ideas for the deliberate use of resources in a future situation—is the element that allows commanders to place forces where they will matter, ready to take meaningful action.

Despite that reality, U.S. military officers, and particularly naval officers, have a low opinion of planning compared to other militaries. In many cases, that skepticism is the product of having seen plans fail during real-world operational experiences. Indeed, that skepticism can be healthy: the expectation that real operations will face the unexpected and require improvisation encourages flexibility and agility that is a strength in execution. If that skepticism causes us to discount planning, however, we will find ourselves in operations without even the framework from which to improvise.

Within Navy staffs, planning is the purview of the N5, who will lead the analysis, development, and synchronization of near-term and long-range plans and policy. Plans cover a variety of challenges, from traditional OPLANS for a major conflict to guidance for theater security cooperation programs.

Planning is a learned skill, informed by a process that is designed to be deliberate, complete, and thoughtful, even if executed rapidly. In recent years, the Navy has invested in a small community of highly educated planners. These officers, graduates of the Maritime Advanced Warfighting School at the Naval War College or of one of the other service equivalents, are qualified to lead the full deliberate planning process for the full range of plans: from a complex OPLAN to a theater security cooperation plan, to crisis action planning (CAP). Given the difficulty of these programs, most major staffs have only a handful of these experts. A good staff officer will learn who they are and add them to their network.

Planning Process

Three themes run through the planning process: ends, ways, and means; guidance; and risk.

Ends, Ways, and Means

Plans will constantly refer to the interplay of ends, ways, and means. Simply put, ends are the military objectives that must be achieved in the light of higher headquarters, or political or national objectives. Ways are the sequence of actions that are intended to achieve these military objectives. Means are the resources required to execute the ways.

Guidance

Plans exist in a framework of guidance. Guidance provides the ends and defines and constrains the means that can be used. As they begin the planning process, it is not uncommon for N5 officers to refer to the policies and direction of the office of the Secretary of Defense, the Department of State, the OPNAV, and the relevant CCDR.

Risk

Every plan involves risk. Skilled commanders understand risk, and accept and manage it as necessary to maximize their odds of success. Planners contribute to this process by finding the sources of risk, finding options to mitigate them, and articulating where risk is being accepted. Risk is binned into two categories:

- Risk to mission. The chance that a force will fail to accomplish its ends.
- Risk to force. The chance that the force will be lost, rendered ineffective, or rendered unable to conduct follow-on tasking.

Planning Function

Even though the planning function is led by the N5, the execution of any major plan will involve the entire staff. Thus, the planning process needs to engage and be engaged by every element of the staff to be successful. Very rarely will the N5 develop a plan without input from multiple staff elements. In that sense, the staff structures associated with plans can be seen as a means to bring together that cross-staff expertise to produce the required products. The three most common are future plans cell, maritime planning group, and operational planning teams.

Future Plans Cell

FUPLANS is the small core of planning experts who provide the staff's long-range operational planning capability. This team normally leads the development of concept of operations plans (CONPLANS), OPLANS, and component supporting plans to CCDR-level OPLANS. The FUPLANS team will scope the planning task, and determine the process to be followed to reach success. Depending on the output, this process will follow the naval planning process outlined in NWP 5–01 *Navy Planning* or the joint operation planning process (JOPP). The team will also determine the type and scope of support required from other staff elements during the process.

Maritime Planning Group

The maritime planning group will function as a planning clearinghouse for plans across all time horizons. In most staffs, where FUPLANS works long-term planning tasks, the maritime planning group conducts contingency and CAP.

Operational Planning Teams

OPTs are the go-to staff answer for short-term planning problems that require cross-staff focus.

Both FOPS (N3) or FUPLANS (N5) can establish OPTs. Each will report to the N-code that established it and will have a slightly different approach depending on which is designated as the lead.

The Power of Planning

The surprise attack on Pearl Harbor came as a shock to the U.S. Navy. In the days afterward, however, Navy leaders quickly established the basic approach to the war in the Pacific. The approach was realistic, well designed, and nested effectively within the overall strategic guidance for the conduct of the war. This rapid strategic orientation was a direct result of a planning process that spanned more than thirty years.

As early as 1907, U.S. Navy planners had perceived a potential threat from imperial Japan. Fresh from its victory over Russia in 1905, Japan looked like a potential long-term challenger. The first war plans were by design basic, intended more to allow a consideration of possible issues than to offer executable naval courses of action.

After World War I, Japan's imperial ambitions became more apparent, and were backed by a growing effort to achieve military parity with established powers such as Great Britain, Italy, and the United States. In response, U.S. Navy planners began to develop plans of increasing sophistication. Competing strategic approaches—rapid movement to decisive battle versus island hopping—were articulated, exercised, and evaluated.

In the late 1930s, the U.S. Navy plan for war with Japan was folded into the nascent joint planning system.

While the U.S. Navy's senior leaders in World War II had been part of the planning effort, most of the officers who worked on these plans left the service long before the war they imagined came to pass. In many cases, their names are forgotten even to specialist historians of the era. Their work, however, identified the factors that would shape operations, the issues that would need to be solved, and the range of possible solutions. They created the intellectual framework for victory in the Pacific, a victory that was as much theirs as if they had accompanied the fleet into Tokyo Bay in 1945.

The Role of the Commander in Planning

The wishes of the leader will not bring victory unless as a commander he has the strategical knowledge and the tactical skill to make a good plan.

> U.S. Navy War Instructions
> Commander in Chief, U.S. Fleet, 1944

In both deliberate and crisis planning, the role of the commander is essential. Any plan adopted by the headquarters must ultimately be approved by the commander. The process through which these plans are shaped, how risk is identified and either accepted or mitigated, and what operational approaches are accepted requires guidance to be given at the different stages. Such engagement at formal decision points is the minimum, and no competent commander should do less. Delegating these decisions to a deputy or senior staff results in plans that do not have the commander's full support or the benefit of their experience.

Because any plan is ultimately the commander's, there are key elements that must be commander's business. These include the overall intent behind the plan, the task organization and command relationships between the units involved, and the key decision points in the plan execution.

The best commanders empower their planning teams as an extension of their own thinking. This approach requires regular contact, and often conversational interactions that allow ideas to be proposed and evaluated by all sides. Over time, this dialogue allows the planners to understand their commander's operational approach—the why as well as the what—and enables them to craft plans that fit the commander's thinking.

Joint Operations Planning and Execution System

The Joint Operations Planning and Execution System (JOPES) is the joint system that sequences the movement of forces and resources in time and space. Once a plan has been approved by a CCDR, and the supporting Navy plan has been developed and approved, the Joint Operations Planning and Execution System team develops the force deployment plan that makes the plan real. As part of the joint planning process, the team receives a time phased force deployment data (TPFDD) letter of instruction outlining the CCDR's guidance for the movement of naval forces. Using this guidance, the relevant JOPES cell sources units to meet plan requirements and transportation and sustainment of these forces. They also develop the reception, staging, onward movement, and integration (RSOI) plans that will be used to integrate units into the force if the plan is executed.

Operational Assessment

Assessment is the critical process of determining if a plan is working. Responsibility for assessments is usually associated with the planning team under the theory that the creators of the plan are best equipped to help determine what it should produce and whether it is on track. These assessments then become inputs to the continuing planning process, allowing the commander and staff to adjust and adapt as required.

For assessment to be effective, the staff needs an understanding of the objective to be achieved, the insight to know what factors would indicate progress toward the objective, and the ability to gather sufficient information available to conduct assessment.

The information required for assessment falls in two categories: measures of performance and measures of effectiveness:

- Measures of performance (MOPs) are sometimes characterized as, "Did we do it right?" They measure whether the plan was conducted as intended. Examples of measures of performance include the number of sorties generated by the force against an adversary, ordnance delivered, and the amount of stores supplied.

- Measures of effectiveness (MOEs) ask, "Did we do the right things?" They should help determine if the operation is on track to achieve the desired ends. Examples of measures of effectiveness include the number of adversary attacks on friendly forces in a period, the cost of an embargoed commodity in an adversary nation, or the willingness of adversary forces to surrender to friendly forces.

How and what to measure in a complex operation is a topic of much debate. The danger in assessments is that many staffs confuse measures of performance and measures of effectiveness. There is also a natural tendency to prefer measures of effectiveness that can be reliably collected and measured. While suitable to fill a spreadsheet or chart, these may or may not be reliable indicators. Furthermore, in any conflict the adversary will work to deny information or to ensure that deceptive information is always available. History is replete with examples, such as the Royal Navy overestimating the number of German U-boats it destroyed in the Battle of the Atlantic during World War II, and nonetheless being told by senior political leaders that it was too pessimistic in its assessments; U.S. forces in the Vietnam War counting enemy dead, ignoring that fraud and uncertainty made accurate numbers essentially impossible to acquire.

Few staffs have the fortitude to tell their commander that relevant, diagnostic measures of effectiveness are not possible, even though that is more the rule in combat than the exception.

CHAPTER 16

Communications

Staffs exist to help commanders make decisions. The life-blood of that decision-making process is the communication of information. Information must be moved to the staff, within the staff, and back out to impact actions. In short, a staff is inseparable from its communications.

Beyond that critical dependence, communications are a limited resource that must be built, maintained, operated, and managed on behalf of the fleet. In peacetime, they are subject to compromise or cyber intrusion. In conflict, they will be attacked.

Navy staffs run on coffee and communications, sometimes simultaneously. *Naval History and Heritage Command*

Despite these realities, many in our Navy still view communications as a service to be provided by narrow specialists, rather than a resource to be managed by commanders. Ignoring the communications officer until something stops working is no more a recipe for success than a commanding officer ignoring the chief engineer until a major casualty develops. The C2 of C2 is itself an art and science, and clearly is commander's business.

Managing the complexities of modern communications is normally the purview of the communications officer or the assistant CoS for communications. Many Navy commands have a communications officer. What is distinctive about staffs is that staff communicators are inherently responsible both for the communications of the staff and for managing the communications of several units. The more senior the staff, the more the management of communications services across a force becomes the focus.

The Limits and Risks of Communications

The Royal Navy ended the largest naval battle of World War I without the clear victory that it had expected. A century later, the reasons for it fighting the imperial German navy to a draw remain controversial. One of the most interesting theories, however, centers on how the Royal Navy understood and constructed its tactical communications.

While wireless had been developed for long-range communications by 1916, it was slow and subject to environmental degradations. Visual communications by flag hoist remained the standard for signals in combat. The first signal book was introduced in 1799, and a later revision was used for Nelson's famous signal at the 1805 battle of Trafalgar: "England expects that every man will do his duty."

In the hundred years before World War I, naval formations grew in size, covering larger areas of the sea. The range and variety of weapons grew, and with them, the complexity of formations and maneuvers. The Royal Navy response was to develop more-complex signal systems. These required a highly trained cadre of signals officers, exquisitely drilled in transmitting tactical signals across maneuvering formations covering several horizon's distance. Opportunities for specialized training as a signal officer were limited, and it was a significant career asset.

In his extraordinary work, *Rules of the Game: Jutland and British Naval Command*, British historian Andrew Gordon asserts that the prominence of the Royal Navy's signals officers skewed its assessment of how tactical communications would work in actual combat. At Jutland the smoke of sustained gunfire, damage to masts and halyards, and the complexities of multiple tactical formations maneuvering simultaneously caused the detailed ballet of visual signals to break down. While such breakdowns were foreseeable, signals officers had assured commanders that they would be overcome in practice. Gordon's conclusion: professional signals officers had incentive to advocate for their own capability, and over a century had produced a fleet dependence on a system too complex to survive combat—a point every staff officer and commander should remember when the staff communications officer (COMMO) assures them that they can plan on communications being up in a crisis.

To support 24/7 operations, most staffs maintain a communications watch. At the numbered fleet or above level, this center, called a Communications and Information Systems Center (CISC) or Navy Communications Systems Coordination Center (NCCC), plans and manages computer information systems and communications for the commander.

A full NCCC includes the following:

- Communications current operations (communications COPS). This watch team is the heart of what most staff officers consider the NCCC. Communications COPS executes the communications plan (COMPLAN) that provides satellite communications (SATCOM), communications security (COMSEC), spectrum management, and communications support to the staff and subordinate commands. They monitor communications status 24/7 and provide situational awareness of the communications architecture to the staff. In the event of an outage, they assess the technical and operational impact of the loss. When needed, they direct shifts in communications in response to new and emerging operational requirements or outages. A competent staff will have written procedures for what actions the watch can direct immediately, when they need to inform other staff elements, and what actions need to be referred to higher authority, such as the operations officer or commander.

- Communications systems plans. The communications plan team works across the life cycle of the staff planning process to ensure that upcoming operations are supported by optimal communications. These planners are usually integrated into future operations planning and various OPTs.

  Communications planning requires the team to consider the adversary threat to friendly communications and computer systems, the physical and environmental limitations of the operating area, and the requirements of the operation. Communications have a similar relationship to plans as logistics: they are easy to overlook, but absolutely determinative to the success of the operation.

  It is important that communications planners understand both the ideal communications for an operation and the minimum thin line of communications required. The communications planners will then create a plan to satisfy as much of the ideal as possible, along with preplanned responses (PPRs) to outages and secondary and tertiary communications paths. The plan will be limited by such things as the expected emission control posture, the availability of limited SATCOM channels, and the communications capabilities of the individual units.

  The planners also are the first link in the critical process spectrum management. The electromagnetic spectrum is a crowded place, with ever-growing demands from civilian, government, and military users. Careless design of the communications plan will produce electromagnetic interference that may impact mission-critical systems.

- Communications systems MOC / headquarters (HQ) support cell. The support cell handles the staff's own communications issues, coordinating the required audio, video, and data networks required to ensure information flows where needed. It is the element that staff officers will interact with most often. During routine operations, the support cell is often collocated with the communications COPS watch.

At the naval component level, the NCCC will interface with the CCMD J6 team on policy and joint communications management issues.

The communications team supporting a shore staff is not generally hands on the communications equipment in the sense of operating a major communications center. Such centers are under commander, U.S. Tenth Fleet, and are generally aligned in support of operations within a major ocean area. There are cases where FCCs have specific transmitters or deployable communications capabilities, but these are exceptions and not the rule.

Major shore staffs have complicated arrangements with their IT systems that often become an additional exception to this rule. Most U.S. Navy shore IT networks are provided and operated by contractors. The Navy–Marine Corps Intranet (NMCI) is the most widespread and best-known example. Overseas shore commands are serviced by the OCONUS (outside contiguous United States) Navy Enterprise Network (ONE-Net) outside the continental United States. Operating these networks as contracted information systems allows the Navy to leverage the experience of major IT firms in enterprise-level systems management. It is also big business, with the most recent operating contract worth in excess of $7 billion.

For a shore staff, this operating model means that the N6 does not operate the command's NIPR and SIPR networks. That does not mean, however, that the COMMO is without influence on the process.

When afloat, naval regulations dictate that the embarked commanders assume control of the flagship's communications. The COMMO (or N6) acts on the commander's behalf in exercising this authority. The staff COMMO has the challenge of integrating ship and staff communicators into a single team that support both while allowing the ship to return to normal operations once the staff shifts flags.

CHAPTER 17

Training, Exercises, and War Games

Victory in combat, as well as safe operations, depends on well-trained forces. As a result, most staffs have a training element, normally coded as N7. The scope of their responsibility varies with the level of staff. In a DESRON, training may be one of many functions that the staff administers. In a staff whose main responsibility is providing ready forces, training may be the main function of the staff. Responsibility for training is generally divided by its level of complexity. For example, in accordance with the fleet training continuum (FTC) and fleet readiness training plan (FRTP), in the surface forces, the TYCOM conducts basic and advance phase training at the unit level. Integrated phase training is conducted at the fleet level.

The fundamentals of training, however, are constant across all levels of the service, and thus across every training office:

- First, there must be training standards. Standards define what each Sailor, unit, and formation needs to be able to do, and how well they need to be able to do it. These standards are captured in a range of documents and instructions.

- Second, there needs to be a system to monitor training standards, tracking the completion of training objectives by individuals, units, and formations.

- Third, there needs to be a plan for achieving standards such that the unit is ready to operate on the timeline required.

Whether a collateral training officer at the unit level or a fleet training office, these functions remain. However, at the staff level, there are added elements of complexity. Training staffs plan for the utilization of limited

191

training resources, including the most critical resource—time. Navy forces are finite resources, and time spent training is time away from operations. Thus, the Navy training process represents a constant tension between efficiency—delivering enough training as rapidly as possible— and effectiveness—training thoroughly and completely to be ready for a complex operational environment. The training staff is at the nexus of these competing demands.

Training staffs often manage attendance at simulators or team trainers, even those provided by outside elements. For example, a DESRON may have six slots per year for an attack team trainer that it will apportion to subordinate units. Training staffs also schedule outside training teams that conduct on-board training within different specialties.

At the fleet level, the training staff often manages training ranges. Pacific Fleet, for example, manages the funding, maintenance, and use of fleet training ranges throughout the Western Pacific, Hawaiian Islands, and West Coast. Modern ranges are complex integrated systems covering hundreds or thousands of square miles. Depending on their purpose, a range may include instrumentation to ensure range safety and allow monitoring of unit performance, systems that emulate threat platforms, and live targets in, on, and under the sea. They are also often shared with other users ranging from fishing fleets to commercial space launch enterprises. A number are in environmentally sensitive areas that require special restrictions and careful monitoring. This behind-the-scenes work concerns operational forces only when they are using a range, and is transparent to most of the staff. It is worth noting, however, that many N7s are managing a series of complex facilities in addition to their usual staff functions.

Limitation on ranges is one of the many reasons that fleet synthetic training is an increasingly critical tool for operational forces. Synthetic training differs from traditional simulators in that the units being trained use their own systems, which are networked to allow complex virtual interactions. Dozens of ships can train battle group tactics together in a secure virtual environment while physically remaining in their homeports or under way hundreds of miles from each other. While the training audience may not be physically under way, coordinating this level of complex training requires much the same level of staff work as real-world train-ing. Savings in time and resources should be folded back into the training, allowing more-challenging and more-thoughtful operational learning.

At every level, the best training staffs do more than simply execute training requirements created by others. Training must be firmly based on current reality. Ties into the intelligence team are critical to understanding the threats that may be faced now and in the near future. Feedback and les-sons learned from real-world operations form an essential check to train-ing success. Furthermore, most large training teams draw from across the various Navy warfare communities, bringing together a range of tactical and operational experiences. These teams can identify where training stan-dards have been overcome by changes in threat or technology, and where interactions between different warfighting tools can offer new solutions to tactical problems.

When training requirements are out of date, cannot be completed, or have been satisfied through other means, the training staff is the starting point for training waivers. Waivers are a sensitive issue in the service. On one hand, a waiver can be a commonsense measure. If a ship regularly con-ducts an evolution as part of normal operations, but has not been observed doing so because of unavailability of an observer, suspending its qualifica-tion seems pedantic. If the unit understands and executes the evolution according to standards, it is. However, IBM Chair Louis V. Gerstner Jr's statement, "People do what you inspect, not what you expect" holds true.[1] Following two collisions in 2017 that killed seventeen Sailors, investiga-tors concluded that routine use of waivers due to demanding operational schedules had contributed to the mishaps. While the ships involved had been operating regularly, they had drifted from the required and safe stan-dard of performance, undetected due to routine waivers. Whereas before these accident waivers could be granted at relatively junior levels, they now can be granted only by senior commanders.

Exercises

Exercises are a specialized element of training, often administered within the same staff element. Exercises fall into three categories, each distinct:

- Field training exercises (FTX). An FTX is an exercise involving actual forces. FTXs train commanders, staffs, and individual units in basic, intermediate, and advanced warfare skills.
- Command post exercise (CPX). A CPX is a specialized type of FTX intended to train the commanders, staffs, and C2 processes within and between headquarters. In a CPX, the forces involved are simulated.
- Table-top exercise (TTX). A TTX is a structured discussion used to assess plans, policies, and procedures. Often conducted in an informal, classroom setting, TTXs usually examine a specific problem through a scenario or series of vignettes.

Each type of exercise can be conducted with other services, making it a joint exercise, or with other nations, making it a combined exercise. While true joint exercises are part of a Joint Staff–administered exercise program, it is common for other services to be folded into Navy exercises by mutual agreement.

Exercises follow a five-phase life cycle that carries the event from design, planning, preparation, execution, and evaluation. The command conducting the exercise will drive each step of the process. For all but the largest exercises, a single staff officer, usually from the N7 team, is assigned as action officer for the entire exercise life cycle. They will typically have a designated representative from each staff code who will define how their function will be represented:

- Phase 1: Design. During the design phase, the N7 gathers the initial interested commands together for a training objectives workshop (TOW). The TOW sets what the goals for the event will be. In many cases, these are well-known and established mission essential tasks (METs) that are always part of an exercise series. However, there can be an element of negotiation in the training objectives. For example, an Air Force unit may attend the TOW and express interest in supporting the Navy exercise, providing that the exercise is designed to offer them a required training event between their aircraft and naval surface units. The TOW is followed by a concept development conference (CDC), where the N7 team will present the broad outline of the exercise. The concept should encompass as many training objectives as possible, balanced against a realistic understanding of resources.

- Phase 2: Planning. The planning stage of a major exercise normally includes two planning conferences; an initial planning conference (IPC) and a mid-planning conference (MPC). Around the time of the mid-planning conference, a master scenario events list (MSEL) will be developed by a separate MSEL development conference (MDC). The master scenario events list is a complete chronological list of events that need to happen during the exercise. For a major fleet exercise, that list can include more than four thousand events, each requiring deconfliction in time, space, and resources.

- Phase 3: Preparation. Preparation includes establishing and testing databases and communications, readying the ranges and physical facilities, and all the other practical steps required for the exercise. During this phase, the final planning conference (FPC) offers the commander a last chance to review and shift the exercise plan and ensure synchronization across the participants.

- Phase 4: Execution. Execution is the fun part: simulated operations or combat under the guidance of the exercise control group (ECG) and the careful observation of the designated umpires or observers.

- Phase 5: Assessment. At the conclusion of the exercise or shortly thereafter, the exercise observers gather to conduct an immediate assessment and feedback session with the training participants. This after action review (AAR) is a key primary venue for learning because it is here that the participants officially learn if they completed the exercise satisfactorily. Technically, after action review is the end of phase 4 rather than the start of phase 5. Phase 5 consists of the detailed analysis and reporting of the events of the exercise, a process that inherently requires time and thought. Unfortunately, few Navy commands have the discipline and focus to concern themselves with the analysis of an exercise that concluded weeks or months before.

Most FTXs are scheduled years in advance, and are driven by the requirement to manage training resources, range time, and unit schedules. In most cases, the FTX is intended to achieve a specific training effect. This required outcome will drive the content of the exercise, which generally varies little from year to year.

One challenging element of major FTXs is the inclusion of free play. Free play is unscripted action between the opposing sides in an FTX. If done properly, free play captures the uncertainty and dynamic challenge of combat better than any other training tool. However, effective free play is challenging, resource intensive, and unpredictable. Simply put, the most efficient training maximizes the number of training tasks or events that the participants complete in a given time. Free play requires that both sides are free to act in the way that best advantages them. That approach may or may not ensure that specific training tasks are actually completed. Realistic free play also requires a significant investment in opposing forces (OPFORs), who must be large and capable enough to be able to realistically represent an adversary. A realistic opposing force, however, comes at the cost of valuable fleet resources and may be able to defeat the training audience, thus preventing them from completing certain specific training tasks. As a result, realistic free play is rare despite its value in developing warfighting

A war game at the Philadelphia Navy Yard, 1920. At the time of the game, many of the ships being represented were in reduced readiness as a post-World War I economy measure. *Naval History and Heritage Command*

excellence. An N7 organization should be the primary advocate for free play as a key part of fleet training.

It is important to note that exercises are not war games. A war game is a structured analytic tool, whereas an exercise is designed to produce a training outcome. The two are often confused, since CPXs, TTXs, and war games often look (and feel) similar in execution.

War games can be significant tools for learning, both for the participants and for the Navy. War gaming is a regular part of the Navy planning process. These games are usually designed and conducted by the N5. Larger war games designed to develop doctrine or test concepts are often led by the fleet N7. At the highest level, the Navy conducts service or Title X games designed to inform the future direction of the entire Navy. These games are usually conducted in partnership with a specific fleet, partnering the fleet N7 team and the Naval War College War Gaming Department as the service's subject matter experts on game design.

It is important to remember that, while exercises and war games are among the most effective tools to improve warfighting effectiveness, any individual event is limited in impact. Building these events over time while synchronizing with experimentation, modeling, and simulations in a coherent campaign of learning is the essential next-level staff work that produces game-changing outcomes.

Training the Fleet and the Staff

Between 1923 and 1940, the U.S. Navy conducted twenty-one expansive at-sea operations that built the skills essential for success during World War II. These annual operations, named Fleet Problems, were larger and more complex than any regularly scheduled exercise currently conducted by the U.S. Navy, and offer a valuable example of what high-end fleet training entails.

Each Fleet Problem started with an operational problem selected by the CNO, almost always an element of the current war plan against Japan that presented genuine uncertainty and complexity. The problems often began with the U.S. side at a significant disadvantage. In Fleet Problem XIX (1938), for example, the scenario assumed a major U.S. Navy defeat

Not every experiment is a success: the airship USS *Los Angeles* moored to USS *Patoka* off Panama during Fleet Problem XII, 1931. *Naval History and Heritage Command*

had already occurred, requiring friendly forces to defend from a position of weakness.

Operational staffs were required to assess the situation, then to conceive, communicate, and execute complex combat operations in response. This linkage between the staff process and operational execution ensured that poor staff work became immediately apparent at sea.

Both forces were led by senior officers. It was assumed that there would be a clear loser—and not a junior officer designated to be defeated, but an officer of stature and accomplishment. Senior officers could and did fail dramatically, were critiqued candidly and publicly, and continued to advance and lead. The critique of a Fleet Problem was often attended by every commander down to the unit level. In 1925, eight hundred officers gathered after Fleet Problem V to hear each of the commanders present their operations and lessons. The record suggests that these were not polished staff briefings, carefully harmonized to avoid contradiction of seniors, but relatively free and interactive events, with each side walking through their choices and assessments.

As a free play event, the unexpected was expected. During Fleet Problem III (1924), an insider sabotaged the battleship USS *New York* by gaining access to its magazine and simulating a catastrophic explosion while the ship was in restricted waters in the Panama Canal. Umpires ruled that not only was the ship lost, but also that the waterway was closed to further transits. Since the point of the problem was to investigate defense of the Panama Canal, the Blue side, representing the U.S. Navy, was ruled to have failed.

The Fleet Problems also stretched commanders to imagine how to use new tools and technologies. Aircraft carriers were integrated into every Fleet Problem, with other units representing aircraft carriers before the first U.S. Navy carrier, USS *Langley*, was placed into service. Circular screens, submarine operations, and advanced base operations— all critical during World War II—were perfected in these events.

In 2015 the original Fleet Problem series was the inspiration for a new series of Fleet Problems designed to hone the fleet's high-end warfighting skills against new challenges. While the present forward-deployed force does not allow the bulk of the fleet to be dedicated to a major training event, the Fleet Problems series continues to serve as an example of what training for large-scale warfighting can be.

CHAPTER 18

Afloat Staffs

N avy staffs were born afloat. In their simplest form, they arose when the first officer commanding more than one warship needed assistance with their task. Today, the Navy has afloat staffs ranging from O6 to O9 commands, comprising teams ranging from a dozen or so to hundreds.

Afloat staffs come in five major varieties: destroyer squadron, amphibious squadron, expeditionary strike group, carrier strike group, and maritime prepositioning ships squadron. In addition, some numbered fleets are able to operate afloat.

Destroyer Squadron

Under the command of an O6 surface warfare officer, a DESRON will function as both operational and administrative command element for groups of surface combatants.

In their ADCON role, the DESRON will be responsible for overseeing and assisting in the overall readiness, staffing, training, and equipping of assigned units.

There are two common operational employment patterns for a DESRON. When assigned to a CSG, the DESRON commander will function as the sea combat commander (SCC) within a CSG CWC structure. Embarked onboard the assigned aircraft carrier (CVN), the DESRON staff will normally provide a watch position in the Tactical Flag Command Center (TFCC) to support this warfare area.

In other cases, DESRONs will command a surface action group (SAG) or task force (TF) on independent operations. In either case, these are usually temporary organizations brought together for a specific operation or deployment. The distinction is that a surface action group is made up of combatant ships, whereas a task force may be units of any variety. Examples of task force operations include UNITAS (Latin for unity), a series of at-sea exercises with Central and South American navies; CARAT (Cooperation Afloat Readiness and Training), a series of annual bilateral military exercises between Pacific Fleet and navies in Southeast Asia; and Pacific Partnership, an annual deployment of Pacific Fleet units into Oceania.

Surface action group operations, once limited to one-off events in support of specific tasks, have become more common in recent years as the surface force deploys more capable weapons and systems that significantly increase the lethality of surface combatants operating independently.

In supporting independent operations of increasing complexity, DESRON staffs will face challenges due to their relatively small size. However, the requirement that they be able to embark a DDG-class combatant with limited space for staffs means that this limitation will likely endure, and that it will provide officers assigned to such staffs the opportunities to work beyond their pay grades.

Amphibious Squadron

Commanded by an O6 Navy officer, an amphibious squadron (PHIBRON) staff usually commands an ARG.

In addition to the PHIBRON staff, a baseline ARG consists of the following:

- At least three amphibious ships, usually including an amphibious assault ship (LHA or LHD), an amphibious transport dock ship (LPD), and an amphibious dock landing ship (LSD)
- Two to three helicopters
- Two assault craft units consisting of air cushion landing craft (LCAC) and conventional landing craft (LCU).

An ARG will embark a Marine expeditionary unit (MEU) of approximately 2,400 Marines and supporting air elements, led by a Marine colonel and staff.

PHIBRONs, like DESRONs, are relatively small staffs, offering staff officers an opportunity to be responsible for major staff functions at relatively junior levels. They also offer the opportunity to team with a Marine

Corps staff to accomplish a common mission. While the C2 lines between the Navy and Marine Corps have been contentious at different moments of our history, the result is the finest example of joint warfighting in the DoD today. Furthermore, as the Marine Corps shifts from its post-9/11 role of operating in the Mideast as excellent—but not amphibious—light infantry, the value of understanding what the Blue/Green (Navy/Marine Corps) team can bring to a high-end maritime fight will be increasingly valuable for developing naval leaders.

Expeditionary Strike Group

An ESG is an ARG led by either a Navy or Marine Corps O7. While the implication is generally that the ESG is a larger and more capable force than an ARG, there is no requirement for a different force structure. In this case, the command element defines the difference. Navy doctrine states that an ESG provides a greater range of amphibious and expeditionary warfare planning capabilities for the execution of a variety of missions, to include the capability to conduct operations ashore and function as a sea base.

To support the deployment of ESGs, the Navy maintains four full-time ESG staffs—one on the West Coast, one on the East Coast, one forward deployed to Japan, and one deployed in the Arabian Gulf. Typically led by an O7 surface warfare officer, their seniority parallels that of their CSG counterparts. They usually deploy in conjunction with a PHIBRON staff, and provide the "greater range of . . . planning capabilities" noted in Navy doctrine. They will also C2 surface combatants and submarines that may be found in an ESG, depending on the task and threat environment. As the Navy contemplates ESG operations in high-end maritime combat, the requirement for ESG staffs to the full spectrum of maritime combat tasks, to include the most sophisticated strike and information warfare missions, has moved these staffs out of their traditional core amphibious missions.

Carrier Strike Group

Commanded by a one- or two-star Navy flag officer, the CSG staff commands a CSG. In addition to the CSG staff, a baseline CSG consists of

- an aircraft carrier,
- a carrier air wing (CVW) with staff,
- five to seven air defense–capable surface combatants,

- submarines assigned to direct support,
- a DESRON staff, and
- an air and missile defense commander (AMDC) with staff.

Recent history will suggest that this baseline is rarely achieved in actual deployed operations. The number of five to seven surface combatants represents the units that are administratively assigned to the CSG, but do not deploy due to their maintenance cycle or because they are used as independent deployers apart from their assigned CSG.

Maritime Prepositioning Ships Squadron

The two Maritime Prepositioning Ships Squadrons (MPSRONs), located in Guam and Diego Garcia, maintain TACON of ships carrying afloat prepositioned military supplies. Each MPRSON consists of fourteen to sixteen U.S. naval ship (USNS) vessels. These vessels are owned by the U.S. military and are operated by Military Sealift Command (MSC) civilian merchant mariner crews. Together, they offer the ability to deliver critical supplies to support the early phases of major combat operations in the region until vessels from the United States can reach the area.

The Maritime Prepositioning Ships Squadrons provide the military command element to these vessels, handing C2 and the integration of these strategic assets into wider military operations.

Numbered Fleet

The U.S. Navy maintains two afloat numbered fleets—Seventh Fleet, which is permanently embarked on USS *Blue Ridge* (LCC 19); and Sixth Fleet, which will sometimes embark USS *Mount Whitney* (LCC/JCC 20). The newly created Second Fleet is sized to allow embarkation of surface vessels in support of operations, but does not have a permanently assigned command ship.

Numbered fleets are usually commanded by a vice admiral and are expected to support a MOC capability. While the details of the MOC function are discussed more fully in chapter 19, it is worth noting that afloat numbered fleets face the challenge of supporting the complexities of a MOC with the restrictions on staff size and communications that a flagship creates.

Senior Third Fleet staff gather in the wardroom of their flagship, USS *New Jersey*, to review plans for an upcoming landing, December 1944. *NARA*

The Afloat Difference

Afloat staffs are U.S. Navy staffs that conduct all or part of their operations embarked on board a vessel.

Putting that obvious statement in writing highlights a fundamental assumption that navies make: the venue of command matters. Many of our joint colleagues find the distinction curious. In other services, command is command, the staff provides support, and that function is the same whether conducted in the field, in garrison, from a tent, or from a hardened bunker. Yet every Sailor instinctively knows that operating from a ship at sea impacts how a staff works. While most of the observations about staffs apply across all levels and venues, it is worth considering how afloat staffs are unique.

Why Put a Fleet Afloat?

Other than USS *Constitution,* USS *Blue Ridge* and USS *Mount Whitney* are the oldest commissioned vessels in the U.S. Navy. Commissioned in 1970 and 1971, respectively, they are unique in that they were purpose-built as command ships. While each has been extensively modified over the decades, they pair an extraordinary communications suite with a ship's infrastructure that is almost fifty years old. Their steam propulsion plants are the last of their kind in the fleet and require specialized knowledge and care. The cost of these platforms, both in supporting their current operations and their possible future replacement, regularly raises the questions of the benefits of a fleet staff being afloat.

So why pay the cost of putting a fleet staff afloat? The Navy usually makes three arguments:

- Survivability. In combat, fixed command centers are high-value fixed targets. The inherent mobility of naval forces makes command ships tougher to find and target.

- Communications flexibility. Even in this age of instant, worldwide communications, geography matters in the communications game. Being able to place a communications node in the ideal location to maximize connectivity between operating forces and to bridge between afloat forces and shore support is helpful in any environment. In high-end combat where an adversary has attacked and degraded friendly communications, it could be decisive.

- Sovereignty. Like all U.S. Navy vessels, command ships are essentially sovereign U.S. territory. Overseas shore-based command centers are subject to the political restrictions of the host nation. They can be evicted, as the French did to U.S. and NATO installations in the 1960s, or their actions can be restricted due to political decisions. During Operation Odyssey Dawn in March 2011, several NATO partners raised concerns about offensive operations in Libya originating from their territory. In response, the Sixth Fleet staff embarked USS *Mount Whitney* and supported NATO operations while under way in international waters.

Semi-Afloat or Deployable Staffs

The perception that fixed command structures may be vulnerable in a conflict, along with the advantages of being embarked on a ship, have caused a number of shore-based staffs to consider how they might be able to relocate to an afloat unit to support operations. Some shore-based staffs already have a rudimentary outline of how such an embarkation might occur as part of their continuity of operations planning (COOP). However, there is a significant difference between securing limited functionality to ensure continuity of routine operations and a robust afloat C2 capability. Few U.S. Navy vessels are both configured to host a large staff and not already in routine use by a staff. A careful survey of the available vessels, an understanding of the fixed limitations of communications and space, and, in some cases, significant augmentation of the ship's normal fit, are essential to make a staff deployment more than a PowerPoint course of action.

At the most basic level, an afloat staff is tied to a ship. The flagship may be a purpose-built vessel (*Mount Whitney*–class LCC/JCC), designed

Everyone bears a hand under way: Sailors from the Seventh Fleet staff and the flagship USS *Blue Ridge* work together to load stores, 2016. *U.S. Navy*

for a flag staff (*Nimitz*-class CVN), or may support a staff as an occasional embarkation (for example, an *Arleigh Burke*–class DDG). Regardless, the ship creates the environment within which the staff works.

First and foremost, an afloat staff is impacted by the act of being afloat. Navies are unique in that Sailors inhabit their weapons system, and are tied to it in a constant, long-term way that is found only in the sea services. The experience of living and working together while conducting deployed operations bonds afloat staffs together in a way that shore commands can only dimly emulate. This phenomenon of being literally in the same boat as the rest of the fleet creates a mindset that is both difficult to quantify and uniquely suited for the command of maritime operations.

The size of an afloat staff is limited by the size of the staff that the flagship can support. That limit may be the number of racks or the number of computer drops available, but there is a limit to what is comfortable and a limit to what is possible with even the largest and most capable ships. These limits are hardly a new phenomenon. Throughout World War II, the Pacific Fleet staff remained quite small for the scope of operations that they were controlling. FADM Nimitz wanted to keep the option for his staff to go afloat, and so controlled its size using possible flagships as a guide.

Afloat staffs also operate with the same communications challenges that subordinate forces experience. Simply, underway naval forces can only communicate in the radio frequency (RF) spectrum, something large shore headquarters, tied into robust fiber optic communications lines, often forget. Add in environmental conditions, competition for limited satellite channels, and, in combat, adversary countermeasures, and naval warfare hinges on managing the flow of information through limited channels. An afloat staff, living in this environment, will have a visceral appreciation of the need to manage the movement of information to afloat units.

It is with good reason that one of the first positions created on afloat staffs in the seventeenth century was the staff communicator who, because the means of communicating involved flag hoists, was known as the flag lieutenant. Communication is so critical to the function of an embarked commander that naval regulations dictate that the embarked commander assume control of the flagship's communications. The COMMO (or N6) acts on the commander's behalf in exercising this authority. The staff COMMO has the challenge of integrating ship and staff communicators into a single team that supports both while allowing the ship to return to normal operations once the staff shifts flags.

Working with a Flagship

While embarked, it is critical to manage the relationship between the staff and the ship's company. The lines between the two, both formal and informal, have been established by long experience and tradition. The running of the ship is the business of the ship's commanding officer, but that commanding officer is responsible to the embarked commander. When the embarked commander is the officer in tactical command (OTC), the ship responds to its direction as would any other unit.

The staff is subject to the regulations, orders, and routine of the flagship, and are required to respect the integrity of the ship's chain of command. Like any long-term guest, the staff is responsible for taking care of where they live and work, both for cleanliness and routine maintenance. This means, for example, that an afloat staff will typically have petty officers trained to maintain damage control equipment, and to integrate into the ship's planned maintenance system (PMS) to care for gear in staff spaces.

Ships with embarked staffs, like all other fleet units, occasionally have failures in maintenance, training, and discipline. In these cases, even if these issues will not impact staff operations and the ship has complete authority in handling these issues, it is an expected courtesy that the admiral or CoS will be informed before reports are sent off the ship. It is never a good idea to allow a senior to be surprised by reading about events on their own flagship in message traffic.

When the staff is a small element within a large ship, it is relatively straightforward to keep the two elements within their professional lanes. On a command ship, where the ratio between ship's company and staff can approach two to one, the relationship can be somewhat more difficult. For these ships, supporting the fleet staff is the mission. That fact does not, however, remove the requirement for the ship to conduct all the essential tasks that make them a whole and complete unit. Generally, drills that will impact staff operations—for example, by securing power or communications—are scheduled when they are unlikely to impact the staff's mission. Routine drills are carefully segregated by space or time to avoid staff areas. At least one command ship had its normal training drill "Set material condition Zebra, main deck and below," avoiding restricting the movement of the staff. For its part, the staff must allow the ship enough time to train.

In an emergency, the reality is that most afloat staffs are little more than passengers. They are, normally, accomplished professionals with significant experience from previous tours, perhaps even in the same class of ship. But rarely are their firefighting qualifications current, few have ever seen the inside of the ship's damage-control lockers, and none has participated in shipboard drills. In extremis, the staff can assist. Staff in World War II routinely found themselves acting as damage-control parties after their flagships were hit. In the late 2000s, a major fire on board a CVN saw the ultimate vertical fire boundary set by staff Intelligence Specialists. Nonetheless, the state of staff training and situational awareness suggests that in an emergency normally the best option for both the ship and the embarked staff members is for the staff to stand aside.

The Great Bomber Raid

USS *Blue Ridge*, under way in the East China Sea: Boom! The door to the intelligence center slammed open under the impact of the fleet intelligence officer. Charging into the space at a run, the N2 proceeded to excoriate the intelligence watch team for failing to provide warning of inbound bombers about to overfly the fleet command ship. As an animated N2 loudly enumerated the ways in which this intelligence failure reflected their personal and professional shortcomings, the watch team stared at him uncomprehending, until it dawned on one petty officer that perhaps, maybe, the captain was referring to a drill the ship was running?

In fact, the ship was running a training combat scenario that would eventually lead to a damage-control problem. The fleet staff habitually turned off the 1MC announcing system in staff spaces, avoiding distractions from their work, and ensuring they had no idea what the ship was doing. The N2 had been jogging topside, where the 1MC was still audible. When the combat information center (CIC) announced the incoming threat, he had no idea a drill was in progress.

Slightly chastened, the N2 resumed his run, but the 1MCs in the staff spaces never were turned on.

Like any command, staffs have watch positions that vary depending on the focus and tasking of the staff. In port, the staff will have at least one staff duty officer, who functions much like the command duty officer onboard a ship. The staff duty officer's focus, however, will typically be on email and message traffic as he monitors the needs of assigned forces on behalf of the commander. Under way, the staff will have a watch officer acting as the commander's representative to ongoing operations.

On a combatant not equipped with flag spaces, the staff watch officer will stand watch in the ship's CIC. On board a CVN, the CSG commander's officer-in-tactical-command functions are largely exercised from the TFCC. TFCCs were added to *Nimitz*-class aircraft carriers in the mid-1980s, giving flag staffs a dedicated CIC-like watch space for the first time. The TFCC is usually near the combat direction center (CDC), which provides a similar CIC function for the aircraft carrier commanding officer.

Fighting Afloat: Staffs and the Composite Warfare Commanders

The CWC concept is core to how the U.S. Navy conducts combat operations at sea below the fleet level. Tactical Navy staffs have the unique requirement to integrate with and support the CWC construct as part of their warfighting roles.

Interestingly, the CWC construct is so foundational to navy operations that it is often overlooked. For example, *Network-Centric Warfare: How Navies Learned to Fight Smarter Through Three World Wars*, Norman Friedman's excellent study of afloat naval combat information systems, does not directly address the concept.[1] Joint Publication 3–32, "Command and Control for Joint Maritime Operations" diplomatically states, "While acknowledged in joint doctrine, the OTC [officer in tactical command] and CWC are Navy and NATO unique constructs."[2]

Indeed, the CWC concept grew from the interplay of the unique requirements of modern naval warfare and the naval C2 culture. During

World War II, the need to integrate an air defense picture and the introduction of radar and other new sensors drove the development of the CIC. While each combatant had its own CIC, the requirement for fleet air defense created a need for a largely more-integrated approach. In the postwar era, the growing speed of air engagements stressed this construct, and it became clear that any complex chain of command would fail to provide the needed speed of decision at scale.

A partial solution was found in the masterpieces of automation that are now the fleet's everyday tools. Machine-to-machine exchange of information through Navy Tactical Data System (NTDS), automated sensor management pioneered by the AEGIS radar program, and rapid all-source intelligence fusion all originated to deal with this challenge. Despite these innovations, in a multithreat environment with air, surface, subsurface, and electronic warfare threats all playing out simultaneously, no single command center could cope with detailed battle management on this scale.

The conceptual solution exploited the Navy's culture of mission command and delegation of execution. Simply put, the CWC concept allows the OTC to delegate specific warfare missions to subordinate commanders in a tactical setting. These warfare area commanders are trained specifically for these missions, embarked on the optimal platform to C2 their warfare area, and are provided with the flow of detailed information that allows them to control engagements. They are provided commander's intent through standing orders and expressed rules of engagement. The OTC receives enough information to monitor the overall battle across all mission areas, allowing the OTC to shift resources and focus as the mission and threat requires. This visibility also allows the CWC system to exploit command by negation. Joint Publication 3–32 notes, "Once such functions are delegated, the subordinate commander is to take the required action without delay."[3] The OTC has the option to intervene, negating an order that a subordinate warfare area commander has taken. Thus, the overall tempo of the fight can proceed at a pace that both matches the demands of modern maritime combat and allows the senior commander on scene to manage across a complex, multi-domain fight.

Most CWC organizations will accelerate and simplify this process by having a series of preplanned responses to possible tactical events. Indeed, the creation, promulgation, and exercising of these responses is a key task of an afloat staff before deployment. Well-crafted preplanned responses are an explicit expression of the commander's intent, and allow subordinates to initiate action independently when circumstances warrant.

In a CSG, the CSG commander is normally the OTC because TACON is rarely delegated below this level. The OTC will also be known as the composite warfare commander (CWC), reflecting the OTC's control over all of the various composite warfare areas. The OTC delegates specific command functions, designating warfare area commanders depending on the mission. In regular conversation, they are known by their radio call signs; for example, the OTC will answer to AB. Normally, these will include the following:

- Strike warfare commander (abbreviation STWC, call sign AP). Normally the carrier air wing commander (CAG), AP coordinates strikes against land targets with either embarked aircraft or Tomahawk land attack cruise missiles (LACMs).

- Air warfare commander (abbreviation AWC, call sign AW). The AWC is normally the commanding officer of a *Ticonderoga*-class cruiser, if assigned. These ships were purpose-built for fleet air defense and are commanded by an O6 surface warfare officer with previous command experience, making them well suited for the task. Generally, AW is the only warfare area commander not embarked on the aircraft carrier.

- Information warfare commander (abbreviation IWC, call sign AQ). The IWC is an O6 from one of the information warfare community designators (18XX) assigned to the CSG staff. The IWC is the newest warfare area commander and reflects the growing importance of information-related capabilities at the tactical level of naval warfare. The IWC's role will vary based on the CWC's direction, but will, at a minimum, include managing the use of the electromagnetic spectrum by friendly forces and the deliberate countering of adversary intelligence, surveillance, reconnaissance (ISR) and targeting efforts.

- Surface warfare commander (abbreviation SUWC, call sign AS). Usually the embarked DESRON commander, the SUWC is responsible for surface surveillance and for engaging surface threats.

- Antisubmarine warfare commander (abbreviation ASWC, call sign AX). The ASWC is responsible for the defense of the force against submarine threats. The ASWC is normally authorized direct liaison with the submarine operating authority (SUBOPAUTH) and the theater undersea warfare commander (TUSWC) to integrate tactical efforts into task force or fleet-level ASW efforts. AX is often also assigned the role of helicopter element coordinator (abbreviation HEC, call sign AL) to allow seamless integration of helicopter assets into the ASW fight.

- Air resources element coordinator (abbreviation AREC, call sign AR). The AREC manages organic aircraft carrier air resources to respond to the tasking from other warfare area commanders. Usually assigned to the carrier air wing strike operations officer, AR promulgates current information on the availability of aircraft to meet CWC requirements.

- Undersea warfare commander (abbreviation USWC, call sign AX). The USWC

- Submarine element coordinator. The submarine element coordinator is usually a submarine officer who advises AX on utilization of submarines that are in direct support of the battle group.

Warfare Area	Abbreviation	Call Sign
Composite Warfare Commander	CWC	AB
Strike Warfare Commander	STWC	AP
Air Warfare Commander	AWC	AW
Information Warfare Commander	IWC	AQ
Surface Warfare Commander	SUWC	AS
Antisubmarine Warfare Commander	ASWC	AX
Air Resource Element Coordinator	AREC	AR

Practicalities of the Composite Warfare Commander Concept

It should be immediately clear to even a novice staff officer that the demands of the various warfare commanders will consistently exceed the available resources. This is especially true for high-demand, low-density assets and for assets that have capabilities across multiple warfare areas. For example, an *Arleigh Burke* DDG can provide decisive effects in the air, surface, information, and subsurface fights, but rarely can it do all effectively at once. The ideal placement of an escort to provide warning of inbound threat aircraft may be the opposite of the likely threat axis from which submarines may be expected. Using a towed-array sonar may place restrictions on the ship's ability to maneuver, complicating operations near another unit. The iron-clad rule is that a unit may be under the TACON of only one commander. The elegance of the CWC concept is that this rule can be honored while at the same time the ship's capabilities can be in the service of multiple warfare area commanders

Assuming that the OTC has delegated effectively, prioritizing limited resources between warfare commanders will be the OTC's foremost task. Routine decisions can be made by the staff watch officer, but complex operational risk is commander's business.

The form and focus of the CWC construct show its lineage as a defensive construct. The CWC was designed to allow rapid action in time-critical defensive situations. Throughout most of the post–World War II era, offensive action was thought of as less time critical, usually launching against fixed land targets on our timeline. With increasing emphasis on fleet engagements in a high-end, contested environment, there is reason to believe that future offensive actions may be characterized by fleeting detections of targets and brief opportunities for engagement. Adapting the CWC system to allow rapid offensive action will be a challenge for future naval staffs.

CHAPTER 19

Fleet Commands and the Maritime Operations Centers

Fleets are a relatively recent development in U.S. Navy history. The early Navy was organized as single ships or squadrons. On the rare occasions when several ships were required to work together—say to suppress piracy—they were formed into a temporary squadron. It was not until the 1880s that the idea of a battle force maneuvering together caused the U.S. Navy to form permanent fleets. After the Cold War, the U.S. Navy tended to deploy and fight as tactical-level formations such as CSGs, ARGs, or surface action groups. The return of great power competition and the need to integrate fires and effects across domains has changed that paradigm, and today the U.S. Navy considers the fleet as its basic combat formation. The requirement to fight as a fleet has placed a renewed focus on the operational role of the fleet staff, and has made duty on a fleet staff a dynamic and challenging professional experience.

The U.S. Navy has nine fleet commanders. Each is entrusted with a unique mission covering a major swath of the world (or, in the case of Tenth Fleet, all of the world). Their structure and their staffs vary in response to the scope and nature of these missions.

Each fleet has a distinctive institutional personality that is known and acknowledged across the Navy. All fleets balance an OTE function and an operational role. The balance between the two determines the fleet commander's focus and thus much of the staff culture. For example, the newly reformed Second Fleet has almost no OTE mission. Third Fleet, its nominal West Coast counterpart, focuses on OTE of West Coast naval forces, having only a limited operational mission. This difference is reflected in how the two staffs invest their time and effort.

Fleet Commands under the Chief of Naval Operations (Echelon One)

Echelon Two	Echelon Three	Organize, Train, Equip role	Operational Area of Responsibility	
U.S. Fleet Forces Command		East Coast forces		
	Second Fleet	None	Atlantic	
U.S. Pacific Fleet		West Coast and Pacific forces		
	Third Fleet	West Coast forces	Eastern Pacific/U.S. West Coast	
	Seventh Fleet	Some role for assigned forward-deployed forces	Western Pacific and Indian Ocean	
	U.S. Naval Forces Japan	Minimal	Defense of Japan	Naval component of U.S. Forces Japan.
	U.S. Naval Forces Korea	Minimal	Defense of Republic of Korea	Naval component of U.S. Forces Korea.
U.S. Naval Forces Europe / U.S. Naval Forces Africa	Sixth Fleet	Minimal	Barents, Norwegian, Baltic, Black Mediterranean Seas; and Africa	Dual hatted in both roles. Sixth Fleet shares staff and is collocated with U.S. Naval Forces Europe (NAVEUR); they are effectively one command.
U.S. Naval Forces Central Command	Fifth Fleet	Minimal	Mideast	Fifth Fleet shares staff and is collocated with NAVCENT: they are effectively one command.
U.S. Naval Forces Southern Command	Fourth Fleet	Minimal	Caribbean, South America, Central America	Fourth Fleet shares staff and is collocated with U.S. Naval Forces South (NAVSO). They are effectively one command.
U.S. Fleet Cyber Command	Tenth Fleet	Organize, train, equip (OTE) for assigned U.S. Navy (USN) forces	Worldwide for warfighting domain	

Fleet staffs also differ in command echelon. Echelon two fleets report administratively directly to the CNO or act as a naval component to a joint CCDR. Echelon three fleets, or numbered fleets, were created in World War II to exercise OPCON over large combat formations. After the Cold War, Navy leaders sought to create a more efficient staff structure. The command functions of the two fleet echelons, however, were too established to unbuild. Instead, the Navy combined the echelon two and three staffs. The result are staffs that straddle both levels. Naturally, many staff do most of their business in one role over the other. Commander, U.S. Naval Forces Southern Command (COMUSNAVSO) and commander, U.S. Fourth Fleet (FOURTHFLT), for example, exists as a single staff working as both an echelon two and three headquarters. Because current U.S. Navy presence in South America is minimal, the operational-level functions of the staff consume little time. Commander, U.S. Naval Forces Central Command (COMUSNAVCENT) and commander, U.S. Fifth Fleet (FIFTHFLT) are similarly a single staff, but in contrast are entirely about operations. They rely on other staffs to provide them with trained and ready forces that they use—and then send home for others to fix.

FFC and Pacific Fleet are different from the other fleet staffs and deserve some explanation.

PACFLT is an echelon two command that both organizes, trains, and equips its forces and commands their operations through two separate echelon three numbered fleets. This arrangement is the traditional fleet structure established during World War II. The passage of time and the search for efficiency have left PACFLT as the last major fleet organized cleanly along these lines. PACFLT also has two distinctive echelon three commands: U.S. Naval Forces Japan (CNFJ) and U.S. Naval Forces Korea (CNFK). These staffs exist to curate the U.S. Navy relationship with these important regional navies. In the event of armed conflict, they become part of the larger U.S. response in support of these treaty allies. PACFLT is also a force provider, since PACFLT ships deploy to other AORs.

In contrast to the traditional arrangement of PACFLT, FFC represents a half-finished experiment. Located in Norfolk, Virginia, FFC was formed from U.S. Atlantic Fleet in 2001. A few years prior, the joint force had established a COCOM in Norfolk, U.S. Joint Forces Command, to control concepts, doctrine, and experimentation. The FFC designation aligned Atlantic Fleet, and these traditional OPNAV roles, to the new CCDR. Hand in hand with this joint alignment, a number of Navy leaders proposed having FFC control all OTE functions for the Navy worldwide, which would be a return to an earlier era when administration of the fleet was vested in a single four-star officer. This vision of FFC as the senior-most fleet was never fully realized. Some OPNAV functions shifted to FFC, and FFC assumed Navy-wide control over some, but not most, OTE functions.

The incomplete transformation of FFC has been complicated by the Inouye Amendment, named after former Hawaii senator Daniel Inouye. Since 2011, each year Congress has directed that "none of the funds available to the Department of Defense may be obligated to modify command and control relationships to give Fleet Forces Command administrative and operational control of U.S. Navy forces assigned to the Pacific Fleet . . . unless changes are specifically authorized in a subsequent Act."[1] The Inouye Amendment reflected both the desire of a powerful senator to defend naval presence in his state and a concern that FFC as a single OTE authority could not effectively care for the majority of the fleet based more than three thousand miles away from its headquarters.

As a result, relationships between FFC and PACFLT are complex and sometimes difficult. Officially, the two fleets are coequals. However, PACFLT Sailors still deride FFC as OPNAV South, while their shipmates at FFC find PACFLT's focus on current operations a hindrance to long-term thinking about OTE issues. Managing the natural friction between them is commander's business, and is something every Navy staff officer needs to understand.

Fleet Administration, Fleet Operations, and Tragedy

The complex relationship between fleet administrative and operational functions became a major topic after 2017 collisions involving USS *Fitzgerald* and USS *McCain*.

Fitzgerald and *McCain* were both forward-deployed naval forces (FDNFs) homeported in Japan. As part of FDNF Western Pacific (WESTPAC), they fell under Seventh Fleet, whose staff traditionally focused more on operations than on readiness. At the time, the readiness of most U.S. Navy ships was managed as part of the optimized fleet response plan (OFRP), a construct administered by FFC. FDNF ships were not tracked as part of this system and kept a different maintenance cycle based on their always-deployed status.

FFC, however, was designated as manning control authority (MCA) for all U.S. Navy afloat forces worldwide. The manning control authority made the final determination of how limited personnel would be prioritized across competing fleet needs. FFC focused on staffing ships that were part of the optimized fleet response plan, reflecting a natural administrative bias toward improving a process for which it was accountable. As a result, ships in the FDNF routinely operated with smaller crews than their counterparts in other fleets, despite the challenging WESTPAC operating environment and their demanding schedules.

Navy investigations officially concluded that staffing levels were not a factor in the two collisions that killed seventeen Sailors. However, a number of commentators, as well as the then–Seventh Fleet commander, disagreed. At a minimum, they asserted, constant staffing challenges in the WESTPAC surface force contributed to the overwork of the FDNF crews and the creation of a culture of risk acceptance that led to tragedy.

Whether or not crew size was a factor in these collisions, the incidents highlight the real tension between fleet operational and administrative roles, as well as the difficulty of coordinating cross–area of responsibility priorities. In the year following the collisions, the Navy shifted manning control authority from FFC to Naval Personnel Command. While the move officially had nothing to do with the collision, it did ensure crew size decisions were made by a staff that had no ties to one particular part of the fleet.

Commanding Operations, Organizing the Fleet: The Maritime Operations Center

The MOC is the shore-based expression of decades of Navy thought on the C2 in modern naval combat. As discussed in chapter 1, the post–World War II Navy had invested heavily in automated combat systems and machine-to-machine communications that allowed afloat units to work together in combat. Navy command centers ashore focused on monitoring broad ocean areas, which was an arrangement consistent with both the limits of the available information systems and the service's preferred style of decentralized C2. With the advent of modern computers, however, some naval technologists envisioned the ability to provide battlespace visibility that was both broad and granular. Such automated insights would allow the centralized coordination of naval forces across a larger area than previously thought possible.

The Joint Operational Tactical System (JOTS), introduced in the mid-1980s, allowed commanders to view a range of tactical datalink feeds in what today would be described as a personal computer–based interactive display. Personalities matter in driving change: within the fleet, it was commonly accepted that JOTS stood for "Jerry O. Tuttle System," after VADM Jerry O. Tuttle, a fierce advocate of naval automated C2 systems in the era. Once JOTS terminals were installed in FCCs, the fleet commanders had a window into the movements of their forces that invited increased control.

While the Navy was contemplating the implications of new technologies, the joint world created a second driver for changing Navy shore command processes. Starting in the 1990s, the Joint Staff began to develop a formalized process for senior staffs to be certified to command a JTF. The expectation that Navy numbered fleets and components would be certified caused the Navy to make naval doctrine and processes compatible enough with joint processes to allow such integration.

At the same time, the U.S. Air Force began to invest heavily in its air operations center (AOC) construct. While the AOCs concept had been in existence for several decades, the Air Force began to pair numbered Air Force commanders—the counterpart to U.S. Navy numbered fleet commanders—with a separate and subordinate command tasked to provide situational awareness and C2 to the numbered Air Force. The Air Force planned a standardized staff structure and systems architecture for the AOCs. AOC C2 systems were designated as weapons systems. This designation in many ways resembled the Navy approach to the AEGIS weapons system and its supporting software. Recognizing that computer systems were often modified by local commands, AOC systems were subject to detailed review prior to changes being made. This step imposed a common software baseline across the force. The designation also allowed the Air Force to fund AOC C2 as a single integrated program rather than as a series of small acquisition programs.

Military effectiveness aside, the existence of the AOCs became a powerful tool for the Air Force to assert more control over joint operations. The agility and flexibility of air power, the argument went, rewarded centralized control enabled by the AOC. In time, most COCOM air components were able to assume control of all air operations across the entire joint area of responsibility. Naval components sometimes struggled to integrate naval aviation into the unfamiliar and much more rigid Air Force air tasking process, a process that usually involved sending naval aviators to the AOC as advocates and interpreters. These Navy integrees were later codified in doctrine as a naval and amphibious liaison element (NALE). Even when their forces successfully integrated with the AOC, many naval commanders had a sense that their control over an essential element of naval combat had eroded.

By the mid-2000s, senior Navy leaders had unified around the belief that the Navy needed to articulate a coherent approach to naval C2 at the operational level; some unified because they believed future warfare demanded it, and some unified because they thought it was necessary to protect Navy interests in the joint arena. In 2007 CNO ADM Gary Roughead issued an "Enabling Concept for Maritime Command and Control." The concept focused at the operational level of war, and set out to build effective, agile, networked, and scalable MOCs. Supported by standardized doctrine, processes, and information systems, these MOCs were intended to enable Navy component commanders (NCC) and numbered fleet commanders to command their own forces at the operational level; operate across fleet areas; and collaborate in a joint, interagency, and multinational environment. Since that time, MOCs have been established at FFC, Pacific Fleet, Second Fleet, Third Fleet, Fourth Fleet, Fifth Fleet, Sixth Fleet, Seventh Fleet, and Tenth Fleet.

Today's Maritime Operations Centers

In contrast to the Air Force solution of creating stand-alone commands for operational-level C2 from the ground up, the Navy elected to develop the MOCs from the existing FCCs. Each Navy fleet command was a bespoke structure, developed organically in response to regional requirements. Rather than upend these unique and often fiercely protected arrangements, the Navy imposed the MOC as an additional layer on the existing headquarters. Initially, and still in some publications, the design was called a Maritime Headquarters with Maritime Operations Center (MHQ w/MOC). Joint Publication 3–32 states that a "maritime operations center (MOC) can be thought of as a loosely bound network of staff entities overlaying the N-code structure."[2]

As this network was being established, several major staffs divided their structure into two elements, placing the operational staff codes in one part and the support codes in another. These two parts are referred to as the MOC and the MHQ respectively, each under a flag officer as director. This use is non-doctrinal but widespread, and underscores the lack of precision and standardization in the MOC process.

The heart of this loosely bound network is a web of functional and cross-functional teams (CFTs). In fact, Navy Tactical Reference Publication (NTRP) 1–02 goes so far as to define a MOC as "the collective name for the boards, bureaus, cells, centers, and working groups that execute the maritime headquarters maritime operations functions."[3] In common usage, these are collectively referred to as B2C2WG (boards, bureaus, centers, cells, and working groups).

The B2C2WG comprise two basic types: permanent and temporary. Permanent structures meet enduring requirements, such as creating, maintaining, and sharing knowledge and situational awareness. These structures tend to exist across all phases of conflict, to be focused on a specific staff code, and often to have permanent spaces and 24/7 watches. The FCC, LRC, and Maritime Intelligence Operations Center (MIOC) are common examples. Temporary structures are established when required by events. These are sometimes referred to as cross-functional teams, or CFTs, reflecting that their membership is usually drawn from multiple staff codes. In principle, these CFTs exist to provide the commander a specific mission-oriented output.[4]

While the terms are often used inexactly, each type of element is intended to have distinct characteristics:

- Board. A board is a group appointed by the commander that meets with the purpose of gaining the Chair's guidance or decision. They are chaired by the commander, deputy commander, or an officer who has delegated decision-making authority. Board composition is determined by who in the staff can inform the Chair's decisions or who must know directly of the decisions. Doctrine divides boards into command boards and functional boards. While the composition of each is often similar, command boards focus on cross-domain issues such as guiding and synchronizing operations across multiple geographic areas or warfare domains or allocation of resources. Functional boards focus on gaining the commander's guidance on a specific mission area, such as targeting or information operations.

- Bureau. A bureau performs a specific function or task, and is an enduring organization with a supporting staff.

- Cell. A cell performs a specific process or supports and enables a specific capability or activity. A cell will always be a subordinate organization within a larger organization in the staff.

- Center. A center is a standing organization with a designated staff. Centers often have their own physical spaces. While they are functional at all phases of operations, they often scale depending on the requirements. For example, an FCC may have six watchstanders during normal operations, may increase to twelve during high-interest operations, and may build to thirty or more during combat or contingency operations.

- Element. An element is formed around a specific function within a designated directorate of a headquarters.

- Group. Sometimes called a working group, a group is an enduring functional organization formed to support a broad function. Normally, groups draw from multiple staff codes and meet on a regularly scheduled basis.

- Office. An office is an enduring organization formed around a specific function. The distinction between an element and an office is that an office typically handles support requirements and does not normally nest within a staff directorate.

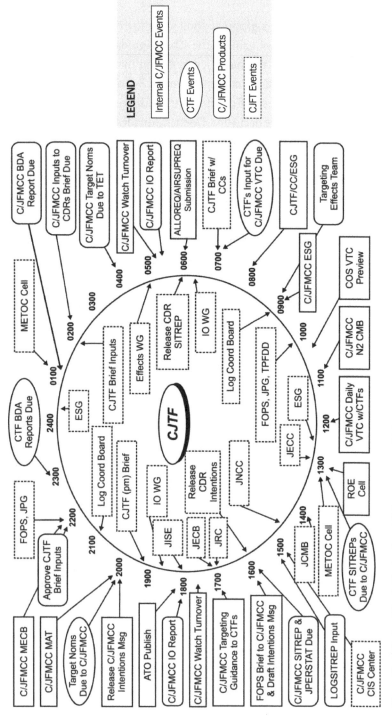

Figure 19-1. Notional Battle Rhythm for a MOC acting as JFMCC from NTTP 3-32.1

- Planning team. A planning team is a functional element established to solve a specific problem. The most common type of planning team is an OPT. Planning teams should dissolve upon completion of their assigned task; however, it is common for a series of standing OPTs to be created during major operations, with each team cycling from one planning problem to another.

Battle Rhythm

How the various staff components come together in time is as critical as the staff structure itself. Every MOC has a battle rhythm. On one level, the battle rhythm is nothing more than a plan for how each staff element schedules its production, communications, and interactions with other elements. More significantly, the battle rhythm is a tool to manage scarce staff resources: personnel, information, and, most critically, time.

Figure 19-1 represents a notional battle rhythm for a MOC acting as a Joint Force Maritime Component Commander (JFMCC) within a JTF. This depiction is significantly simplified, but serves to suggest the complexity of these interlocking parts that must be tailored to the needs of the mission and the commander. Beyond the basic flow chart of products and outputs, there are other considerations that need to be deliberately addressed:

- Commander's guidance. Where in the process does the commander get a vote? If the battle rhythm has the commander approving a developed product, the press of operations is unlikely to allow major shifts. It may be better to show the commander early thoughts and build based on their expressed intent.

- Watch turnovers. Watch or team turnovers offer both challenges and opportunities. The challenge is that the oncoming team will inherently have less awareness of recent events than the team that has shaped them over the past hours. When this loss of situational awareness will have less impact on operations is a key consideration in the timing of turnovers. Turnovers also often represent a formal communication of information, sometimes in the form of a brief. These moments offer leaders a chance to talk to multiple teams, and for representatives from one team to communicate to another—but only if their timing allows that contact.

- How fast can we operate? Many operational events—a lost aircraft, an attack, new orders—drive actions inside the decision cycle of the MOC battle rhythm. The battle rhythm needs to be able to pause, shift, and come back together in response.

- Time for the commander and seniors. The battle rhythm must preserve enough open time for the commander to command. Command requires time to think and to take initiative; a full schedule of meetings, however well crafted, will leave the commander less effective. The same holds true for the senior staff, who must have time to assimilate information and guide their own teams in order to serve the commander effectively.

Once the MOC is in high-tempo operation, inefficiencies and misalignments will become apparent. Savvy staff officers watch for the work arounds—the places where the mission is being accomplished through some means outside the normal MOC process. For example, if the operations officer is walking directly into the deputy commander's cabin multiple times per watch in search of guidance, there may be a need for a more regular touch point. At the least, guidance given in these informal interactions needs to be shared through the established processes to avoid creating an information asymmetry within the staff.

If this seems complicated, that is because it is. Navy Tactics, Techniques, and Procedures (NTTP) 3–32.1 comments that the "MOCs will have more than one line of operation or tasking," an admission up front that fragmentation of the command process is inherent in the MOC structure.[5] Managing that complexity is essential to the commander's success. Doctrinally, "the commander establishes and maintains only those CFTs that enhance planning and decision making within the HQ."[6] The key phrase is that the MOC structure should be as complex as required— but no more complex than required.

Maritime Operations Center Governance

Many MOC directors use a seven-minute drill to review and authorize component parts of the MOC staff. The drill is usually conducted as part of the MOC Governance Council, a board of senior staff representatives who approve the overall MOC battle rhythm. New B2C2WGs are briefed in this forum when they are proposed, and often each B2C2WG is briefed and reviewed before major staff exercises.

The lead staff code for the B2C2WG briefs the purpose of the team, its linkages to other parts of the staff, and how it supports the commander's decision-making requirements. A standard seven-minute drill would include the following:

1. The name of board or cell
2. The lead staff code
3. Where it physically meets and when it fits in the MOC battle rhythm
4. Its purpose
5. What inputs are required and from what parts of the staff
6. When these inputs are required
7. What the B2C2WG will produce
8. When the product will be delivered
9. What other staff codes will be required to provide memberships

While it is often expected that all these answers will fit on a single slide, it is more important that the requirements be clearly articulated. For example, if there is a requirement for the N2 to provide a representative to the B2C2WG, is that a 24/7 embed or a liaison who attends one meeting a day? What skill set do they need to bring? Will the products they are expected to provide require additional personnel within the Maritime Intelligence Operations Center dedicated to support? The N2's requirement for personnel, IT systems, and spaces will be impacted in ways that simply listing "N2" on the slide will not express.

Maritime Operations Center Standardization

Despite layering the MOCs on existing fleet staff structures, the enduring goal of MOC development has been full interoperability between MOCs and with joint structures. Each MOC is required to conform to a minimum 80 percent commonality to the MOC standard baseline. Commander, U.S. Fleet Forces Command, and commander, U.S. Pacific Fleet, jointly govern the MOC standard, though practically, Fleet Forces, as the larger administrative staff, drives the process. The two fleets together approve resourcing strategies to staff, train, and equip the MOCs; to prioritize resources; and to approve fleet headquarters (HQ) requests for non-standard support.

Naval Information Forces (NAVIFOR) is tasked to provide to each MOC the systems identified through this process as the MOC core baseline. OPNAV N2N6 is assigned as the resource sponsor for this effort within the Navy staff. The reality is that the suite of information systems installs, updates, refreshes, and support for the MOCs is historically prioritized below afloat requirements, meaning that MOC systems standardization is often more aspirational than real.

Maritime Operations Center Certification

Each fleet headquarters that is designated as a MOC is required to be certified once every two years. Certification follows an assessment led by the MOC training team, an element under the FFC directorate for fleet and joint training. Assessments follow an established schedule generally determined years in advance and are usually conducted in conjunction with a major staff exercise that offers the assessment team a chance to see the MOC in crisis rather than day-to-day operation. Some months prior to the assessment, the MOC training team will conduct an assist visit, often tailored to the concerns of the supported command and informed by previously identified deficiencies.

While well-intentioned and sometimes useful, the MOC certification process offers significant challenges for staff officers involved.

The first challenge is that the MOC standard represents a Christmas tree, with each staff function and warfare community adding elements that *may* be needed under some circumstances. The major exercise that forms the basis for the certification may not have a need for each of these elements. Nonetheless, there will often be a demand for these staff functions to be demonstrated, with the associated cost in time and resources.

The second is that the MOC certification process represents a closed loop between the MOC education teams and the assessment teams. In principle, this relationship should allow lessons from the observations to impact the training process; the reality is more often the reverse, with the assessment teams expecting school solutions less suited for operational problems.

Most major exercises draw heavily on reservists and augmentees to supplement the permanent MOC staff. Real-world operations continue during these exercises, requiring some part of the full-time staff to continue in their normal roles. As a result, the team being observed and assessed is rarely the team that conducts daily fleet operations.

The last factor is that no command ever fails. The MOC assessment is not suited to officially conclude that a three- or four-star command that supports daily real-world operations that it is not competent to perform its basic functions, nor would such an assessment be palatable in present Navy culture.

The result is that the MOC assessment event is often viewed more as theater to be endured than as a reflection of normal operations. Good staff officers will understand the level of investment their commander intends, and focus on leveraging the process for the training that will actually improve their teams.

The Maritime Operations Center Director

Central to the MOC process is the director of the MOC (MOC-D or DMOC). The MOC-D is intended as the single individual who is entirely focused on ensuring that the MOC as a whole is functioning as required. The MOC-D is designed by the commander, and is often a second hat for the operations officer. The N3 is usually already overworked, but has such a central role in the MOC process that shifting the job to another staff code rarely makes sense.

A MOC-D should not be confused with the DMO (director of maritime operations). The former refers to MOC functions, while the latter refers to directing operations across the entire fleet.

Joint Roles

Most fleet commanders are assigned command roles under one or more joint commands. The two most common are the following:

- Joint Force Maritime Component Commander (JFMCC) or Theater Joint Force Maritime Component Commander (T-JFMCC). In joint doctrine, a JFMCC is simply the maritime commanders under a joint commander. When used for fleet commands, the phrase is most often applied to the naval component under a combatant command. The designation "theater" before JFMCC is a Navy reaction to the Air Force asserting that their major staffs would coordinate all air operations within a theater. When the Air Force started referring to "theater joint force air component commanders" to emphasize that they were the one and only within a CCMD, Navy answered by designating JFMCCs as "theater." The JFMCC role is important because it carries the responsibility of commanding operations for maritime forces assigned to a specific CCMD.

- Joint Task Force (JTF) commander. Many fleet commanders are designated as JTF commanders or components. JTFs are a joint construct to align forces for a specific task or operation. In many cases these JTFs are designated in advance, but remain inactive until needed. How much a commander's JTF role impacts their staff will vary. In some cases, the JTF role is buried in a joint plan, little noted and never exercised. In other cases, the JTF role is regularly activated and exercised, and will form a significant part of the staff's work load.

Maritime Operations Centers and the Challenges of the Future

The MOCs grew to support the Global War on Terrorism and regional operations in the Balkans and Libya. Today, with the nation's renewed focus on more traditional military threat, the MOCs find themselves facing new challenges. Creating solutions to support these complex operations and emerging missions will be a key focus of MOC staff officers in the coming years. These solutions include the following:

Creating a Maritime Fires Process

Throughout the past three decades, U.S. airpower has been used against fixed targets in a largely permissive threat environment. Most application of military power was coordinated through the joint fires process, and MOC structure and battle rhythms were accordingly tailored to maximize the integration of supporting naval forces into it. The joint fires and joint targeting processes are products of an Air Force–centric centralized approach to application of airpower, and prizes coordination and accuracy over speed and flexibility. Combat in the maritime environment, where every target is mobile and fleeting, requires a different approach that remains a work in progress.

Enabling Fleet Maneuver

In a high-end maritime fight against a peer adversary, the fleet is the Navy's basic maneuver element. Commanding and controlling operations on this scale requires a different approach that integrates dynamic maritime maneuver with critical fleet-level and joint support capabilities.

Commanding Information Warfare

Resilient C2, space, and cyber capabilities will be essential in any future maritime fight. Coordinating these tools in support of dynamic operations requires a combination of the broad view of the battlespace that the MOC offers with a level of tactical responsiveness that is faster than current staff processes. Current MOC doctrine describes Space Support Working Group and an Information Warfare Working Group, for example, but neither offers a mechanism for these warfighting domains to come together in a way that maximizes their power and reach. As doctrine evolves, several approaches have emerged:

- Combined N2N39. In 2008 PACFLT combined its intelligence and information operations elements under a single staff element within the MOC. Several other fleets have followed suit. The result allows an intimate cross-functional relationship between these two disciplines.

- N6 in MOC. Several fleets have moved their N6 from the MHQ to their MOC. This shift focuses the fleet communicators on their role in support of operations, and allows more seamless integration with the N2 and N3.

- Information Warfare commander (IWC) in the MOC. Some elements of the information warfare (IW) community have advocated for an IWC in the MOC. While unifying information warfare capabilities in execution is essential, merging the MOC and CWC concepts at the fleet level raises C2 and organizational issues that have not been fully explored.

Planning for Reduced Communications

The MOCs have grown in a world environment of uncontested communications. No future adversary will allow our forces the unchallenged use of the electro-magnetic spectrum that has enabled our communications-heavy style of command. MOC doctrine acknowledges this challenge; it remains for individual staffs and officers to ensure that this reality is central to plans and processes going forward.

Updating Maritime Operations Center Standards

The MOC standardization guidance notoriously lags fleet requirements. That is not for lack of effort on the part of the professionals responsible. The fleet moves fast to meet a rapidly changing world, and is often too busy to capture those efforts in text. Nonetheless, investing the time in ensuring the various responsible offices understand what is working in the fleet now pays off in the long-term spread of best practices throughout the Navy.

Whether at sea or on staff, naval professionals apply their initiative and ingenuity and make it work.

CHAPTER 20

Office of the Chief of Naval Operations

O ver a thirty-year career, most naval officers will serve in the staff of the CNO. Duty on the Navy staff, known colloquially as OPNAV, is a rite of passage. It is also the most dreaded of Washington, DC, staff duty for Navy officers. Why? The traditional wisdom is that the following is true:

- OPNAV is, as a general rule, not operational. Post the Goldwater–Nichols Act, the CNO's primary duty is to OTE the naval forces that CCDRs use. The only ship that reports directly to the CNO is USS *Constitution,* the U.S. ship of state. Wags sometimes refer to the CNO as the "Chief of No Operations," though generally not in the CNO's presence.

- OPNAV is tied to the budget cycle. The budget cycle is unfamiliar to most naval officers and can appear to be a frustrating and arbitrary black box. Furthermore, the budget runs on five-year cycles, which means that success is always tentative and that tangible results are often not seen until long after any individual staff officer tour has ended.

- OPNAV does not offer joint duty credit.

- It is also usually not seen as novel or exotic.

It is all true. However, like so much traditional wisdom, it is only half the story.

- OPNAV is all about the Navy. A tour there offers a graduate-level education in a core element of the service.

- The CNO, as one of the Joint Chiefs of Staff, has a seat at the table (literally) for the most consequential decisions that the U.S. military makes, both strategic and operational. While not its primary focus, OPNAV supports this role.

- Budgets matter. Plans without resources are nothing more than hopes. Officers who understand the budget are the ones who can turn ideas into reality—and are always in demand.

- OPNAV is full of senior Navy mentors, ready to help promising young professionals.

- OPNAV tours are not bound by joint rules for minimum assignment length. It is easier for a detailer to shift an officer to a new opportunity or to make them available for their next career milestone than if they are encumbered in a joint billet.

As discussed in chapter 21 on the SECNAV, the OPNAV staff is one of two service staffs within the DoN. The OPNAV staff is the CNO's staff, and it takes its tone and focus from the CNO. The CNO is appointed for four years, meaning most OPNAV staff officers experience one or, at most, two CNOs in a full tour.

The CNO's principal deputy is the VCNO. In contrast to the CNO, the VCNO is not assigned for a fixed period. Most serve two to three years, and it is not unusual for them to subsequently advance to a senior fleet or joint assignment. Where the CNO is the face of the Navy to the Joint Staff, Congress, and the public, the VCNO will normally focus on the internal business of the Navy. The VCNO will monitor the process that turns CNO strategic guidance into budget reality, and will oversee most flag officer assignments and senior-level disciplinary issues.

Where the VCNO is executive officer for the entire service, the director, Navy staff (DNS) answers for the functioning of the OPNAV staff. DNS is one of the most challenging senior staff jobs in the U.S. Navy. The scope is broad, and the DNS, as a three-star or civilian equivalent, is a peer to the DCNOs who lead most of the OPNAV staff.

Beyond the VCNO and DNS, the CNO has the special staff that is common to most large staffs. Two unique direct reports, however, are worth noting:

- Director, Naval Nuclear Propulsion Program (OPNAV N00N). Commonly referred to as naval reactors (NRs), director, Naval Nuclear

Propulsion Program is, by law, a four-star admiral appointed for a term of eight years—the longest senior officer appointment in the U.S. military. N00N also has arguably the most complicated chain of command in the U.S. military. N00N is at once a direct report to the CNO, serves as code SEA 08 under NAVSEA, and as deputy administrator of the National Nuclear Security Administration (NNSA) under the U.S. Department of Energy. These three relationships give NR total responsibility of all aspects of Navy nuclear propulsion, from research, design, construction, testing, operation, maintenance, through the ultimate disposal of the nuclear plants at the end of their service lives. For most OPNAV staff officers, the uniqueness of NR's command relationships is little more than a curiosity. NR has a very specific role, within which it neither invites nor accepts outsiders.

- President, Board of Inspection and Survey (CNO N09P). Commonly known as INSURV, the Board of Inspection and Survey conducts regular inspections of U.S. Navy ships to ensure they are properly maintained. The board dates to 1868, and was permanently established in law by Congress in 1882. Because the board is grading the work of the fleet and shore establishments and is required to report annually to Congress, its position reporting directly to the CNO is an essential part of ensuring that it is free to make independent assessments.

The CNO also acts as an echelon one commander. In general, the CNO has ADCON over all U.S. Navy forces that are not designated to report directly to the SECNAV. These ADCON relationships are critical in establishing the CNO's control over the Navy and endure even when these forces have a separate command relationship with a joint commander. For example, U.S. Naval Forces Central Command (NAVCENT) is under the COCOM of U.S. Central Command (CENTCOM). The CNO, however, retains an ADCON relationship. See chapter 13 for a discussion of the nuances of these relationships.

CNO is also the echelon one commander for a range of more specialized activities, ranging from the Naval Safety Center to the U.S. Navy Band.

In a number of cases, OPNAV staff elements also have command authority. There are at least two reasons for such a dual-hat arrangement. First, in some cases it is necessary to have command authority in order to perform a function. For example, the OPNAV N1 is also designated as chief of naval personnel, in which role they are the echelon two commander of the labor force, personnel, training, and education shore establishment. In both roles, the N1 answers to the CNO as the echelon one commander. In other cases, the separation was the result of a past effort to reduce the number of billets assigned to the OPNAV staff. Staffs tend to grow, and headquarters reduction reforms are a regular effort by both Congress and the Office of the Secretary of Defense (OSD). Removing an element or function from OPNAV into a separate command often counts as a reduction in staff billets, even if the total Navy end strength remains the same.

In support of the roles and missions given to the CNO, the OPNAV staff performs eleven major functions:

1. Field a naval force capable of carrying out tasking from higher authority.

2. Investigate and report on Navy readiness.

3. Establish Navy strategy and policy, and issue guidance.

4. Align actions of Navy organizations.

5. Plan and program in support of the Program Objective Memorandum (POM).

6. Plan and coordinate Navy employment.

7. Translate maritime strategy into strategic guidance and priorities.

8. Integrate requirements.

9. Determine fiscal distributions and allocations.

10. Conduct operational test and evaluation.

11. Conduct and manage all aspects of intelligence assessment throughout the DoN.

A full list of the missions, functions, and tasks of the OPNAV staff fills more than twenty pages. Nonetheless, most OPNAV functions relate to the organization, training, and equipping of naval forces. Indeed, OTE is so central to OPNAV that it is worth considering the basics of the Navy planning, programming, budgeting, and execution (PPBE) process before introducing how the staff supports these roles.

When staffs were smaller: ADM George Dewey leads the Navy staff on a formal call on President Theodore Roosevelt, 1905. *Naval History and Heritage Command*

The PPBE process is simply the process by which the DoD handles money. PPBE was introduced to DoD in the early 1960s by Secretary of Defense Robert McNamara, who was appointed by President John F. Kennedy to bring business management practices to the DoD. It is sometimes called the world's last five-year plan, with DoD being characterized as the world's last true planned economy. While everyone loves to hate the PPBE process, the reality is that the DoD manages almost $800 billion of the taxpayers' money each year. Any process able to coordinate resources on such a scale would inherently be large, complex, and imperfect.

OPNAV's role in the PPBE allows the CNO to set strategy and priorities, and then influence how these are made real by spending its limited money on the highest priorities. While the process has many parts, it pivots around the Program Objective Memorandum (POM). At its most basic, the POM is a recommendation to the Secretary of Defense on how the Navy intends to allocate the money it is given to meet the guidance it has been given in the defense planning guidance (DPG). The POM covers a five-year period, which is referred to as the Future Years Defense Program (FYDP). While there are budget plans covering more than five years into the future, the PPBE process forces resource decisions within the FYDP to match some agreed reality. Outside the FYDP there are no such constraints—which means that, outside the FYDP, plans are at best loose outlines and at worst little more than vague hopes.

It is worth noting that there is one POM for the DoN covering both the Navy and the Marine Corps. This POM is approved by the SECNAV. How large a role the SECNAV plays in the process varies from one SECNAV leader to another.

Building the POM is a complex process. As the POM goes through its annual life cycle, different OPNAV staff elements lead or provide input to the process. Each step involves knowing, understanding, and influencing guidance from higher headquarters and Navy leadership. Each step also involves negotiation between different stakeholders within the Navy.

Not all stakeholders have the same needs or influence. A resource sponsor acts as the designated advocate for resources, capabilities, and programs within a specific portfolio. The resource sponsor is charged with integrating the desires of individual capability providers—for example, program offices and systems commands—into a suite of investments that will yield capabilities that support the CNO's vision. For example, OPNAV N4 serves as the resource sponsor for operational logistics and supply chain support, a task that covers providing operationally suitable logistics support for such disparate elements as ordnance, fuels, combat logistics, and salvage platforms.

The requirements sponsors have a trickier job. Certain issues—for example, maintenance and readiness—are important across multiple portfolios. A requirements sponsor is charged with advocating for these service-wide requirements. However, because these issues cut across portfolios, the resources supporting them are controlled by other elements. In staff terms, a requirements sponsor is someone who is charged to have opinions about how other portfolios spend their money—never a popular place to be.

In the PPBE process, as in any complex negotiation, information is power. Few secrets in the Pentagon are more carefully protected than a service's internal budget discussions. A host of outside entities—other services, Joint Staffs, Congress, the media, and—yes—even foreign countries—want to know what the Navy is thinking about its own future. Informing each of them is also a key OPNAV function. Once decisions are made, it is important to convey them in a clear, consistent narrative that communicates their importance.

Defending the Navy Budget—Arleigh Burke on Words

Op-00/rw

7 Nov 56

MONTHLY MEMORANDUM FOR ALL DEPUTIES

Subj: "Savings"

1. It is noted in many reports pertaining to the most economical operations that sometimes, in order to obtain men and money for other activities or the operating forces, the word "savings" is used. It usually happens in a statement which says, "If _____ is done, there will be a savings of _____ personnel and a savings of $ _____ in funds." If these reports are distributed outside the Navy, as they frequently are, even though they are not so addressed, they are frequently taken to mean that the Navy budget can be reduced by that amount. This is especially true when the budget is under discussion or when the report pertains to budgetary matters.
2. Therefore, it is requested that all hands be alert not to use the word "savings" when what is meant is that in order to obtain money or men for use by one activity, another activity can be reduced by so many dollars and men.

ARLEIGH BURKE[1]

The bulk of the OPNAV staff works for one of the DCNOs, known collectively as the N-codes. While their responsibilities parallel those of their counterparts in other major staff, each has a number of unique roles, given their position within the Navy.

OPNAV N1:
Deputy Chief of Naval Operations for Manpower, Personnel, Training, and Education

N1 is the single sponsor for military personnel issues and handles Navy labor force, and training integration. This includes directing recruiting, organizing, training, and educating military personnel and supervising labor force, training, and education requirements for the other OPNAV resource sponsors. N1 also leads language, regional expertise, and culture (LREC) programs for the Navy. In addition to an echelon one staff role, the N1 has an echelon two command as the chief of naval personnel.

OPNAV N2N6:
Deputy Chief of Naval Operations for Information Warfare

N2N6 was formed in 2009 as part of the stand up of the Navy Information Warfare (then called Information Dominance) community. The N2N6 is the Navy lead for intelligence, surveillance, and reconnaissance, cyberspace operations electromagnetic spectrum maneuver warfare; counter command, control, communications, computer, intelligence, surveillance, and reconnaissance (C-C4ISR); and electronic warfare (EW). The N2N6 is designated as the director of naval intelligence (DNI), which conveys specific status within the larger defense and national intelligence communities, and is the Navy's designated liaison to the Office of the Director of National Intelligence (ODNI) on Navy requirements. In addition to acting as an OPNAV resource sponsor, the N2N6 handles specialized intelligence budgeting processes, managing the Navy part of the Military Intelligence Program (MIP) and acting as a resource sponsor within the National Intelligence Program (NIP).

OPNAV N3N5:
Deputy Chief of Naval Operations for Operations, Plans, and Strategy

The N3N5 plans and coordinates the employment of the Navy. Since the Navy functions as a force provider to the joint force, this responsibility largely consists of supporting Global Force Employment (GFM) plans and responding to ad hoc requests for forces rather than conducting operations. N3N5 also manages the optimized fleet response plan and is responsible for the Navy's afloat anti-terrorism/force protection (AT/FP) policy. While in recent years many of N3N5's strategy responsibilities have shifted to the newly established N7, N3N5 retains the responsibility for coordinating the Navy International Engagement and Security Cooperation effort. This portfolio includes coordinating Navy international engagements with other DoD staffs, providing regional affairs expertise to CNO and other senior OPNAV leaders, and planning and executing international engagement events. Prominent among these is the biennial International Seapower Symposium (ISS), a CNO-hosted gathering of heads of Navy (HoNs) from more than one hundred foreign partners.

OPNAV N4:
Deputy Chief of Naval Operations for Fleet Readiness and Logistics
N4 handles the breadth of operational logistics and supply chain support for the Navy. The N4 is both a resource and requirements sponsor whose portfolio includes fleet readiness, logistics (including combat logistics force and other Military Sealift Command vessels), shore readiness, Navy expeditionary medical services, and environmental programs.

OPNAV N7:
Deputy Chief of Naval Operations for Warfighting Development
N7 was established in 2020 in an effort to align the Navy's strategic development to the requirement of strategic competition and high-end warfighting. N7 develops the intellectual framework for prioritizing and aligning Navy warfare development and creates strategic guidance for fleet design, architecture, requirements, and resource decisions. In addition to strategy, N7 guides the Navy's professional education and the war gaming efforts.

N7 is an anomaly in the OPNAV staff in having no resourcing responsibilities. The intent in this construct is to allow Navy strategy to develop apart from the resource sponsors' interests in the strategy supporting their particular capabilities. In a staff where control of resources is the main tool of influence, the long-term relevance of the N7 will depend on the extent to which the CNO empowers it.

OPNAV N8:
Deputy Chief of Naval Operations for Integration of Capabilities and Resources
N8 builds the Navy plan and programs in support of the POM. The N8 conducts capability analysis, administers the interface between the Navy

and the PPBE system, and monitors the execution of the Navy budget. It also administers the Defense Readiness Reporting System—Navy (DRRS-N). The three main elements of N8 are worth knowing:

- N80 Programming Division creates the POM from the disparate inputs submitted by the resource sponsors. It is hard, detailed work, but is the critical shop where all the ideas come together into a single Navy plan and narrative.

- N81 Assessment Division is the Navy's modeling and operational analysis team, conducting assessment in support of budget decisions. N81 analysis provides the footnotes that allow Navy leaders to present their budget choices as objective and well-informed in discussions with Pentagon leadership.

- N82 Fiscal Management Division handles the actual spending or execution of money. N82 is dual-hatted as Deputy Assistant Secretary of the Navy for Budget (FMB), and does most of its work in that hat on behalf of both the Navy and Marine Corps. Reflecting the importance of that role, it is more common to hear N82 referred to as FMB than N82.

OPNAV N9:
Deputy Chief of Naval Operations for Warfare Systems

N9 is the resource sponsor for warfare systems, which gives it the role of advocating for most of the Navy's requirements. A distinctive feature of the N9 organization is the four directorates known collectively as the High Nines:

- N95—Expeditionary Warfare
- N96—Surface Warfare
- N97—Undersea Warfare
- N98—Air Warfare

The two-stars who run each of these staff elements are the main advocates within OPNAV for their community's capabilities. They will be hand selected and closely aligned with the senior leaders in each of their communities. They are also recognized as single-issue voters, charged with protecting specific equities.

Because the High Nines naturally think and work as single communities, CNOs have established various mechanisms to knit their plans into a single coherent narrative. The team that creates this case has moved around the staff in response to personalities and perceived needs. At present, the task falls on the Warfare Integration Directorate (N9I), who is tasked to turn the High Nines' program requests into a single budget narrative.

OPNAV Watches

Given that CNO directly controls no operations, it surprises many new OPNAV arrivals to find that the staff maintains a robust 24/7 watch. The watch construct has changed over the years as senior DoD leaders have similarly questioned why the services maintain what look like redundant operations watches in the Pentagon. Today, OPNAV watches nest within the larger Joint Staff watch structure to support the CNO as a member of the Joint Chiefs of Staff, principal naval advisor to the President, and advisor to the SECNAV. The reality is that naval culture makes it inconceivable that the CNO would not have a watch, whatever construct is used to justify it. The OPNAV N3N5 runs these watch functions with support from the N2N6 and N4 on their areas of specialization.

The Navy Operations Center (NOC) Watch Cell is located within the National Military Command Center (NMCC). Located in the Pentagon in the Joint Staff area, access to the NMCC requires specific authorization. The NOC Watch Cell is relatively small, sized to directly support the Joint Staff functions that are the focus of the NMCC.

Outside of the NMCC, the NOC maintains a larger watch team within the nearby Resource and Situational Awareness Center (RSAC). The RSAC contains all the service watch elements that the Joint Staff did not consider critical enough to place in the limited physical space of the NMCC. This includes the Navy Crisis Action Team (NCAT), which actually monitors current U.S. Navy operations worldwide whether a crisis is in progress or not. The RSAC also includes the CNO Intelligence Plot (CNO IP), which maintains awareness of global maritime threat intelligence to support the CNO and NMCC.

Arleigh Burke on Choosing Battles within the Pentagon

Op-00 Memo 0215-59

26 May 1959

Subj: Controversies in the Pentagon

1. There are many controversies within the Pentagon in which the Navy is necessarily deeply and directly involved. There are a few controversies in which the Navy is not directly, but is indirectly involved, and there are, also, a few controversies in which the Navy is neither directly nor indirectly involved.

2. I would like to point out that it is CNO's policy that we do not have to become involved in all controversies in the Pentagon.

ARLEIGH BURKE[2]

The organization and functions of the OPNAV staff are complex and beyond the scope of a single chapter. To under them more fully, it is worth consulting three further categories of resources.

First, take advantage of the OPNAV action officer (AO) course. At the time of the writing, this two-day class is required of all new OPNAV AOs, but many avoid it nonetheless. It has a strong focus on the basics of the PPBE process and will include the most updated guidance for the staff.

Second, consult one of the several guides to the Navy PPBE process written for the OPNAV and service staffs. The RAND Corporation's *Navy Planning, Programming, Budgeting, and Execution: A Reference Guide for Senior Leaders, Managers, and Action Officers*, available online, is an excellent starting point. While published in 2015, its tips for maneuvering effectively within the process remain relevant and insightful.

Finally, skim one or more histories of the OPNAV staff listed in the Further Reading section of this guide. While these do not provide immediate guidance, they offer a view of how the staff has evolved in response to changing needs and different leadership, which is a key starting point for staff officers thinking about how the staff can meet future needs.

Future needs are what the OPNAV staff is all about. COPS are critical, and offer glamour and immediate rewards, but ensuring the Navy is organized, trained, and equipped for an uncertain future is work that offers lasting impact. Approached with a learning attitude and a sincere interest in making the Navy better, an OPNAV tour will offer unique and valuable experience essential to any naval professional worthy of the title.

Office of the Chief of Naval Operations under Fire

The morning of 11 September 2001 found the Navy Command Center in new spaces. The watch had moved across the Pentagon only weeks prior, trading the cramped but historic watch floor for a new facility designed for the digital era. When the second hijacked airplane hit the south tower of the World Trade Center, it was apparent that America was under attack. The team on watch, under senior watch officer CDR Patrick Dunn, started notifying the senior Navy leadership, established communications across the Navy to raise force protection levels, and prepared for what might come next. The CNO Intelligence Plot watch team under CDR Dan Shanower gathered to review what was known.

At 9:37, American Airlines flight 77, under the control of terrorists, hit the southwest wall of the Pentagon. The plane disintegrated into a cloud of debris as its kinetic energy carried it—and 5,300 gallons of aviation fuel—through the first two rings of the buildings and into the Navy Command Center.

Those working in the building who were not immediately killed struggled to escape from spaces that filled instantly with black, oily smoke. Some fled through the hole punched through the outer wall by the airplane's landing gear. Shipmates in other parts of the building proved the maxim that "every Sailor is a fire fighter," using their damage-control training to find and assist their colleagues.

Those who escaped did not huddle in shock. They realized war had come to America, and that America would need its Navy for whatever might come next. They rallied with senior Navy leaders, moved to alternative watch locations, and reestablished the watch. By midday, the CNO was established in an alternative Navy Command Center at the Washington Navy Yard. The CNO Intelligence Plot was re-created in Marine Corps intelligence spaces in the Navy Annex. The survivors of the on-watch intelligence team who had escaped their smoke-filled spaces through a hole punched in the wall by debris formed the core of that first watch.

The next week would see hundreds of acts of dedication, commitment, and innovation. The year 2001 was the beginning of the digital era and Navy information warriors seized the cutting edge of available technology to quickly network the suddenly dispersed OPNAV staff. Within forty-eight hours they had reestablished all critical C2 links, tied the Navy into the joint C2 architecture, and installed the Navy's first classified desktop video teleconference system.

And in the midst of contributing to a sudden global fight, OPNAV took care of its own. Forty-two Navy personnel, both military and civilian, were among the one hundred twenty-five Pentagon personnel who died that morning, all of them within the Navy Command Center. For weeks afterward, the long work days would pause for some of the surviving OPNAV staff to travel the short distance to Arlington National Cemetery to lay another shipmate to rest.

Today, the Navy Command Center sits near the Pentagon spaces it occupied for less than two months, every sign of the destruction of that day repaired. Inside the building only a small chapel marks the point where flight 77 first hit the building, the names etched inside a mute reminder of the OPNAV staff who remain forever on watch.

CHAPTER 21

The Secretary of the Navy Staff

I n every naval officer's life, there are banner days when their name appears in a message from "SECNAV WASHINGTON DC" that begins with the words, "I am pleased to announce the following Line Officers on the Active-Duty List for promotion to the permanent grade of _____." Even at a basic career level, the SECNAV matters. And yet, among U.S. Navy officers, the role and responsibilities of the SECNAV are probably the least understood part of their chain of command. The ignorant will explain that the SECNAV used to be a member of the cabinet, replaced after World War II by a single DoD and a single cabinet secretary. The secretaries of the military departments became secondary figures, relegated to the vague world of man, train, and equip (MTE; now called organize, train, equip, or OTE). The CNO, while stripped of authority by joint reforms, still at least could pretend to have an operational role in their position as a member of the Joint Chiefs of Staff.

Here is the reality—the SECNAV controls the U.S. Navy. Title 10 U.S. Code § 8013 states that the secretary is "responsible to the Secretary of Defense for the functioning and efficiency of the Department of the Navy" and "has the authority necessary to conduct all affairs of the Department of the Navy."[1] With the exception of a few specific roles carved out in law for uniformed leaders, authority in the Navy flows from and through the SECNAV. Even the CNO "performs duties under the authority, direction, and control of the SECNAV and is directly responsible to the SECNAV except as otherwise prescribed by law."[2] It follows that understanding how to work with the Office of the Secretary of the Navy (sometimes called the Navy Secretariat)—or to be one of the officers who are part of it—is an essential skill for a Navy staff officer.

The relationship between the secretary and the CNO—and thus between the Secretariat and the OPNAV staff—has varied significantly over the years. Different secretaries have interpreted their positions differently, exercising little control, detailed control, or focusing their control on specific areas of personal or professional interest. The relationship between OPNAV and the Secretariat will naturally reflect the relationship between these seniors.

The relationship is also complicated by the legal relationship between the secretary's staff, OPNAV, and Marine Corps headquarters. Title 10 U.S.C. 8014 establishes that the secretary's staff is not a higher headquarters for the Navy and Marine Corps. Rather, the SECNAV has three subordinate staffs with separate functions, headed by the under secretary, CNO, and CMC, respectively. The SECNAV's staff, however, often acts as if they are a higher headquarters rather than a staff with separate and equivalent functions. This dynamic is complicated by the order of precedence within the DoN; the under secretary, the various assistant secretaries of the Navy, the GC, and only then the CNO and the CMC.

A smart staff officer who handles issues that impact both OPNAV and the Secretariat will work to avoid getting caught between the two. Even with the closest of relations, the OPNAV and Marine Corps headquarters staffs are significantly larger than the secretary's staff, giving them an ability to simply produce more products and manage more issues.

An Expansive Secretary: John Lehman Jr.

The Chief of Naval Operations really runs the Navy. Why do you want to be Secretary of the Navy?
    —*Common question put to John Lehman before his appointment*

In 1981, John Lehman very much wanted to be the SECNAV. Ronald Reagan had just been elected President, in part on a promise of restoring U.S. military dominance over the Soviet Union. Lehman, a successful investor and reserve naval aviator, believed the U.S. Navy was in serious need of a new direction, and the new administration agreed.

Lehman knew that recent SECNAVs had functioned as organizational leaders, deferring to the CNO on major issues of strategy and force design. His small staff could not out-produce OPNAV, but he exploited the bureaucratic high ground. Shortly after taking office, he established a Naval Policy Board made up of his under secretary and assistant secretary, the CNO, CMC, and selected uniformed seniors. From this board flowed strategic direction—starting with an admission that the Soviet Navy was in a position to challenge U.S. Navy dominance, that maritime superiority was the United States' official goal, and guidance for programs and investments designed to achieve that superiority. Ultimately, this board drove:

- The maritime strategy, which was the most influential public statement of the need for and use of U.S. naval forces in half a century.
- The naval build-up of the 1980s, which was building toward a six-hundred-ship Navy.
- A strategy of forward operations, which put U.S. Navy forces close to the Soviet homeland, shifting a potential fight from the high seas to the Soviets' backyard.

Lehman's toughest bureaucratic exercise, however, was not reappointing ADM Hyman Rickover to another tour as head of the Navy Nuclear Power Program. Rickover had reached statutory retirement age in 1962, but had been reappointed with congressional support every two years since. Exercising his authority over senior officer appointments, Lehman navigated Congress, the Secretary of Defense, and a fiery confrontation with Rickover in front of President Reagan to ensure an orderly transition in the leadership of the program.

Lehman was on a mission to restore the U.S. Navy, knew the scope of his authority, and was prepared to use it in ways few of his predecessors were. His term as SECNAV remains an example of what is possible if the authority of the office is used expansively.

When they do think of the secretary, most staff officers think of the seven functions that, by law, may not be delegated outside of the Secretariat:

1. Acquisition
2. Auditing
3. Comptroller and financial management

4. Information management

5. Inspector General

6. Legislative affairs

7. Public affairs

Secretary of the Navy Staff Organization

The SECNAV also holds some interesting minor authorities. For example, the SECNAV names commissioned vessels of the U.S. Navy; while the CNO will make recommendations, the final prerogative is the SECNAV's alone. The natural result is that the organization of the SECNAV staff centers on the key, non-delegable functions.

Under Secretary of the Navy

The Under Secretary of the Navy is the secretary's principal assistant and carries the SECNAV's full authority. The UNSECNAV is the Navy's chief operating officer and chief management officer, as well as conducting oversight of Navy intelligence and sensitive activities.

Assistant Secretary of the Navy (Research, Development, and Acquisition)

The Assistant Secretary of the Navy (Research, Development, and Acquisition) (ASN RD&A) handles all acquisition functions, but neither determines requirements for systems nor does operational testing.

Assistant Secretary of the Navy (Financial Management and Comptroller)

The Assistant Secretary of the Navy (Financial Management and Comptroller) (ASN FM&C) handles the DoN's money, to include acting as comptroller.

Assistant Secretary of the Navy (Energy, Installations and Environment)

The Assistant Secretary of the Navy (Energy, Installations and Environment) (ASN EI&E) handles energy, installations, safety and occupational health, environment, and strategic sourcing.

Assistant Secretary of the Navy (Manpower and Reserve Affairs)

The Assistant Secretary of the Navy (Manpower and Reserve Affairs) (ASN M&RA) administers all DoN personnel, whether active duty, retired, reserve, civilian, or family members. This includes such diverse functions as health affairs, non-appropriated fund activities, and the board for the correction of naval records.

General Counsel of the Navy

The general counsel (GC) of the Navy acts as the secretary's lawyer. While the GC and JAG's areas of interest overlap somewhat, the GC has the lead on specific areas of law to include acquisition law, business and commercial law, property law, civilian personnel and labor law, environmental law, intellectual property law, intelligence and national security law, law pertaining to cyberspace, ethics and standards of conduct, and Freedom of Information Act (FOIA) and Privacy Act law.

Staff Assistants Who Specialize in More-Limited Areas

One echelon down are staff assistants who specialize in more-limited areas. A number of these special assistants are senior uniformed officers. In some cases, such as chief of naval information (CHINFO), the officer assigned also reports to the CNO as an additional duty. In these cases, the support relationship with the CNO is clearly outlined and subordinate to the relationship with the SECNAV.

Deputy Under Secretary of the Navy

The Deputy Under Secretary of the Navy (DUSN) acts as the principal civilian advisor on defense and foreign policy; intelligence; and a host of sensitive activities. The DUSN is also the DoN's security executive and leads the DoN security enterprise.

Chief of Naval Information

The chief of naval information is the senior PAO for the U.S. Navy. Usually an active-duty flag officer from the PAO community, the chief of naval information manages the conveying of all aspects of the Navy story to the American people.

Chief of Legislative Affairs

The chief of legislative affairs (CLA) ensures that the Navy speaks to Congress with one voice. It provides a single point for all DoN communications with Congress. This includes developing, coordinating, and processing responses to congressional investigations, handling congressional travel, and providing members and committees with information on the actions, plans, and programs of the DoN.

Chief of Naval Research

The Chief of Naval Research (CNR) leads the Navy's research and development efforts, to include the Office of Naval Research and the Naval Research Laboratory.

Chief Information Officer

The chief information officer (CIO) provides policy and governance oversight for information management and IT across the DoN.

Chief Learning Officer

The chief learning officer (CLO) was introduced in 2018 to provide a single senior official to oversee the Navy's institutions of higher learning. As of 2022, the position was vacant and is likely to be disestablished.

Judge Advocate General

The judge advocate general (JAG) provides legal and policy advice to the SECNAV and advises the CNO in the provision of legal services within the Navy.

Naval Inspector General

The Naval Inspector General (Naval IG) inspects, investigates, and inquires into any and all matters of importance to the DoN in order to maintain the highest level of integrity and public confidence.

Auditor General

The auditor general (AUDGEN) of the Navy leads the Navy Audit Service, an all-civilian organization that conducts independent internal audit functions for the DoN.

Director, DoN Sexual Assault Prevention and Response Office

The director, DoN Sexual Assault Prevention and Response Office (DoN-SAPRO) is the principal advisor to the secretary on the prevention of and response to sexual assault, domestic abuse, and sexual harassment.

Director, Office of Small Business Programs

The director, Office of Small Business Programs (OSBP) promotes acquisition opportunities where small business can support the needs of the DoN.

Director, DoN Special Access Program Central Office

The director, DoN Special Access Program Central Office (DoN-SAPCO) is responsible for the execution, management, oversight, administration, security, information systems and networks, IA, and records management for special access programs (SAPs) under the responsibility of the DoN.

Director, Naval Criminal Investigative Service

The director, Naval Criminal Investigative Service (NCIS) leads NCIS, a civilian federal law enforcement agency responsible for investigating felony crime, preventing terrorism, and protecting information within the DoN.

Why the Naval Criminal Investigative Service Reports to the Secretary of the Navy

Staffs have their current form for specific reasons, both mundane and profound. How NCIS came to report directly to the SECNAV is worth remembering.

The Tailhook Association, a private association of current and former naval aviators, hosts an annual gathering for its members. While the event was part professional development, featuring panels, exhibits, and mentoring, the DoD inspector general later concluded that, in the 1980s, the gathering was "the scene of much drinking, general rowdiness and wild parties." [3] The most extreme "rowdiness" centered on several dozen hotel rooms, misnamed as hospitality suites, rented by squadrons and organizations near the convention. Around these suites, "a loosely formed group of men . . . lined the corridor . . . and 'touched' [assaulted] women who passed down the corridor." [4] At the 1991 convention in Las Vegas, the female flag aide to a senior naval aviator, herself a Navy helicopter pilot, was sexually assaulted by this gauntlet—a gang made up largely of fellow aviators.

The victim reported the assault to her commander, then, seeing no action was being taken, reported it three weeks later in a letter that reached the VCNO. The VCNO ordered the Naval Investigative Service (NIS) to investigate the potential criminal activity. NIS quickly determined that a number of women had been assaulted during the event. Given the scope of the criminal activity reported, NIS conducted a massive investigation, interviewing more than 2,100 people, most of them junior officers.

After its conclusion, the NIS investigation was itself the subject of an investigation, as voices outside the Navy perceived that the Navy had not held its members accountable for their actions. A key criticism was that NIS did not interview any of the senior officers who attended. At the time, the commander of the NIS was a Navy JAG flag officer who reported directly to the VCNO. Both the VCNO and the commander of NIS "were well aware that the Secretary of the Navy, the Chief of Naval Operations, plus a large number of active duty and reserve flag officers were in attendance at Tailhook 91."[5]

The DoD IG wrote, "Although NIS agents did not develop any leads suggesting that senior officers were involved in or had knowledge of the assaults, it does not appear . . . that was information they were attempting to develop and, thus, the absence of such information is rather predictable. . . . NIS took no steps to inquire systematically of the 2,100 witnesses . . . whether they observed any admirals (or the secretary) in the vicinity of the gauntlet."[6]

Stated clearly, the Navy failed to establish the culpability or innocence of its most senior officers who were at the site of an organized sexual assault because it did not ask.

Following the Tailhook 91 scandal, Congress replaced the Navy admiral commanding the newly renamed NCIS with a senior civilian law enforcement officer and moved the agency directly under the SECNAV.

Simply put, NCIS reports directly to the SECNAV because, decades ago, senior uniformed leaders failed to demonstrate that they could be trusted with law enforcement authority over their own ranks, a failure of integrity now permanently etched into the organizational structure of the DoN.

CHAPTER 22

Type Commanders, Systems Commands, and Program Executive Offices

YCOMs, SYSCOMs, and PEOs are often overlooked in discussion of Navy staffs. While their work is more specialized than that of an operational staff, each provides for essential Navy needs though a staff process. Each also offers staff officers a unique environment to learn the material side of operating, training, and equipping naval forces.

Type Commanders

Each major warfare community—air, surface, submarine, expeditionary, special warfare, and information warfare—has a type commander, or TYCOM, responsible to OTE its forces. They provide the fleet with ready forces, administering all aspects of maintenance, modernization, and readiness for their assigned units. Each will also maintain a close relationship with the OPNAV High Nine who represents their community's requirements. Since the TYCOM touches the waterfront and the flight line, they are the source of ground truth into the requirements process. Thus, TYCOMs exist in uncomfortable tension between operational needs, which are always expansive, and resources, which are always limited.

Since 2001, TYCOMs have been arranged on a lead-follow basis. Prior to 2001, the Atlantic Fleet (now Fleet Forces Command) and Pacific Fleet each had a subordinate and coequal TYCOM for each major warfare area. While in principle the two TYCOMs within each community were supposed to coordinate training and standards, there was often divergent guidance. Over time, this variance accumulated and built the perception that the East and West coasts were two separate navies. There was also a perception that having two TYCOMs for each community was duplicative and inefficient.

A logical answer would have been to eliminate half of the TYCOMs. That arrangement, however, would have bifurcated responsibility between the TYCOM and at least one of the two responsible fleets. The answer instead was to make one of the two TYCOMs in each community junior to the other. The junior TYCOM would follow the lead TYCOM. Whether lead or follow, the TYCOM is an echelon three command under their respective fleet commanders. Lead TYCOMs are generally three-star commands, and the follow TYCOMs are generally two-stars. The existence of a follow TYCOM ensures that each major fleet has a community-focused command concerned with the needs of its forces.

Who is lead and who is follow can vary:

H	Lead	Follow
Surface	Commander, Naval Surface Force Atlantic (COMNAVSURLANT)	Commander, Naval Surface Forces, U.S. Pacific Fleet (COMNAVSURFPAC)
Air	Commander, Naval Air Force, U.S. Pacific Fleet (COMNAVAIRPAC)	Commander, Naval Air Force Atlantic (COMNAVAIRLANT)
Submarine	Commander, Submarine Force, Atlantic (COMSUBLANT)	Commander, Submarine Force, U.S. Pacific Fleet (COMSUBPAC)
Expeditionary	Commander, Navy Expeditionary Combat Command (NECC)	None
Special Warfare	Commander, Naval Special Warfare Command (NSW)	None
Information Warfare	Commander, Naval Information Forces (NAVIFOR)	None

TYCOMs acting in a lead role will sometimes refer to themselves without a geographic limitation in title. For example, commander, Naval Air Force, U.S. Pacific Fleet (COMNAVAIRPAC) will refer to itself as commander, Naval Air Forces (COMNAVAIRFOR). Navy Expeditionary

Warfare and Navy Special Warfare, leading smaller communities, have been single TYCOMs since their creation. When the information warfare community was established, it declined to establish a follow TYCOM. While there is a NAVIFOR element that assists U.S. Pacific Fleet units, the lack of a subordinate information warfare TYCOM element under U.S. Pacific Fleet has been a source of friction in integrating information warfare capabilities.

TYCOMs also often serve as the Navy-wide lead for a warfare enterprise. For example, the commander, Submarine Force, U.S. Pacific Fleet also leads the Undersea Warfare Enterprise (UWE). A warfare enterprise is a collection of senior stakeholders who form a board of directors that monitors and guides the performance of their warfare area. These stakeholders are, in many ways, the remnants of a decades-departed CNO's effort to govern the service more like a business enterprise. The formal OPNAV elements of the effort have long eroded; how active and influential the individual enterprises are, varies with the community and the personalities of the senior officers involved.

While the responsibilities of each TYCOM are largely intuitive and established, there are two notable exceptions:

- U.S. Navy aircraft carriers fall under Naval Air Forces. Other aviation capable ships do not; this is a dynamic that creates variance between platform types.
- Electronic systems installed on other platforms remains unclear. For example, is a radio installed on a destroyer the responsibility of SURFOR or NAVIFOR? Some instructions suggest that all electronics systems should be administered by NAVIFOR, but practice suggests that the platform TYCOM has decisive control.

Systems Commands

The six SYSCOMs are responsible for the design, construction, and maintenance of ships, aircraft, and weapons. For most of the Navy, SYSCOMs operate in the background, occasionally appearing to provide technical assistance to repair a material casualty or to evaluate or install a new piece of equipment. In fact, the responsibility of actually building the Navy requires an enormous, diverse, and technically skilled enterprise. NAVSEA

TYCOM planning in action: USS *Stout* prepares to drydock for a maintenance availability, 2021. *U.S. Navy*

alone employs more than 70,000 people and consumes almost 25 percent of the overall Navy budget. SYSCOM staffs are heavily civilian, with a small cadre of military members providing operational experience to complement their engineering and acquisitions expertise.

The current DoN systems commands are

- Naval Sea Systems Command (NAVSEA)
- Naval Air Systems Command (NAVAIR)
- Naval Information Warfare Systems Command (NAVWAR) (known as SPAWAR until 2018)
- Naval Facilities Engineering Command (NAVFAC)
- Naval Supply Systems Command (NAVSUP)
- Marine Corps Systems Command (MCSC)

Each SYSCOM is an echelon two command under the CNO. However, the SYSCOMs also report to the ASN (RD&A). Since the ASN is responsible for acquisition within the DoN, most of the SYSCOM's attention is directed to their SECNAV senior.

Program Executive Offices

Under the SYSCOMs are program executive offices (PEOs). PEOs bear the responsibility for cost, schedule, and performance of major acquisition programs. For example, there are PEOs for aircraft carriers and for the *Columbia*-class SSBN program. PEOs are a creature of DoD-wide acquisition rules that sought to standardize the competence and oversight of major DoD acquisitions. Thus, their role and responsibilities flow largely from joint and DoD instructions and public law. Like the SYSCOMs, PEOs have a dual chain of command to both the CNO and to the ASN (RD&A).

The Defense Acquisition Workforce Improvement Act (DAWIA) created specific requirements for positions of responsibility within DoN acquisitions programs, as well as standards for professional certification. Most of the officers assigned to a SYSCOM are part of the Navy acquisition community (called acquisition professional membership since 2020) or are looking for the opportunity to earn acquisition experience. Officers generally elect this career path as O4s, and spend much of their following years in SYSCOM and PEO billets. Acquisition experience is critical if the Navy is to take full advantage of the talent and capability in America's industrial base, but it also creates a separate professional ecosystem that is relatively insular from Navy operational forces.

CONCLUSION

Arleigh Burke, "Bad Staff Officer"

ADM Arleigh Burke is rightly revered as a U.S. Navy legend. As commodore of Destroyer Squadron 23, the Little Beavers, in the Pacific during World War II, he led more than twenty surface engagements over four months of sustained combat. He relentlessly incorporated the hard-won lessons of previous engagements into his squadron's tactics. At the battle of Cape St. George, he commanded the most successful destroyer action of the war, sinking three Japanese destroyers and damaging another in a five-ship-on-five-ship night action.

In 1944, however, Burke was pulled from squadron command to staff duty. CNO ADM King wanted to pair senior aviator admirals with surface line chiefs of staff and vice versa. It was not a popular idea. As the new policy was implemented, Burke was assigned as CoS to VADM Marc Mitscher, a stoic, taciturn aviation pioneer who did not believe that he needed a destroyer Sailor helping run his ships.

Fresh from successful command of a DESRON, Burke had to throw himself into learning carrier operations while establishing himself as a numbered fleet CoS, handling both administration and combat operations, all under the skeptical eye of an accomplished commander and his established staff team.

And Burke struggled. His letters to his wife, Bobby, during this period were full of self-doubt:

"I don't know my job."
"I feel lost and I don't think I'll like [the staff]."
"I'm afraid [Mitscher] is going to be terribly disappointed when he finds how stupid I've been."

"Professionally this is the best of all the staff jobs—Actually I'd rather not have it because I'd rather fight battles than plan them—and I don't think I'll be particularly good at planning them."

"I don't think I'll be able to do a bang up job—I'm sort of out of water here."[1]

Burke thought the taciturn Mitscher was freezing him out of staff discussions, trying to push him to request a transfer.

Burke, of course, succeeded in his tour. He learned carrier operations, and taught Mitscher's staff to emulate the clear, succinct doctrine and battle orders that had enabled the Little Beavers. He came to respect and like Mitscher, describing him to his wife as "a good hard fighting little shriveled up pleasant man."[2] Mitscher grew to trust Burke, increasingly relying on him through battles in the Marianas, Leyte Gulf, and Iwo Jima, all the way to the end of the war. After the war, when Mitscher became DCNO for Air,

The "good hard fighting little shriveled up pleasant man" and his chief of staff. *U.S. Naval Institute photo archive*

he paid Burke the compliment of asking him, one of the Navy's premier surface warriors, to be his deputy—an honor Burke declined.

Burke's knowledge, attention to duty, and gentle humor made him a valued advisor to commanders and presidents. Burke eventually served an unprecedented three tours as the CNO, leading the Navy through the introduction of nuclear power, submarine-launched ballistic missiles, and establishment of the Cold War nuclear deterrent force.

For Navy staff officers, Burke's example holds two important truths: First, while Burke is revered as a combat leader, his most lasting impact on the Navy came through, with, and in command of Navy staffs. And second, even Arleigh Burke had to learn the role.

May you be as successful in your journey.

NOTES

Introduction

1. Alfred Thayer Mahan, *Naval Administration and Warfare: Some General Principles with Other Essays* (Boston, MA: Little, Brown and Company, 1908), 11.
2. Title 10 U.S. Code §8062.

Chapter 1. What Is a Navy Staff?

1. "Standard Organization and Regulations of the U.S. Navy," OPNAVINST 3120.32D CH-1, 15 May 2017.
2. FADM Ernest J. King, *U.S. Navy at War, 1941–1945: Official Reports to the Secretary of the Navy* (Washington, DC: Office of the Chief of Naval Operations, 1946), 188.
3. Martin van Creveld, *Command in War* (Cambridge, MA: Harvard University Press, 1985), 269.
4. Ibid.
5. *The Navy Department: A Brief History until 1945* (Washington, DC: Naval Historical Foundation, 1970), 2–3.
6. Geoffrey S. Smith, "An Uncertain Passage: The Bureaus Run the Navy," in *In Peace and War: Interpretations of American Naval History, 1775–1984*, 2nd ed., edited by Kenneth J. Hagan (Westport, CT: Greenwood Press, 1984), 84.
7. John T. Kuehn, *America's First General Staff: A Short History of the Rise and Fall of the General Board of the Navy, 1900–1950* (Annapolis, MD: Naval Institute Press, 2017), 4.
8. BG J. D. Hittle, *The Military Staff: Its History and Development*, 3rd ed. (Harrisburg, PA: Stackpole Company, 1961), 70.
9. Albert A. Nofi, *To Train the Fleet for War: The U.S. Navy Fleet Problems, 1923–1940* (Newport, RI: Naval War College Press, 2010), 9–10.

10. RADM Julius Augustus Furer, *Administration of the Navy Department in World War II* (Washington, DC: Department of the Navy, 1959), 125–29.

11. Ibid., 159–62.

12. E. B. Potter, *Nimitz* (Annapolis, MD: Naval Institute Press, 1976), 16.

13. Trent Hone, *Learning War: The Evolution of Fighting Doctrine in the U.S. Navy, 1898–1945* (Annapolis, MD: Naval Institute Press, 2018), 302–3.

14. COMINCH Order 192200, dated 19 February 1943. I am indebted to Dave Kohnen for providing this key document from his forthcoming biography of FADM King.

Chapter 2. The Commander

1. Carl Solberg, *Decision and Dissent: With Halsey at Leyte Gulf* (Annapolis, MD: Naval Institute Press, 1995), 118–26.

2. Christopher Nelson, "A Navy Planner Speaks—Captain David Fields on the Challenges and Future of U.S. Navy Planning," U.S. Naval Institute *Proceedings*, December 2020.

3. Ibid.

4. *Sound Military Decision* (Newport, RI: U.S. Naval War College, 1942), 210; emphasis in original.

5. Lewis A. Coser, *Greedy Institutions: Patterns of Undivided Commitment* (New York, NY: Free Press, 1974).

6. FADM Ernest J. King, quoted in James C. Bradford, "Henry T. Mayo: Last of the Independent Naval Diplomats," in *Admirals of the New Steel Navy: Makers of the American Naval Tradition, 1880–1930* (Annapolis, MD: Naval Institute Press, 1990), 275–76.

7. VADM Hank Mustin Oral History (Naval Historical Foundation, 2001), 176.

8. ADM Scott Swift, "Fleet Problems Offer Opportunities," U.S. Naval Institute *Proceedings*, March 2018.

Chapter 3. The Staff Command Triad: Deputies, Chiefs of Staff, Executive Directors, and Senior Enlisted

1. David Alan Rosenberg and Deborah L. Haines, *Arleigh Burke: The Sailor at War, 1921–1945*, unpublished manuscript, 274.

Chapter 4. The Personal Staff

1. OPNAVINST 1306.3C, "Guidance for Use of Enlisted Aides," 31 January 2019.

Chapter 5. Special Staff

1. Rosenberg and Haines, *Arleigh Burke*, 462.

Chapter 6. Getting Started as a Staff Officer

1. Reclama is a request to a senior or an element with authority to reconsider a decision, and is sometimes used as a verb.
2. Rosenberg and Haines, *Arleigh Burke*, 145.

Chapter 7. Communicating as a Staff Officer

1. *Department of the Navy Correspondence Manual*, SECNAV M-5216.5 CH-1, May 16, 2018, 4-1 (first two quotes), 4-2 (last quote).
2. Bravo Zulu messages are a naval tradition, passing the commander's thanks for a job well done. Savvy staff officers know that they usually come about because someone on the staff suggests it and then writes the message for the boss. It is not a bad thing to be an officer with a reputation for pointing out excellence and helping the commander recognize it.
3. National Aeronautics and Space Administration, *Report of the Columbia Accident Investigation Board*, 26 August 2003, vol. 1, 191.
4. Edward Tufte, *Beautiful Evidence* (Cheshire, CT: Graphics Press, 2006), 64–65.
5. NASA, *Report*, vol. 1, 192.
6. CDR Christopher Nelson, "A Naval Strategist Speaks," U.S. Naval Institute *Proceedings*, May 2019.

Chapter 9. Civilian Personnel

1. Robert G. Albion, "Brief History of Civilian Personnel in the U.S. Navy Department," U.S. Navy, October 1943.
2. Office of Federal Procurement Policy (OFPP) Policy Letter 11–01, "Performance of Inherently Governmental and Critical Functions," effective 12 October 2011.

Chapter 12. Intelligence

1. Edwin Layton, *And I Was There* (New York, NY: William Morrow, 1982), 357.
2. CAPT Dale Rielage, "Build Human-Machine Dream Teams," U.S. Naval Institute *Proceedings*, May 2017.

Chapter 13. Operations

1. Navy Tactics, Techniques, and Procedures (NTTP) 3-32.1, Maritime Operations Center (April 2013), 3-1.

Chapter 14. Maintenance, Logistics, and Readiness

1. ADM J. O. Richardson, *On the Treadmill to Pearl Harbor* (Washington, DC: Naval History Division, 1973), 437.

Chapter 17. Training, Exercises, and War Games

1. Louis V. Gerstner Jr., *Who Says Elephants Can't Dance?* (New York, NY: Harper Business, 2002), 250.

Chapter 18. Afloat Staffs

1. Norman Friedman, *Network-Centric Warfare: How Navies Learned to Fight Smarter Through Three World Wars* (Annapolis, MD: Naval Institute Press, 2009).
2. Joint Publication 3–32, "Command and Control for Joint Maritime Operations," II-15.
3. Ibid., viii.

Chapter 19. Fleet Commands and the Maritime Operations Centers

1. H.R. 2863, Department of Defense Appropriations Act, 2006, SEC. 8106.
2. Joint Publication 3–32, "Command and Control for Joint Maritime Operations," II-12.
3. Navy Tactical Reference Publication 1-02, "Navy Supplement to the DoD Dictionary of Military and Associated Terms," June 2012, 2-51.
4. "Navy Tactics, Techniques, and Procedures (NTTP) 3–32.1," *Maritime Operations Center*, April 2013, 1–4.
5. Ibid.
6. Ibid., 1–10.

Chapter 20. Office of the Chief of Naval Operations

1. Rosenberg and Haines, *Arleigh Burke*, 134.
2. Ibid., 443.

Chapter 21. The Secretary of the Navy Staff

1. Title 10 U.S. Code § 8013.
2. Title 10 U.S. Code § 8033(c).

3. Department of Defense Office of the Inspector General, "Tailhook 91 Part 1–Review of the Navy Investigations," September 1992, 2.
4. Ibid., 3–4.
5. Ibid.
6. Ibid., 17.

Conclusion. Arleigh Burke, "Bad Staff Officer"

1. Rosenberg and Haines, *Arleigh Burke.*
2. Ibid., 241.

FURTHER READING

One of the most powerful questions to ask a mentor is what you should read. Every leader worth following has been shaped by the thoughtful and sometimes brilliant minds they have encountered in books. The list below may be a useful starting point.

Staff History and Development

Trevor N. Dupuy. *A Genius for War: The German Army and General Staff, 1807–1945*. New York, NY: Prentice-Hall, 1977.

Julius Augustus Furer. *Administration of the Navy Department in World War II*. Washington, DC: Department of the Navy, 1959.

J. D. Hittle. *The Military Staff: Its History and Development*. Harrisburg, PA: The Stackpole Company, 1961.

John Kuehn. *America's First General Staff: A Short History of the Rise and Fall of the General Board of the U.S. Navy, 1900–1950*. Annapolis, MD: Naval Institute Press, 2017.

Alfred T. Mahan. *Naval Administration and Warfare: Some General Principles, with Other Essays*. Boston, MA: Little, Brown, and Company, 1908.

Charles E. White. *The Enlightened Soldier: Scharnhorst and the Militarische Gesellschaft in Berlin, 1801–1805*. Westport, CT: Praeger, 1989.

Leaders and Their Staffs

Kathleen McInnis. *The Heart of War: Misadventures in the Pentagon*. New York, NY: Post Hill Press, 2018.

Phillips Payson O'Brien. *The Second Most Powerful Man in the World: The Life of Admiral William D. Leahy, Roosevelt's Chief of Staff*. New York, NY: Dutton, 2019.

E. B. Potter. *Nimitz*. Annapolis, MD: Naval Institute Press, 1976.

Robert E. Stoffey. *Fighting to Leave: The Final Years of America's War in Vietnam, 1972–1973*. Minneapolis, MN: Zenith Press, 2008.

Craig L. Symonds. *Nimitz at War: Command Leadership from Pearl Harbor to Tokyo Bay*. New York, NY: Oxford University Press, 2022.

Milan Vego. *Operational Warfare at Sea: Theory and Practice*, 2nd edition. New York, NY: Routledge, 2017.

Sandy Woodward. *One Hundred Days: The Memoirs of the Falklands Battle Group Commander*. Annapolis, MD: Naval Institute Press, 1992.

Office of the Chief of Naval Operations and the Pentagon

Rosa Brooks. *How Everything Became War and the Military Became Everything: Tales from the Pentagon*. New York, NY: Simon and Schuster, 2016.

Thomas C. Hone. *Power and Change: The Administrative History of the Office of the Chief of Naval Operations*. Washington, DC: Naval Historical Center, 1989.

Fred Kacher and D. A. Robb. *The Naval Officer's Guide to the Pentagon*. Annapolis, MD: Naval Institute Press, 2019.

Mara Karlin. *The Inheritance*. Washington, DC: Brookings Institution Press, 2022.

Peter M. Swartz. *Organizing OPNAV (1970–2009)*. Alexandria, VA: Center for Naval Analyses, 2010.

Planning

Jeffrey R. Cares and Anthony Cowden. *Fighting the Fleet: Operational Art and Modern Fleet Combat*. Annapolis, MD: Naval Institute Press, 2021.

B. A. Friedman. *On Operational Art: Operational Art and Military Disciplines*. Annapolis, MD: Naval Institute Press, 2021.

Trent Hone. *Learning War: The Evolution of Fighting Doctrine in the U.S. Navy, 1898–1945*. Annapolis, MD: Naval Institute Press, 2018.

Edward S. Miller. *War Plan Orange: The U.S. Strategy to Defeat Japan, 1897–1945*. Annapolis, MD: Naval Institute Press, 2013.

U.S. Naval War College. *Sound Military Decision*. Newport, RI: U.S. Naval War College, 1942.

Command and Control

Norman Friedman. *Network-Centric Warfare: How Navies Learned to Fight Smarter Through Three World Wars.* Annapolis, MD: Naval Institute Press, 2009.

Norman Friedman. *Seapower and Space.* London: Chatham, 2000.

Andrew Gordon. *Rules of the Game: Jutland and British Naval Command.* Annapolis, MD: Naval Institute Press, 1996.

Michael A. Palmer. *Command at Sea: Naval Command and Control since the Sixteenth Century.* Cambridge, MA: Harvard University Press, 2005.

Martin van Creveld. *Command in War.* Cambridge, MA: Harvard University Press, 1985.

Timothy S. Wolters. *Information at Sea: Shipboard Command and Control in the U.S. Navy from Mobile Bay to Okinawa.* Baltimore, MD: Johns Hopkins University Press, 2013.

Naval Intelligence

Patrick Beesly. *Room 40: British Naval Intelligence, 1914–1918.* New York, NY: Harcourt, Brace, Jovanovich, 1982.

Edwin Layton. *And I Was There: Pearl Harbor and Midway—Breaking the Secrets.* New York, NY: William Morrow and Company, 1985.

Bruce E. Pease. *Leading Intelligence Analysis: Lessons from the CIA's Analytic Front Lines.* Los Angeles, CA: Sage, 2021.

Roberta Wohlstetter. *Pearl Harbor: Warning and Decision.* Stanford, CA: Stanford University Press, 1962.

Staff Communications

R. Brown and S. Leonard, eds. *Why We Write: Craft Essays on Writing War.* Johnston, IA: Middle West Press, 2019.

Stephanie D. H. Evergreen. *Presenting Data Effectively: Communicating Your Findings for Maximum Impact,* 2nd edition. Los Angeles, CA: Sage, 2018.

Janine Kurnoff and Lee Lazarus. *Everyday Business Storytelling: Create, Simplify, and Adapt A Visual Narrative for Any Audience.* Hoboken, NJ: John Wiley and Sons, 2021.

Herbert and Jill Meyer. *How to Write: Communicating Ideas and Information.* New York, NY: Barnes and Noble Books, 1994.

Mark Monmonier. *How to Lie with Maps,* 3rd edition. Chicago, IL: University of Chicago Press, 2018.

Steven G. Rogelberg. *The Surprising Science of Meetings: How You Can Lead Your Team to Peak Performance.* New York, NY: Oxford University Press, 2019.

Edward R. Tufte. *Visual Explanations: Images and Quantities, Evidence and Narrative.* Cheshire, CT: Graphics Press, 1997.

Thinking, Strategy, and Organizations

Benjamin F. Armstrong and John Freymann. *Developing the Naval Mind.* Annapolis, MD: Naval Institute Press, 2022.

Ian Brown. *A New Conception of War: John Boyd, the U.S. Marines, and Maneuver Warfare.* Quantico, VA: Marine Corps University Press, 2018.

Janine Davidson. *Lifting the Fog of Peace: How Americans Learned to Fight Modern War.* Ann Arbor, MI: University of Michigan Press, 2010.

Richards J. Heuer Jr. *Psychology of Intelligence Analysis.* Washington, DC: Center for the Study of Intelligence, 1999.

Morgan D. Jones. *The Thinker's Toolkit: 14 Powerful Techniques for Problem Solving.* New York, NY: Three Rivers Press, 1998.

John F. Lehman. *Oceans Ventured: Winning the Cold War at Sea.* New York, NY: W. W. Norton and Company, 2018.

Scott A. Snooks. *Friendly Fire: The Accidental Shootdown of U.S. Black Hawks over Northern Iraq.* Princeton, NJ: Princeton University Press, 2002.

Steven T. Wills. *Strategy Shelved: The Collapse of Cold War Naval Strategic Planning.* Annapolis, MD Naval Institute Press, 2021.

Exercises and War Gaming

Jeff Appleget, Robert Burks, and Fred Cameron. *The Craft of Wargaming: A Detailed Planning Guide for Defense Planners and Analysts.* Annapolis, MD: Naval Institute Press, 2020.

Craig C. Felker. *Testing American Sea Power: U.S. Navy Strategic Exercises, 1923–1940.* College Station, TX: Texas A&M University Press, 2007.

Albert A. Nofi. *To Train the Fleet for War: The U.S. Navy Fleet Problems, 1923–1940.* Newport, RI: Naval War College, 2010.

Peter P. Perla. *The Art of Wargaming: A Guide for Professionals and Hobbyists*. Annapolis, MD: Naval Institute Press, 1990.

Working with Allies and Partners

Victor D. Cha. *Powerplay: The Origins of the American Alliance System in Asia*. Princeton, NJ: Princeton University Press, 2018.

Mira Rapp-Hooper. *Shields of the Republic: The Triumph and Peril of America's Alliances*. Cambridge, MA: Harvard University Press, 2020.

INDEX

ABOUT THE AUTHOR

CAPT Dale C. Rielage, USN (Ret.), is a former surface warfare and naval intelligence officer with eleven tours on Navy and Joint staffs afloat and ashore, including as an N-code director in two Maritime Operations Centers, and as special assistant to the Chief of Naval Operations. He is the author of dozens of articles on maritime and security issues and is the recipient of first prize in the 2017 U.S. Naval Institute General Essay Contest.

The Naval Institute Press is the book-publishing arm of the U.S. Naval Institute, a private, nonprofit, membership society for sea service professionals and others who share an interest in naval and maritime affairs. Established in 1873 at the U.S. Naval Academy in Annapolis, Maryland, where its offices remain today, the Naval Institute has members worldwide.

Members of the Naval Institute support the education programs of the society and receive the influential monthly magazine *Proceedings* or the colorful bimonthly magazine *Naval History* and discounts on fine nautical prints and on ship and aircraft photos. They also have access to the transcripts of the Institute's Oral History Program and get discounted admission to any of the Institute-sponsored seminars offered around the country.

The Naval Institute's book-publishing program, begun in 1898 with basic guides to naval practices, has broadened its scope to include books of more general interest. Now the Naval Institute Press publishes about seventy titles each year, ranging from how-to books on boating and navigation to battle histories, biographies, ship and aircraft guides, and novels. Institute members receive significant discounts on the Press' more than eight hundred books in print.

Full-time students are eligible for special half-price membership rates. Life memberships are also available.

For more information about Naval Institute Press books that are currently available, visit www.usni.org/press/books. To learn about joining the U.S. Naval Institute, please write to:

Member Services
U.S. Naval Institute
291 Wood Road
Annapolis, MD 21402-5034
Telephone: (800) 233-8764
Fax: (410) 571-1703
Web address: www.usni.org